φΔθ - 7/6 Estrella

Valla Walla Wood.

THAT REMINDS ME —

THAT REMINDS ME—

by

ALBEN W. BARKLEY

DOUBLEDAY & COMPANY, INC., GARDEN CITY, NEW YORK

To THE PEOPLE OF KENTUCKY, *without whose confidence and good will I could not have rendered to them and to the nation the service which I have attempted in their behalf, this book is dedicated.*

IN THE PREPARATION of this book, I have had the invaluable assistance and co-operation of Mr. Sidney Shalett, who has enjoyed a wide experience in literary and journalistic fields. He has, with rare judgment and fidelity, accomplished the arduous task of arranging and co-ordinating my dictated material into orderly sequence. He has spent more than a year in painstaking research and investigation to assure accuracy. This has been extremely valuable because I have written largely from my memory without benefit of diary or private journal. He has shown a sympathy and an understanding which have made it a pleasure to have him associated with me in this undertaking. He has, at the same time, felt the true spirit behind my first efforts as an author. For all this, I acknowledge my obligation and extend to him my sincere gratitude and appreciation.

CONTENTS

ILLUSTRATIONS

THAT REMINDS ME ——

CHAPTER I

Looking Backward—and Forward

As I WRITE THIS, another birthday is approaching. Some would say I am going to be seventy-seven years old; others would think of it as seventy-seven years young. I lean toward the latter viewpoint. Birthdays always remind me of the fellow in my home state of Kentucky who, feeling particularly spry one morning, remarked to his young son that he felt "like a two-year-old." "Horse or egg?" the boy inquired. In my case I would rather kick up my heels than cackle.

Looking back on my three quarters of a century—forty-seven years of which have been spent in public service—I am bound to say that it has been a good life. A good life and a full one. I have had my moments of sorrow and disappointment, as have all who are born to this earth, but there has been no prolonged period when I have not found life filled with joy and zest. I have been proud, too, of the opportunities given me to serve my country.

There is a famous culinary concoction called "burgoo," of which I often partook when I toured the political hustings in certain parts of the Blue Grass State. A "burgoo" is a cross between a soup and a stew, and into the big iron cooking kettles go, as we sometimes say in Kentucky, a "numerosity" of things—meat, chicken, vegetables, and lots of seasonings. These memoirs are going to be somewhat like a "burgoo," made up of a "numerosity" of ingredients. The recipe is largely in my head, for I have never kept a diary or journal; I have had far too busy a life for that. Whatever I write here is entirely from memory, except where I quote from records, letters, or speeches.

As I stir the kettle of my memories, my thoughts go back a long way. I remember my boyhood days, living in the little log house on the farm which my father rented, and working alongside him, planting tobacco, threshing wheat, and clearing timber—man's work at a boy's age. It is not true, as my children sometimes yarn, that I did not wear shoes until I was sixteen. However, I do recall one year when there was an early heavy frost. It came suddenly before Father had made his annual trip to town to purchase my usual winter footgear—a pair of high leather boots with red tops and brass-tipped toes. Since I had outgrown my boots of the previous season, I had to walk barefooted to school. I remember hopping, like a bluejay following the plow, in the tracks of the older boys just ahead of me to keep my feet out of the frost.

I vividly remember the struggle to get an education: how I worked as a janitor to put myself through Marvin College, a small and now extinct institution in Clinton, Kentucky. A sign on the old Marvin dormitory—now a hotel—proclaims, "BARKLEY SWEPT HERE." Earlier I learned the three R's in country schools from such wonderfully patient and inspirational teachers as "Miss Lizzie" Lowe—later the wife of our good family physician, Dr. George T. Fuller—and "Miss Gertie" Backus. Both of them were kind enough to encourage me in my ambitions and even to predict, somewhat generously, that I might someday become President of the United States. Alas, for the predictions of these fine ladies, I did not quite make the presidency. But, after my long career of public service, beginning with the post of prosecuting attorney of McCracken County, Kentucky, and progressing through county judge, congressman, and senator, the people of the United States did bestow upon me the second-highest honor in American political life—the office of Vice President. Yes, all of these things—and many more—I remember, and all of them I enjoyed.

Lest this begin to sound like the lugubrious prelude to a self-written obituary, let me hasten to say that I am not thinking of departing this mortal vale, as the poets have it, at any time soon. There are many things I want to do, many places I have not seen yet, and I am going to do my best to round out my program. In fact, I have practically a guaranty that I will live to be over 100. On a 1948 trip to Egypt I rode out to see the Pyramids by moonlight, and an old Arab fortuneteller took me in hand. For the bargain sum of $2.50 he predicted I would live to be 100, and for another $2.50 he raised it to 105. As I left him, he told me, "Stay out of airplanes," and I had to say to him, "Now wait a minute, old fellow, you're hedging on your guaranty!" At least it is comforting to have a bona fide Egyptian soothsayer on your side.

Every time I get to thinking about longevity, incidentally, I am reminded of an old neighbor I have in Kentucky, who is ninety-nine years old and going strong. Some years ago, when he was a young man of only ninety-two, he was vigorous, physically and mentally, worked regularly, and walked straight as an Indian. One day a neighbor asked him, "To what do you attribute your good health and longevity?"

"Well," my old friend answered, "before my wife and I were married, we entered into an agreement. Any time I railed at her, nagged at her, or picked a fuss with her, she would take her knitting, go out into the kitchen, and knit until it was all over. On the other hand, any time she would pick a fuss with me, I would put on my hat, go outdoors, and stay there until the atmosphere was once again serene."

"But what's that got to do with your health and longevity?" the neighbor inquired.

"Why," said the nonagenarian, "I've spent most of my life in the open air."

A lot of characters come to mind as I review what I like to think of as my two generations in public life. I have met and, in many cases, have been privileged to work intimately with some of the towering figures of the century—Woodrow Wilson, Franklin Delano Roosevelt, Winston Churchill, and many of the titans of Congress. Of these men, of kings and of great generals and statesmen, of men with great nobility of mind and spirit but lesser public fame, of some of the buffoonery in public life which I have also known, I shall have more to say as this account progresses.

In so far as the Washington scene is concerned, I suppose in my time I have known all the personages whom history will set down as famous, and some whom their fellow men have called infamous. I have always hesitated—I suppose it is part of my personal creed—to judge any fellow human as infamous, unless he be a proven and incorrigible wrongdoer. A friend of mine, hearing that I was going to have a go at setting down my observations of public life, jestingly said to me: "Alben, I'll bet you wind up with a book that has all heroes and no villains!" I had to agree that he might be more right than wrong. It was Shakespeare who had Mark Antony saying over the body of Caesar that "the evil that men do lives after them; the good is oft interred with their bones." I prefer to look at it the other way around and think that the *good* men do will live after them, and the evil, if any, should be interred with their bones. In all my life I have disliked but few men and hated no one.

In fact, I am not a bit like the character in one of my favorite stories, Uncle Beauregard, from down around Flat Lick, Kentucky. This, by

the way, was a story I introduced to former President Harry Truman
when he was having one of his earliest running battles with critics of
his administration, and he enjoyed it hugely.

Uncle Beau, who lived to be an old, old man, was in church one
Sunday when the preacher delivered a ripsnorting sermon against hate.
"Is there any man among you who can say he is without hate?" the
preacher exhorted. Whereupon Uncle Beau rose and quavered, "I'm 104
years old and I don't hate nobody! I haven't an enemy in the world!"

"Praise be!" the preacher exclaimed. "Tell us, old man, *why* you
haven't an enemy in the world?"

Uncle Beau's eyes lit up with fiendish glee; he shook his cane and
cackled triumphantly, "I've outlived 'em all!"

In my observations of life I have always been particularly fascinated
by two recurring themes.

One is the fleeting quality of mortal fame. This personal precept, I
hope, has helped me in keeping my hat size down to something approximating normal, and in keeping my sense of perspective at times when
temporary developments and blandishments might otherwise have in-
duced me to swell up like a mule that has eaten a peck of dried apples.

Perhaps it is wise, if you are ambitious, to regard yourself and everything pertaining thereto with the utmost gravity. In the last presidential
campaign the opposition circulated the ugly insinuation that Adlai E.
Stevenson was a congenitally witty man. This is no new "indictment" in
politics. Almost a century ago a definitive, if slightly embittered, rule
was laid down by United States Senator Thomas Corwin, a man of
both wisdom and wit, who always felt he might have risen to the presidency if his enemies had not hounded him with allegations that he was
just too blamed funny. Riding along one day with a young friend named
James Garfield, who later became the twentieth President of the United
States, Senator Corwin delivered this sage advice: "Never make people
laugh. If you would succeed in life, you must be solemn—solemn as an
ass. All the great monuments are built over solemn asses." I do not sub-
scribe to this theory, but, out of the bitterness of his disappointment,
Senator Corwin thus anathematized all monuments and memorials.

I am proud, incidentally, to note that the author of the above philosophy, though he was elected to the Senate from Ohio, was born in Bourbon County, Kentucky. For this I forgive him even the fact that
he was a Whig turned Republican.

For my part, every time I get to taking myself too seriously, I remind
myself of several stories.

One was told me by a prominent Englishman, who was explaining to me why governmental problems are more complex in the United States than in his country. "There are at least fifty-seven varieties—like those famous pickles—of you Americans, and every one of you has different ideas," he said. "In my country, there are only four kinds of people with four ideas. There are the Scots, who won't wear rubber heels because they give. There are the Welsh, who pray on their knees—and prey on everyone else. There are the Irish, who don't know what they want and are willing to fight for it. And finally, there are the English, who are self-made and worship their creator!"

The moral, so far as I am concerned, is that every time I get to thinking of myself as a self-made man, I remember not to get too enthusiastic about my "creator."

The second story is an incident which happened to me in Lisbon shortly after World War II. As you get to know me better through these pages, you will learn that I am an inveterate collector of all sorts of things—canes, gavels, antiques, souvenirs, gimcracks; anything that strikes my fancy. I am particularly partial to my collection of more than a hundred canes, which I began picking up in 1931 while recovering from the effects of having proven to myself the hard way that it is not a good idea to fall asleep at the wheel of an automobile.

Anyway, while in Lisbon, I wanted to acquire a Portuguese specimen for my cane collection, and I asked a young attaché of our embassy where I might look. "You'll have to go to a junk shop, and I'll be glad to take you," he replied. On the way we passed places where four exiled former kings were staying; also the temporary abodes of a lot of fallen royalty and deposed statesmen. He pointed them all out to me. We got out at the place where I was to look for my cane, and, on the corner, was standing a handsome, distinguished-looking man. The attaché presented me to him.

He was one of the exiled former kings—a generation ago, I had been entertained by his father. As we left him to walk into the shop, the young attaché murmured, "Senator, you found your junk sooner than we expected." A youthfully cruel remark, perhaps, but one that was not without significance.

Still another experience—one that happened closer to home—occurred during one of my early races for Congress. I was campaigning through my district, and my son, David, known as Bud, was chauffeuring me. At this particular time there was some sort of schism within the Baptist church in my home town, Paducah, which had got into the newspapers.

We pulled into a filling station in a town in a not too distant corner of my district, and, while the attendant was gassing up the car, I thought I'd get in a little campaigning. Getting out of the car, I stuck out my hand, and said, "My name's Barkley."

The attendant wiped off his hand on the seat of his overalls, shook mine, and said, "Barkus?"

"No, Barkley," I said. "Alben Barkley."

"Glad to know you, Mr. Allen," he said.

"No!" I said again. "The name is Barkley." I added hopefully, "Barkley —of Paducah."

His face brightened up, and he said, "Oh yes—Paducah. That's where the Baptists are having all that trouble, isn't it?"

As we drove away, I said to my son:

"Bud, I don't believe that man knew me."

The second theme which has often preoccupied me and which will probably run like a contrapuntal passage through this narrative is the manner in which Fate often moves in small and seemingly accidental or coincidental ways to influence great decisions in the lives of men and nations. The outcome of a great siege in the history of early Rome was decided by the cackling of a flock of sacred geese which betrayed the invaders. Napoleon might never have lost the Battle of Waterloo had not Blücher, who became lost on his way to reinforce Wellington, encountered a young Belgian cowherd who set him on the right road. George Washington, whom I regard as one of the few indispensable men in the history of America, was on his way to become a British midshipman when his mother's tears led him to unpack his knapsack and stay home, where, of course, he went on to become the father of his country. Both Abraham Lincoln, President of the United States, and Jefferson Davis, President of the Confederacy, were born in Kentucky, a few years and a few miles apart. Would history have been different had Lincoln's parents moved to Mississippi, as Davis' parents did? Or if Davis' parents had migrated to Indiana and then to Illinois, as did Lincoln's?

Nothing in my own life, of course, is in any wise of comparable significance so far as history or general interest is concerned. From where I now sit, however, I like to speculate on how certain events, little twists of fate, have arisen to influence happenings which were of major significance in my life. For instance—as I will later relate in more detail—I might never have met and married my lovely present wife, Jane, had not a last-minute event in her daily life forced her to change her vacation plans.

I have already mentioned how two of my beloved early teachers, Miss Gertie and Miss Lizzie, were convinced that one day I might be President of the United States. I have no bitterness, no rankling disappointment—I am just not made that way—about the fact that I never became President. In fact, when President Truman in 1951 made a surprise appearance in the Senate to present me with a gavel made of wood taken from a White House timber, I jokingly said in my response that, since I had disappointed my early teachers by not going to the White House, it was very kind of the President to bring a piece of the White House to me. But, as this story unfolds, readers may share my interest in speculating how, if certain events—not necessarily large ones—had gone differently, the predictions of Miss Gertie and Miss Lizzie might well have come to pass.

I must admit I had a strange feeling on the afternoon of January 20, 1953, as I stood on the temporary platform in front of the United States Capitol, where for forty years I had served as representative, senator, and Vice President. That, of course, was the day of the inaugural ceremony at which the first Republican President and Vice President in twenty years were sworn in. When the ceremony was over, I was no longer the "Veep."

Sometimes irreverent thoughts come into your head on solemn occasions. Dean Acheson, the much-abused Secretary of State of the Truman administration, whose keen wit, fine character, and devotion to duty I admire highly, told me that when newspaper reporters asked him after the inaugural ceremony if he had any comment, he could not resist the temptation to reply, "Yes! For the first time in four years, I am able to tell you to go jump in the lake!"

As for me, for a moment during the ceremony I thought of the story I sometimes use about the beautiful Frenchwoman who died suddenly, leaving as her principal mourners a husband and an ardent admirer. At the funeral the husband made an appropriate showing of grief, but the admirer was inconsolable. He sobbed, beat his breast, and rolled on the ground. Finally the husband put his arm around the poor fellow's shoulder and soothingly said, "Do not take it so hard, my friend. I shall marry again."

That word, "Veep," by the way, may go down in history as the Barkley-inspired contribution to the English language. Credit for its origination, however, must go not to me but to my grandson, Stephen Truitt. We were having a family conversation one night about what a tongue twister it was to be addressed as "Mr. Vice President," and Stephen, then ten, spoke up. "Gramps," he said, "V.P. stands for Vice President. Why not stick in a couple of little *e*'s and call it 'Veep'?" I mentioned this story at a press conference a week later, when some newspapermen were asking what they should call me. They printed it and the name has stuck ever since. It has been so associated with me that my successor, Mr. Nixon, graciously declined to appropriate the nickname, saying that it had been bestowed upon me rather affectionately, he thought, by the American people. Wherever I go, though I am no longer in office, many people still yell, "Hey, Veep!" and I must admit I get a warm feeling when I hear it.

The word has even been included in some of the newer dictionaries. I was amused recently when I picked up a little twenty-five-cent vest-pocket dictionary which Jane, my wife, had bought to aid and abet her in the pursuit of scrabble. It contained an explanatory note, calling attention to the addition of a number of "up-to-date" words, such as canasta, cortisone, orlon, jet-propulsion, Veep, and hydrogen bomb. Except for the latter I thought I was in pretty good company.

Getting back to my feelings on leaving public office, I felt even more disoriented when I awoke the morning after. The excitement of the previous day was over, and for the first time for as long as I could recall I had nothing in particular to do. I said to Jane, "I have a feeling I haven't had in forty years."

"What's that?" she asked.

"Well," I said, "I haven't got a job; I haven't got a salary; I haven't got an office; I haven't got a secretary; I haven't got a car; I haven't got a chauffeur; I haven't got anything."

"Well," she said, "you've got me."

"That," I answered, "makes up for all the losses."

Then my wife said, "I've got a job for you. You know those two old split-bottomed chairs out in the kitchen? They've needed repairing for a long time. I'd like you to take them down to the Institute for the Blind and have them fixed."

So I carried the two old chairs down to the lobby of our Washington apartment, went outside and hailed a taxi, and did as I was told. Already I felt better!

Since leaving public office, it seems to me I have been busier than before—or at least as busy—what with speechmaking, television appearances, writing, and other occupations. I have had no time to get rusty or to start feeling sorry for myself.

It is not without a certain feeling of trepidation that I now undertake the telling of my life story. I am reminded of one of my favorite expressions—one which I borrowed from a great American, the late Chief Justice Charles Evans Hughes. In writing the historic decision in the so-called "sick chicken" case which invalidated the National Industrial Recovery Act in the early days of the New Deal, Mr. Chief Justice Hughes declared that the law had a "fatal infirmity." Though I regretted his decision—I had helped draft the NRA legislation and believed in it—I liked his phrase, and I have used it many times.

It has always been interesting to me to reflect on why people write books. Sir Walter Scott wrote many of his successful novels because of financial reverses which compelled him to find a way by which to pay his accumulated debts. For this the world is indebted to him. Many persons write books as a profession. Others write them to gratify the wishes of their family or friends. I suppose I might say that I have been influenced by several of these considerations. Having had a long public career and having lived through an important and tragic period of our history and that of the world, I feel that it is not out of place for me to record some of my own recollections.

Now, as I begin to set down my own narrative, it is my hope that readers will be tolerant if I expose too many "fatal infirmities."

I hope that readers will accept these memoirs in at least the same spirit that a certain Southern butler displayed when his employer, during the arid days of prohibition, presented him with a bottle of the local product known as "white mule." A few days later the employer asked him how he had liked it.

"Well," said the butler, "it was just exactly right."

"What do you mean, 'just exactly right'?" the employer asked.

"It was just exactly right," the butler repeated. "If it had been any better, you wouldn't have given it to me. And if it had been any worse, I couldn't have drunk it."

Anyhow, let us get on with the story.

CHAPTER 2

Born in a Log House

I WAS BORN on the farm of my grandfather, Alben Graham Barkley, in Graves County, Kentucky, near a little place now called Wheel, located between the larger communities of Lowes and Fancy Farm. My birth actually took place in a log house, thus making it practically inevitable that I should one day enter politics and come to be regarded as a natural aspirant for the White House. Many worthier men have had similarly hopeful environments and many log houses have suffered from similar disappointments.

I have never engaged in any foolishness or coyness about my age. As a matter of fact, my first memory of ever evoking merriment from an audience occurred when I was about nine years old and accompanied my father to a tobacco warehouse at Lowes. Some men who were lounging around the warehouse asked me when I was born, and I brightly replied: "I was born on the twenty-fourth of November, 1877, at 3:30 o'clock in the morning." They laughed uproariously and wanted to know how I remembered the hour so well.

The community of Wheel was named after an influential farmer of the same name, who founded a semi-secret agricultural organization known as the Wheelers. This society was pledged to work for the interests of farmers, who in those days had no parity programs and little else to aid their economic situation. My father was an active member, and I can recall how he used to talk enthusiastically of plans discussed at the meetings of the Wheelers. Eventually the population of the community dwindled so that Wheel lost even its rural post office. It now is served by the nearby larger and prosperous town of Fancy Farm. The unusual name of the latter community, by the way, was derived from the well-kept country place of an early settler, John Peebles. A post-office inspector had stopped at the Peebles place in 1845, while investigating whether a post office was needed in the growing settlement, and he was so impressed with its trim, neat appearance that he proposed the name of "Fancy Farm" for the new post office.

The log house in which I was born was not an ordinary cabin; it was a two-story affair, with its second story reached by an outside staircase, and in its day it was considered something of an architectural curiosity. It always surprised strangers to whom Grandfather, a congenitally hospitable man, would give a night's lodging. Once, one wanderer, whom Grandfather put up for the night, after clambering down the outside staircase, came into the kitchen for breakfast, and Grandfather spoke a hearty "good morning" to him. Apparently unaccustomed to being greeted in the morning by people with whom he had spent the night, the stranger pointed upward defensively and said, "Don't ye remember? I spent the night up thar."

Grandfather's two-story log house is gone now and not even a picture of it remains. I do, however, have some relics of my birthplace, thanks to the kindness of two old friends, Mr. and Mrs. Fred Biggs, who now have a home on the site where the two-story log house stood. The Biggses' thoughtfulness is illustrative, to me, of the sort of neighborliness that prevailed among the people with whom I grew up. A few years ago I drove out to see them with my son, David, who is a farmer and businessman at Paducah. It was a sentimental pilgrimage for me. I wanted to show him the land, at least, where I was born. While I was pointing out some old oak trees which I knew my grandfather had planted more than a hundred years ago, Mrs. Biggs came up to me and said, "Senator, there was an antique dealer around here the other day, trying to buy a door and a mantelpiece which I believe your grandfather made. I told him, 'No, I don't think I'll sell these. I imagine Senator Barkley would like to have them.'"

I remembered the old door and mantel well, and I knew that my grandfather indeed had made them. I was prepared to buy them from Mrs. Biggs, when she said she wanted me to have them as a gift. The handhewn mantel has been installed in my son's house. The old door, hanging on the same long iron hinges that Grandfather placed upon it, is going into my own home, Angles, at Paducah.

On the same visit I asked Mrs. Biggs what had happened to the old wide brick walk which led from Grandfather's front porch to the stile which the ladies used when they wanted to get into a wagon or mount a horse sidesaddle. Grandfather actually had made the bricks, which was not uncommon in those days. "Look down," she said. "It's under the grass you're standing on." Before I left, we arranged for a truck to come and get a load of those hand-made bricks, which I have had laid as a walk in the front yard of my Paducah home.

It was customary for children to be born at home in those days, as there were no hospitals in the country, and even in the cities few women went to hospitals to be delivered. All my brothers and sisters also were born at home, and, for that matter, so were my own three children. The first of our family to be born in hospitals were my grandchildren, of whom I have seven.

My paternal grandmother, Amanda Louise Girand Barkley, was the midwife at my birth. That's how I happened to be born at my grand-parents' house, for when my mother knew that her "time had come"—I was the first of eight children—she walked over to my grandparents' house a quarter of a mile away. Grandmother Amanda had had plenty of experience in such matters; in addition to helping out with the "neighbor women," she attended the birth of all her own grandchildren, who were not inconsiderable in number, as she and Grandfather raised six children of their own.

The Barkleys are an old family, as are the families with which they have been linked. I am always cautious when I get to rambling about my ancestors, for it reminds me of the little boy who inquired of his father, "Daddy, what's an ancestor?" When the father replied, after some embarrassing hesitation, "Well, son, *I'm* an ancestor," the boy asked, "Why do people brag about them?"

Anyhow—without bragging—the first ancestral Barkley I have been able to pin down was one Roger de Berchelai, one of the Norman followers of William the Conqueror, who invaded and conquered England in 1066. Roger de Berchelai's ancestors probably were Norsemen who had settled in France. Over the years the spelling of the family name has evolved through Berchleigh, Berkeleye, Berkley, Berkeley, Barclay, Barkley, and other variations.

The first of the family to come to America was John Berkelley, who settled in Virginia about 1618. We don't know much about him, except that he must have come over with a family, for he was reported to have been the father of ten children when he was killed by Indians in 1622.

Then there was a Sir William Berkeley—I am glad they did not know about that "Sir William" business when I first ran for office in Kentucky —who showed up as the Crown-appointed Governor of Virginia around

1642. Old Bill was a tyrant whose highhanded acts led to a couple of bloody uprisings; the less said about him the better. There were lots of other Berkeleys, Barkleys, etc., of nicer stripe who began immigrating and propagating, until branches of the family were settled all over the Eastern seaboard and Southern states.

I do not wish to belabor this ancestor theme, but I do want to tell a story on myself about it. Soon after I first went to Congress in 1913, I accompanied the Interstate and Foreign Commerce Committee on a fact-finding trip to Virginia shipping centers. We took a side excursion over to old Jamestown, site of the first permanent English settlement in the New World. I found an old graveyard and said to my colleagues, "I think I'll see if I can't find me an ancestor." They kidded me about it, but I had not gone twenty feet before I came across the grave of an ancient Berkeley. My old friend, Sam Rayburn, the Squire of Bonham, Fanning County, Texas, who came to Congress the same year I did and later served as Speaker of the House longer than any other man in history, was on that committee with me. He has always accused me of planting that ancestor there just to impress my colleagues.

My direct lineage is traced to Henry Barkley, a Scotch-Irish Presbyterian, who settled in Rowan County, North Carolina, in 1740. His son, Robert, who fought in the American Revolution, was the great-grandfather of my own grandfather, the first Alben.

Whence came the name "Alben" no one knows. It does not appear in the family records before Grandfather bore it. But here I am going to confess something which I have kept to myself all my life. I was not born Alben William Barkley. The name my parents bestowed on me at birth was Willie Alben Barkley—not even William, but "Willie"! They intended all along to call me Alben, after Grandfather, and did so, but the "Willie" was—from my viewpoint—a misbegotten gesture of recognition toward two uncles—one on my father's side, the other on my mother's—who were both called "Willie." They were not even rich uncles! Anyhow, I kept the "Willie" business as quiet as possible, and, as soon as I was old enough to assert myself, I firmly let it be known that my official name henceforth was Alben William Barkley and no foolishness! I have been known as such ever since.

All of which leads me to shake my head in sorrow over the crimes that otherwise well-intentioned and loving parents perpetrate on defenseless babies in the matter of Christian names! Just imagine the tribulations I would have had, a robust, active boy, going through a Kentucky childhood with the name of "Willie," and later trying to get into politics! Why,

I doubt that anyone called Willie Alben could have been elected assistant superintendent of the county poorhouse! In fact, I think one of the graver shortcomings of my long career as a lawmaker was my failure to introduce a bill making it mandatory for parents to postpone the naming of their children until the youngsters are old enough to pick out a name for themselves.

At any rate, all facetiousness aside, I was called Alben and not Willie. My mother lived to be almost ninety, and I never remember her once using the hated name. Father had a rather peculiar pronunciation of my name. He called me "Ah-ben," dropping the *l*. The nearest anyone else has ever come to that pronunciation was the Grotonesque broad-*A* twist put on it by Franklin Roosevelt.

The reason why I remember so well the pronunciation given my name by "Poppy"—in the manner of country children of that day we used to address our parents as "Mommy" and "Poppy"—is because it was my duty, as the oldest boy in the family, to get up in the winter mornings and start the fire in the fireplace. I can still hear Poppy's voice calling, "Ah-ben, Ah-ben, get up and make the fire!"

One thing about Poppy, though, he never was one of those up-with-the-rooster farmers. He worked hard and long but never thought it was necessary to begin stirring at 4 A.M.; he was content to wait until daylight at least, and was perfectly willing for us children to do the same. All my life I've never been a particularly early riser; in that respect I'm not in the least like former President Truman, who used to enjoy those 6 A.M. walks.

In fact, I have always said that the "best sleeping" is during that last luxurious hour in the morning, when you know you ought to be up and under way. Sleep is a great medicine, and I attribute a large part of my good health to the fact that I have always been able to relax and sleep anywhere—in a plane, in an automobile, in the old days even in a wagon jolting over country roads. Poppy, when he was provoked at me, used to vow that I could even sleep while riding Old Selum, our family horse, to the barn.

This ability to sleep anywhere has served me well, particularly during World War II years, when sometimes even the majority leader of the United States Senate was unable to get a hotel room. Once during this period I remember spending the night in a chair in the lobby of the Peabody Hotel in Memphis. I have also slept on benches in airports and railroad stations all over the country. Only twice has this talent for easy slumber betrayed me. Once was the time I dozed off at the wheel of my automobile while driving through West Virginia and woke up in the hospital with a damaged right knee and several broken ribs. The other experience went back to my young manhood when I was traveling from Emory College at Oxford, Georgia, to my home in Clinton, Kentucky, and had to change trains in Martin, Tennessee. I fell asleep on the unyielding bench in the depot, and when I woke up my valise was gone. It contained most of my worldly possessions at that time, including my spare collar and the souvenir gavel I had bought while visiting the scene of the "Battle Above the Clouds" on Lookout Mountain near Chattanooga.

I have no personal remembrance of my grandfather Barkley, as he died when I was less than three years old. Somewhere in the dim recesses of my memory I have a vague recollection of attending his funeral. It must have made a tremendous impression on me, for it seems to be the earliest event in my life which I can remember. I have a picture of Grandfather, though, and Grandmother often used to describe him to me. The picture, taken in his Sunday suit, shows him as a man of medium size, with long, heavy hair hanging over his ears and chin whiskers trimmed in the fashion of Lincoln, only longer.

He was a well-to-do farmer who owned his own place, and he was an elder in the Presbyterian church. I am told that he was a man of considerable humor. He also had a temper; though a small man, he once had to be physically restrained from taking out with his fists after a larger neighbor who made the mistake of remarking slightingly that "men from North Carolina have no hair on their chests."

He and my grandmother were married in Christian County, Kentucky, and, immediately after the ceremony and wedding feast, the new bride climbed up behind her husband on his horse and rode double with him to Gibson County, Tennessee, where they lived for some years and where my father and several others of their children were born. Later they moved to Graves County, Kentucky, my birthplace.

Grandmother was a remarkable person. Though living in an age when women were inclined to let the menfolk do most of the talking for the family, Grandmother was never bashful about expressing herself, particularly on politics and religion. She had ample background in both. Her great-grandfather was William Stevenson, the first ruling elder of the Fourth Creek Presbyterian Church in Iredell County, North Carolina, a man who could pray and sing so loudly that he became widely known as "Little Gabriel." Little Gabriel also was the great-grandfather of Adlai Ewing Stevenson, who became Vice President of the United States in

Grover Cleveland's administration and who was the grandfather of the Adlai of more recent fame.

It has been suggested that I inherited my speaking voice from Little Gabriel. Some commentators have implied that my tones are not exactly dulcet. In fact, before I delivered the keynote address at the 1936 Democratic convention in Philadelphia, some Eastern writer heralded me (in advance) as "the greatest hog-caller who ever came out of the Blue Grass State." He went on to say that, when I spoke, "nature pauses in a kind of stunned silence; little dickey birds fall out of the trees, and, as far away as California, the natives catch the rolling echoes of the matchless Barkley voice and hasten to the earthquake cellar."

I have always felt this reporter exaggerated somewhat; for one thing, in all modesty, I could name at least a dozen better hog callers than I in the state of Kentucky. It certainly is true, however, that my father, who, like Little Gabriel, was a Presbyterian elder, was known as the loudest "amener" in Graves County; also, both Father and my aunt Betty, his sister, were the heartiest laughers I have ever known, with the exception of Franklin Roosevelt, who could make the White House plaster reverberate.

Once, after F.D.R. had returned from one of his wartime trips abroad, we had one of our regular conferences—I was Senate majority leader then—in his bedroom. After our business was finished, I told him a story I had just heard about the fellow who came up to the preacher and said, "Reverend, that was a damn good sermon you preached this morning!"

The minister replied, "I appreciate your compliment, but not your language."

"Yes, sir," the fellow went on, "it was such a damn good sermon that I put $100 in the collection plate."

"The hell you did!" said the minister.

Roosevelt roared so lustily that he was heard all over the second floor of the White House. As I left, the Secret Service man standing at the head of the stairs—quite a distance from F.D.R.'s bedroom—remarked, "That must have been a good one you told the Boss!"

Most of my early boyhood memories go back to Lowes, a crossroads community settled in 1837 by Levi Lowe and his wife, Mourning Ann Cook Lowe. They were emigrating westward from Virginia, and on the way their second son was born. They stopped at Lowes because they found a good spring there—in all the 117 years of Lowes's history the spring has never been known to run dry—and the town has been there ever since.

In its early days Lowes had a flavor all its own. There was not much doing in the way of amusement, so the people used to have fairs on an old fairground located three miles northeast of town on what is now known as the Kansas neighborhood. One of the primitive "amusements" of which I have heard—this was long before my time—was the custom known as "goose-pulling." Two long poles were set into the ground, and a goose with a greased neck was strung between them. The men of the community would mount their horses and ride at full speed toward the goose, attempting as they passed under it to pull off its head. The goose, for as long as it survived, loudly and understandably made known its objections to the whole procedure. A prize was awarded to the man who finally pulled off the goose's head: the goose, now long beyond caring, was usually the prize. This rather barbarous custom, however, was entirely out of character in Lowes, which was a community of hard-working, churchgoing people, and it has been long since outlawed, along with the betting on horse races and other forms of wagering which used to take place at the old fairground. The fairground has gone too.

There is also a story—or maybe a legend—which old-timers at Lowes still recount about a certain citizen who is supposedly buried in a round grave, six feet deep and lined with bricks. The tombstone on the grave of this gentleman, who died in 1860, bears the epitaph, "MEET THE DEVIL." The story goes that the party in question was a two-fisted drinker and general rounder, and, before his death, he expressed the wish that he be buried standing up, with a hatchet in one hand and a bottle of whiskey in the other, ready to be either belligerent or sociable, whichever the circumstances called for, when he met up with the satanic party who he was sure was going to greet him.

But Lowes today is quite a different place. Four generations after Levi and Mourning Ann Lowe stopped and remained there because of the pleasant and copious spring their descendants still run the general store at the crossroads, which is a remarkable example of unbroken family mercantile ownership. I remember the old sign, "Dry Goods and Notions"—as a boy, I used to wonder what those "notions" were and what would happen if I walked in and said, "Gimme a penny's worth of notions!" To this day Lowe's store is the community's principal business establishment, and one can still go there and buy anything from a licorice stick or a twist of chewing tobacco to a bolt of gingham or a box of shotgun shells. Or one can simply enjoy some good conversation with the neighbors around the potbellied stove, as I do every time I drive through Lowes.

To me, however, Lowe's store is memorable as my boyhood source of what we used to call "crawly sugar." "Crawly sugar" was thick brown sugar, and we called it that, not because it was infested with any form of animal life, but because, when you placed a cup of it in a plate, it would seem to move and shift around as if it were alive. This "crawly sugar" came in huge hogsheads, big enough for a large boy to get into. Mr. Lowe knew the weakness of us youngsters for sweets, and he also knew that we country boys got precious little of such treats. So when a hogshead had been emptied and rolled out behind his store, he would let us climb into it and scoop out with our Barlow knives whatever crumbs of sugar we could find between the cracks. It was a great treat when Old Man Lowe would roll out the sugar barrel.

In my boyhood one of Levi's grandsons ran the old livery stable in Lowes. On the first Monday of August 1891, the day the people of Kentucky voted on ratifying a new state constitution, he paid me the first quarter I ever earned for tending horses all day while the people who had ridden in from the country were voting. That shiny quarter bedazzled my youthful eyes and for a while I thought I was a Croesus, but, alas, a fool and his money are soon parted! I fell under the spell of a siren song chanted by some lady of the town in front of a homemade stand where the first pink lemonade I had ever seen was being sold for a nickel a glass. *"Come and get your red lemonade; Made in the shade, and stirred with a spade; the best lemonade that ever was made!"* she sang, and before night fell I had squandered twenty cents on the enticing brew. The formula for this delectation, I do believe, actually called for dragging one real lemon through the tub—but it was cold.

My last nickel went that day for the privilege of listening through a sort of trumpet or earphone device while squeaky music emanated from a mysterious black cylinder revolving on some new contraption invented by an Eastern fellow named Edison.

Getting back to Grandma Barkley, I recall another of her cousins and childhood playmates, James A. McKenzie, onetime member of Congress from Kentucky and later United States Minister to Peru. Cousin Jim secured the removal of the tariff from the Peruvian bark from which quinine was made and was known forever after as "Quinine Jim." "Quinine Jim" was quite a figure—a tall, handsome man with a set of gray chin whiskers and a voice like the *vox humana* stop on a church organ. As a boy, I remember hearing him speak once at a political gathering.

I am a Candidate for
COUNTY ATTORNEY
Of McCracken County

Would be Grateful for Your Vote
and Influence

SUBJECT TO THE DEMOCRATIC PRI-
MARY, MARCH 30, 1905.

Respectfully yours

Alben W. Barkley

The beginning of a long career of public service. Candidate Barkley pictured on his campaign card when he ran for county attorney in 1905.

Seven years later the young Kentucky lawyer moved into national politics. He won and took his seat in Congress in the same year Woodrow Wilson became President.

ALBEN W. BARKLEY

Of McCracken County, Democratic
Candidate for Representative in

CONGRESS

From First District of Kentucky

Primary Election Aug. 3, '12

YOUR VOTE AND INFLUENCE
WILL BE APPRECIATED

Democratic Speaking!

CONGRESSMAN

Alben W. Barkley

Will Speak in the Interest of the State
Democratic Ticket at the

COURT HOUSE

Monday, Nov. 5, 1923

At Two o'Clock

COME OUT AND HEAR HIM

Ladies are especially invited to hear him discuss the issues of
Kentucky's Gubernatorial Campaign.

Alben Barkley was a dependable and effective speaker for the Democratic party from his earliest political days. A 1923 handbill announces his support of the party's candidate for governor.

Freshman Congressman Barkley leaving the White House in 1913 after seeing President Wilson.

After fourteen years in the House of Representatives, in 1926 Alben Barkley was elected to the Senate. He is seated in his new office in the Senate Office Building.

Statesman and party workhorse:
Senator Barkley campaigns for himself and Franklin Roosevelt in 1932.

When Barkley became Senate
majority leader, Vice President
Garner, who presided over the
Senate, said, "You and I are a team
—you're the pitcher and I'm the
catcher." They always remained
warm personal friends.

President Roosevelt always enjoyed
a story or a quip from Senator Barkley. Here they are together at the
Jackson Day Dinner in Washington,
1938.

Wide World

Senators Kenneth McKel
Alben Barkley, and J. Hamil
Lewis as they listened to deb
over confirmation of Ha
Hopkins as Secretary of Co
merce in 1939.

Senator and Mrs. Bark
chatting with Secretary of A
culture Henry Wallace in C
cago just prior to the 19
Democratic Convention,
which Wallace became 1
presidential nominee.

Wide World

Acme

Barkley, talking with Roosevelt in December 1943, after the President's return from the Teheran Conference.

Roosevelt, Speaker Rayburn, and Senate Majority Leader Barkley on the way to the 1945 inaugural.

Harris and Ewing

President Truman greeting Senator Barkley's mother at Barkley Field in 1945.

The one and only Barkley mustache. The senator arrived back in Washington early in 1947, after a brief holiday, with a new adornment, but it disappeared shortly afterward.

Acme

The Democratic Convention in Philadelphia, 1948, nominated Barkley the running mate of his old friend and senatorial colleague, Harry Truman.

The winning smile was still there as the Vice President-elect chuckled over a newspaper headline on November 3, 1948.

Although seeking no office himself, the seventy-two-year-old Veep again turned out for the party in 1950. He barnstormed seventeen states in a chartered plane, made forty-two speeches. Here he is shown after an overnight hop, sitting on his berth in the plane, studying the day's work ahead of him.

Life Photograph by Lisa Larson © TIME INC.

The top Democrats in Washington in 1951—President Truman with Senate Majority Leader McFarland, House Majority Leader McCormack, Speaker Rayburn, and the Veep.

At a political rally at the Barkley home in Paducah, September 1952, presidential nominee "Cousin Adlai" was photographed as he ate fried chicken with the Veep.

Jack Anderson

There had been a little dissension in the neighborhood at that time, and there was some talk, which the local Republicans were eagerly encouraging, about a possible split in the Democratic party. Cousin Jim got a big hand right off the bat when he opened his speech with the sonorous and heartening declaration, "My friends and fellow Kentuckians—any man who is too good to be a Democrat ought to die and go to heaven!"

With such a background Grandmother never let me forget that I had politics in my blood. She used to talk to me for hours about my politically prominent kinfolk and tell me that if I tried hard I someday might amount to something myself, politically speaking. I can still hear her as she used to say, "Alben, when I was a girl I used to play barefoot in the creek with Cousin Adlai, the Vice President, and Cousin Jim, who's gone to Congress. We used to squish the mud up through our bare toes. . . ." To this day I'm not sure what the mud had to do with the story, unless it was some form of subconscious warning on the hazards of political life.

In any event, that link through my grandmother's family makes me a distant cousin of the 1952 Democratic nominee for President, whom I later came to know quite well, as I will relate in a further chapter. I first met Adlai Stevenson in Washington when he was a fairly obscure young assistant to the late Secretary of the Navy Frank Knox. We were at some function together and when I saw him in the crowd I spotted him instantly as a Stevenson because of a rather peculiar physical characteristic. All Stevensons seem to have a distinctive way of walking—it is a sort of loping canter. When I saw him that night I said to myself, "There goes a man who walks just like Cousin 'Bub' Stevenson down home."

Sure enough, it was Cousin Adlai, whom up to that time I had never met.

CHAPTER 3

Growing Up in the Country

WHILE I am proud, of course, of being a Southerner, I have always taken equal pride in the fact that I have no geographical prejudices. I may beam and lift my more or less mellifluous baritone in song when I hear the strains of "My Old Kentucky Home," but my heart beats fast when "America the Beautiful" is played. This, of course, is the way it should be in this wonderful country of ours.

I have always regarded myself as fortunate in being brought up in a part of Kentucky where no sectional or racial animosities were bred into me. This freedom from prejudices was rather remarkable, since Graves County is in the so-called "Jackson's Purchase" portion of the state, which had strong Southern sympathies during the Civil War.

At any rate, for years after the Civil War, a candidate for political office in our part of Kentucky who had not had at least one limb shot off while fighting for the Confederacy might as well have whistled down a rain barrel. There's the classic story of the hapless candidate for coroner of Graves County who was attending a speaking at Pilot Oak. That is the community which gave McKinley (Rep.) only 4 votes out of 496 when he ran for President in 1896 against Bryan (Dem.). This particular candidate was being opposed by three visibly maimed Confederate veterans. The first one, wearing his gray uniform coat, stood up and proudly called attention to the empty sleeve denoting the arm he had lost in the battle of Cynthiana. The next had lost a leg at Chickamauga; the third, an eye at Perryville.

When the final candidate, hopelessly outclassed, got up to make his appeal, he took the only course. "I never got wounded; I never even fit in the war," he said. "But, if physical disability is to be regarded as an indispensable qualification for the office of coroner, I hereby announce, unqualifiedly and unequivocally, that I am the most completely ruptured son-of-a-gun who ever ran for public office!"

I also remember a Civil War story that I used to hear Irvin S. Cobb tell when he was a newspaper reporter and I was a struggling lawyer in Paducah. It seemed that two Confederate veterans were reminiscing about the days during the war when Paducah was being fought over by the Northern and Southern forces. "I remember," one veteran said, "when we pushed those damyankees all the way across the Ohio and up into Illinois!" The other old soldier regretfully corrected him. "I was there, old friend," he said, "and I'm afraid that wasn't the way it happened at all. Those Yankees drove *us* out of Paducah and almost to the Tennessee line." The first veteran reflected a bit, then sourly remarked, "Another good story ruined by an eyewitness!"

At any rate, I never acquired any of the prejudices sometimes associated with certain sections of the South. I am proud to say that my record in both the House and Senate has been that of a progressive liberal. Some of my worst political battles have occurred because of my championship of civil-rights legislation and my unalterable opposition to poll taxes as a qualification to voting, to filibustering, and other trappings of political negation.

When I was a boy in Kentucky, I would go out and work on the farms of neighboring farmers. Sometimes I would work in the wheat fields as a thresher; then I would labor with shovel, spade, and ax, digging stumps out of the fields so that crops could be planted. Often Negro men and boys would be hired also and would work beside me. In that way I learned that you do not judge a man's character by the color of his skin.

As a matter of fact, I was nine years old before I ever saw a colored person. He was a young fellow named Silas, who showed up at our house one day and told us his folks had worked for Grandfather Barkley when my grandfather had lived in Tennessee. Silas brought his banjo, on which he was expert, and played for us. From then on he came frequently and became a favorite with all of us.

One of the finest, hardest-working men I have ever known was a Negro farmer named Matt Vincent, who lived up the road from us after our family moved to Clinton. Often I worked with Matt at stump-digging, and during the lunch hour we would sit together in the stump hole that we had dug, he eating the lunch which his wife had prepared for him and I eating the sandwiches which my mother had fixed me. He would tell me of his daughters, in whom he took great pride, and of how he intended to give them the best education possible for them to obtain. He did so, and they grew up to become outstanding schoolteachers in the community. As Matt Vincent and I sat there, eating together and talking, there was no question of social equality; it was simply a matter of two persons, one white and one black, getting acquainted and developing a mutual respect for each other.

In the wheat fields I worked with other Negro men, and I learned from them the words and tunes of folk songs which I doubt that you will find written down anywhere. They would make up these songs as they worked, chanting them to monotonous, mournful tunes, and it would provide a rhythm which set a steady pace for the swinging of the scythes which sheared the stalks of wheat. Some of these stanzas have remained in my memory for more than sixty years. One, in particular, began:

See dat dummy, comin' down de line,
(In de evenin'!)
See dat dummy, comin' down de line,
(In de mornin'!)
See dat dummy, comin' down de line,
He had to run sideways to keep from flyin'!
(Mah Baby!)

The pattern was repeated with infinite variations:

Striped-legged britches an' a pigeon-tail coat, Got hair on his chest lak' a damn billy-goat; Catching rabbits ain't no sin, Open yore mouth and shove 'em in; See dat jaybird a-sittin' on de limb, He winked at me an' I winked at him; When I die, won't yuh bury me deep? An' tell all mah wimmen I'se gone to sleep . . .

and, finally, always sung with great feeling, the concluding stanza:

See dese DIA-MONDS on mah breast,
(In de evenin'!)
See dese DIA-MONDS on mah breast,
(In de mornin'!)
See dese DIA-MONDS on mah breast,
An' tell all mah wimmen I'se gone to rest!
(Mah Baby!)

Some of the most wonderful folk tales I have ever heard—stories which I have repeated over the years—were learned from the Negroes with whom I worked. One, in particular, that was told me in my boyhood by an old Negro man concerns a house that was supposed to be haunted. It had not been lived in for years, and the owners, anxious to sell it, decided to hire an old Negro to spend the night in it, in order to disprove the troublesome legend for the benefit of would-be purchasers.

The old man built himself a fire on the second floor, and, with his Bible in his lap, settled down in front of it for the night. Around eleven o'clock the door creaked and opened. He looked over his shoulder. There was no one there. He began reading his Bible with great fervor.

Then he heard footsteps and a little dog walked in the room, walked right up to the fire, licked out his tongue, took a few hot coals in his mouth, and chewed them up. Then the dog turned to the old man and said, "Is Henry here yet?" The old man said not a word; he just read that Bible harder than ever.

In a little while the door opened again, and in came another dog, a larger one. It went to the fire, swallowed a whole mouthful of coals, and, in a louder voice, asked, "Is Henry here yet?" The old man, shaking like he had been dipped in the pond in December, still said nothing. The only sound was the chattering of his teeth as he steadily applied himself to the Scripture.

Then another dog came in, and another and another, each a little larger than the one before. Each one refreshed himself at the fireplace, and each one asked the question, "Is Henry here yet?"

Finally, an enormous dog, about the size of a small lion, stalked in, sauntered up to the fire, licked out a whole burning log, chewed it up and swallowed it, and, in a terrible, deep voice, demanded of the old man, "Is Henry here yet?"

This was more than the old man could stand. He grabbed up his Bible and headed for the door. As he left, he shouted back over his shoulder, "No, Henry ain't here yet—but if he comes here, you tell him I've been here, but I'm gone!"

I was about fourteen years old when I began working in the wheat fields. Father and I would go out together at a season when the work on our own farm could be left to my younger brothers. We did it to augment the family's meager income, for we would be paid a dollar a day each for our labor, plus two dollars for the use of our team and wagon. We would stay away from home a week at a time, sleeping either under our wagon, in the farmer's hay loft, or in the new-made straw pile. At an even earlier age I began using an ax and handling my end of a crosscut saw with my father. He was a great woodsman and believed in clearing his fields and hills of trees and stumps. I suppose in my time I have split as many rails

as Abraham Lincoln, though I have received less credit for it—and, of
course, was never elected to the White House with rail-splitting as a
slogan.

Many years later both the wheat-threshing and the woodcutting experiences served me well when I made a trip to Soviet Russia in 1930.
Our party had obtained a couple of American Model-T Fords, driven
by Russian chauffeurs, and we were touring in the interior to inspect
collective farms and rural villages. At one place I saw Russian farmers
threshing wheat by methods as primitive as those which I had practiced
in the fields of Kentucky forty years earlier. I could not resist it, so I
got out of the car, took off my coat, and joined them for a few minutes,
taking a hand at the threshing.

At another place I saw workers sawing logs by an extremely peculiar
method: the log was placed horizontally on a high platform, and two
men—one standing on the platform, the other on the ground—would saw
it vertically from one end to the other. I had never before seen logs cut
in this manner, and again I took off my coat and took a hand in the
sawing operation.

In both instances none of the Russians spoke any English and I, of
course, knew no Russian. But they gathered that I was a visiting American
and I seemed friendly, so they showed by broad grins and approving
sounds that they enjoyed and appreciated the gesture. It gave me hope
for a while that, through exercise of good will, an understanding might
be reached with the Russian people. In this hope, of course, I was wrong,
for events have shown all too tragically that understanding may never be
reached until the Russian people shake off the yoke of their dictatorship.

As a further digression, this discursion concerning Soviet Russia makes
me remember the illuminating conversation I had that same year with
Lloyd George, who had been Prime Minister of England in World War
I and was still a member of the House of Commons. I had stopped off
in London on my way to Russia, and I called on him, whom I had met
when I visited England during the First World War. At this time the
United States had not yet granted diplomatic recognition to Russia, but
Britain had done so soon after the Bolshevik Revolution, which over-
threw the rule of the Czar. "Why," I asked of Lloyd George, "did you
recognize Russia so promptly?"

He answered, "We looked upon Russia as a sick man flat on his back,
and we thought it was better to extend the hand of friendship then,
rather than wait until he got well and strong."

I asked further, "Does this mean that you approve of everything that has gone on and is going on in Russia?"

"By no means," Lloyd George replied; and he added, "You may recall that our famous Lord Nelson was blind in one eye. Well, whenever he wanted to look at something that he did not want to see, he always put his telescope to his blind eye."

That was an apt illustration, but I think that, in view of subsequent history, it would have been much wiser to put the telescope to the good eye.

For most of my early life in Kentucky our family lived on small farms which my father, John Wilson Barkley, rented. One year Father was renting fifty acres or so on the Martha Sellars place. He was able to employ a hired hand that season—he was a man named Boyd Watson, and Father paid him fifty cents a day and board—and with this extra help he brought in a record tobacco crop that yielded $600 cash. With this money he was able to graduate from the tenant-farmer class by making a down payment on fifty acres of his own, part of a tract near Lowes known as the Coleman place. That purchase of his own farm was one of Father's proudest achievements.

My father was a strong, hard-working man, much like Grandfather Alben in both habits and appearance. He was a farmer most of his life, and, like his father, an elder in the Presbyterian church. He was married at the age of twenty-two to seventeen-year-old Electra Eliza Smith, daughter of a Confederate soldier who died of injuries received with Morgan's cavalry.

Father never had it easy during any of the years on the various farms which he worked. Thinking back on how he toiled, I am reminded of the story of the Negro preacher who called on a hard-working parishioner, a farmer, each year, soliciting increasingly larger contributions for the church. One year, when he got the proposed levy past a point which the farmer thought he could bear, the preacher sought to persuade him by arguing, "Your farm's been good to you, and the Lord's been good to you. Part of this land belongs to the Lord. You're in partnership with Him, so you ought to give Him His share." To which the farmer replied, "I acknowledges that the farm is paying off, that the Lord's been good to me, and that He is my partner. But did you ever see this place when the Lord was looking after it Hisself?"

I think my father would have enjoyed this story, though both he and my mother were highly religious people and they gave us a strict, old-fashioned upbringing. There was lots of fun, but little of what might be called frivolity in our home. I never saw a pack of cards, for instance, in Father's house, and to this day I have never taken up any card games—a circumstance which in later life used to cause such good friends as Vice President "Cactus Jack" Garner to growl at me occasionally.

Father would not work on Sundays unless there was some dire emergency. Stove wood had to be split on the previous day. The only breach of this rule that I remember occurred one Sunday when our tobacco crop, which represented a whole season of work and income, was threatened by a sudden freezing spell. Father, after wrestling with his conscience, asked the neighbors to help him save the crop. If we had lost it, of course, all of us would have gone hungry all winter.

On Sundays my mother would not even touch the cookstove, unless the preacher happened to be coming for dinner; in that case, we figured, as the old country saying goes, that "the ox was in the ditch."

My mother was a fabulous cook. I still get lyrical at memories of her egg custard pie. It was a special sort of egg custard pie, with a delicate and fragrant seasoning; it was not fluffy and airy and void of substance, in the manner aspired to by some of these modern, calory-conscious cooks, but it was a substantial, solid creation that stuck to your ribs and gave strength to the body as well as delight to the gustatory senses. Mommy was equally good on cakes and preserves and many other dishes. In fact, I never think of the table she set without remembering the story I once heard Father tell when I accompanied him on a wagon trip to the store to lay in a winter's supply of goods for the family. Despite Father's devoutness he had a sense of humor and was a good teller of stories, many of which I still remember and use.

As Father told it, it seems that a countrywoman of the same school as my mother had invited the preacher over for an old-fashioned Sunday dinner, not knowing he had what we used to call dyspepsia. The ten-year-old boy of the house—I was about that age myself when I heard Father tell the story—incredulously watched the minister decline helpings of soups, ham, hominy grits, fried chicken, roast goose, sausage, vegetables, biscuits, homemade bread, preserves, cake, and pies. Finally the boy spoke up and said, "Maw, you reckon the old fool would suck a raw egg?"

In such a household as ours the only "likker" permitted past the threshold was a small bottle of corn which had been rendered completely unpalatable, even poisonous, by the liberal addition of camphor balls. This was for external use only: to be rubbed on the chest when "the croup set in."

If there is anything to the old belief that a dram of whiskey is good for snakebite, the lack of it in our ménage almost cost the nation its future Vice President, for at the age of six I was bitten by a copperhead and almost died. We were living at the time in a log cabin; I remember it well, for it was the most primitive cabin we ever lived in—a crude affair with a stick-and-dirt chimney; it was a wonder the place did not burn down every time we lit a fire. Our chickens roosted under the floor of the cabin, and they were being bothered by rats. I was told to crawl under there and chase out the chickens so they would roost in the trees. When I did so, a copperhead, which, of course, we had not known was also lurking under the floor, got me. I did not know exactly what had happened, but, in a short time, I began feeling queer. I opened my mouth to yell for Poppy, but my tongue fell out and hung there like that of a snake, and I lost consciousness.

Luckily "Uncle Jimmy" Breckinridge, who owned the big farm on which my father then rented a tract, lived nearby, and, though a church-going man himself, he happened to be more "liberal" in some respects than my father. Uncle Jimmy just happened to have a pint of whiskey laid by, and Father, putting down his scruples in the face of an emergency, borrowed it, poured most of it down my throat, and I came back to life. That was my first—and last—snakebite. It also was my first, and for many years my last, drink of whiskey. Despite the popular conception of Old Kentucky as a state populated entirely by julep-drinking colonels, with a distillery in every county, there actually is a great deal of dry sentiment in the state, and a large number of counties still exercise local option against the sale of spirits. I was a teetotaler during most of my life. While I now occasionally enjoy participation in a mild sociable potion, I have never liked either the taste or the effect of strong alcoholic beverages.

On the subject of prohibition, I might sum up my record at this point. During World War I, I not only supported the national prohibition amendment, but, in one of the earlier phases, when the House was having difficulty in drafting acceptable legislation that would deny use of grains for alcoholic beverages in order to conserve food for war purposes, it was I, then a freshman congressman, who finally worded a rider to the bill in such fashion that it passed the House. I also joined Senator Morris Shepherd of Texas in sponsoring legislation making the District of Columbia dry, and I not only voted dry but stayed dry all during the prohibition era.

Years later, feeling that the prohibition law had not been a successful experiment and that the American people wanted a change, I supported the plank in the 1932 Democratic platform which called for the submission of an amendment repealing the Eighteenth Amendment. "A wise man may change his mind, a fool never does," I said at the time. I have always felt that the people have a right to modify or nullify actions previously taken in amending their Constitution.

Prior to the 1932 Democratic convention, incidentally, my views on prohibition caused a flurry that is amusing in retrospect. I had been selected to serve as keynoter for the first time at this convention which nominated Franklin D. Roosevelt for his first presidential race. Some of the delegates were fearful that I was an incurable dry. A Louisville lady associated with the Women's Organization for National Prohibition Reform, came to my defense with these words: "Of old, he was so dry that he fairly crackled. Now, to us, to read between the lines, he seems safely moist, courageously standing for Governor Roosevelt." Whether this description was appropriate is now immaterial. I felt that the democratic process required that the people be again allowed to pass upon this important question.

I never think of this lady's summation of my position without being reminded of the story of the old Negro well digger who worked for a devout Methodist lady. One day he collapsed while digging, and she revived him with a few drops of medicinal spirits, which might as well have been administered with an eye dropper. When he came to, he remarked, "You know, Miz Cole is a fine lady. But she so afraid she might do wrong, she afraid to do what's right!"

I might digress further to observe that, for a Kentucky congressman, I started off my career with a certain number of what might be considered political liabilities. First, some persons might consider my advocacy of prohibition rather odd for a congressman coming from the state which produces the finest bourbon whiskey in the world. While this is true, it is also true that prior to the Eighteenth Amendment a large majority of the counties of Kentucky had voted against the sale of liquor under what was known as the county unit plan. Since repeal of the Eighteenth Amendment a substantial majority of Kentucky counties have voted under local option to outlaw liquor. My stand on the question, first in voting for the submission of the Eighteenth Amendment, and later for an amendment to appeal it, was a matter of principle and not of expediency.

Second, as I will relate in a later chapter, I once strenuously opposed legalized betting at the race tracks—possibly an atypical trait for a man representing the proud mother state of the Kentucky Derby.

Third, I even gave up, some twenty-five years ago, the use of tobacco, another product in which Kentucky takes pride. I did smoke for many years, beginning, naturally enough, with a corncob pipe, graduating through a French brier pipe and into a meerschaum, and finally taking up cigars. I stopped smoking while a member of the House because I was extremely thin at the time and I wanted to gain weight. I had noticed one day that the son of Speaker Champ Clark, Bennett Clark (later a senator and now a member of the United States Court of Appeals in the District of Columbia), who was then serving as parliamentarian of the House, was putting on some weight. I asked him how he managed it, to which he replied, "I have quit smoking and drinking coffee." "Well," said I, "I think I will try half of it—the smoking." This I did. I have never smoked since. Eventually I added a considerable number of pounds to my weight, as a glance at my generous waistline before I reduced it to some extent, would have revealed.

Getting back to my early days, I had the rugged life of a country boy. In addition to the work I have already described I used to help Father with the plowing. As a matter of fact, I rather enjoyed that experience. There is a sort of thrill that comes to a barefoot boy when he plows up the ground, turns it over, and steps into the fresh furrow with his bare feet. There is a good feel and a good smell to the earth. I like to remember the way the birds—all sorts of birds, blackbirds, robins, and bluejays— and the chickens would follow along behind me and pick up the worms as I turned over the dirt with the plow. Our old mule, Nell, was smart, too: when she heard the dinner bell, no matter where we were, Nell would stop her plowing, turn around, and head straight for the barn, where she knew her oats would be waiting.

I also used to work in the tobacco fields with Father, and I liked that less. I can still feel the itchy stickiness of the gum from the tobacco leaves. It pervaded your hands, face, nostrils, eyebrows, ears, and hair. You had to scour it off with ash-and-lye soap. Making that soap was Mother's department: she saved fat drippings and pork scraps from the kitchen and kept an ash hopper out in the yard. That was just one of the many things that she and many other sturdy women of the country did: she also made most of our clothes, and kept geese—and plucked them—to make our feather beds and pillows. A feather bed, of course, was considered the only thing fit to sleep on; my mother would not have had a regular mattress in the house as a gift. As long as I live, I shall never forget the soft, sinking sensation of first settling down on a feather bed. Of course, it was a little hot in the summertime.

This constant tobacco-gum stickiness and the abrasive effects of the lye and ashes must have had considerable effect, not only on my hide, but upon my youthful subconsciousness. I remember the first cake of store-bought soap I ever used. I bought it myself about the time I began noticing the girls: it made me smell a little fancier than Mamma's home-made soap. I used to hide it from my brothers and sisters, and by careful hoarding I could make one cake last me about a year.

I also remember when Father took me into Mayfield to buy my first suit of clothes with long pants. I observed with awe how clean the clerks looked—they dressed better on weekdays than we did on Sundays—and I determined then and there to become a store clerk. Some years later I did clerk briefly in Mr. Jim Rudy's shoe store in Paducah, but I was not a conspicuous success. One day a man with the biggest feet I had ever seen came into the store. As we used to say in the country, he had "about a foot-and-a-half of his leg turned under." He said to me, "I'd like to see a pair of shoes that would fit me." I answered, "So would I." Shortly after Mr. Rudy and I agreed that my future lay elsewhere.

I was twelve years old, by the way, when I got that first long-pants suit. Children get long pants much younger now. I remember it so well, not only because of my being impressed with the neat appearance of the clerks at Mayfield, but because the storekeeper, in recognition of the fact that Father was purchasing a whole suit for me, threw in a pair of red suspenders, a more liberal gift than the stick of peppermint candy which usually accompanied the purchase of a pair of overalls or boots.

Up to that time I had always worn—for dress-up occasions—knee pants and long stockings. The stockings were knitted for me—and for all the other children and Father too—by Mother. She not only carded her own wool and knitted the stockings, but she dyed them as well. They were colored brown from a dye which Momsy made from the juice of sumac berries, which I would be sent into the woods to gather.

I suppose the only garment Mommy ever made for me which I did not appreciate was a certain overcoat. It was of a nice gray herringbone material, but she lined it with yellow Canton flannel, and the boys at school teased me unmercifully about it. They would call me "yellow-hammer," after a bird we have down in Kentucky, a sort of gray bird with yellow feathers under its wings. I tried to fight them, then to bribe them with apples, to make them stop their teasing. But there were too many for me to lick, and the bribery, I learned, did not help—a valuable lesson for me, incidentally. At any rate, the trouble I had with it made me despise that coat.

In addition to helping Father with these man-sized chores which I have detailed, I also put in many an hour assisting my mother in taking care of the younger children and helping out with the housework. Even if we could have afforded it, there were no maids in the country in those days. Not only did I rock the younger children to sleep and change their diapers, but I spun yarn, washed dishes and clothes, and even ironed the flatwork. I got to be rather expert at ironing, and even today, if I do not have time to take a wrinkled suit to the tailor before keeping an engagement, I get down the ironing board and iron and do a pretty fair job of pressing. Of course in Mom's kitchen we used a couple of cast-iron flatirons that we heated on top of the wood stove, and the kitchen table served as the ironing board.

Another custom of those days was the system of calling out all the able-bodied male citizens of the community once a year to work on the roads. It was a community enterprise, and no one got paid. A road overseer was appointed for the different districts, and it was his job to see that the men turned out with their own plows, hoes, scrapers, teams, or whatever they could bring, and patch up the dirt roads, which were all we had to serve us.

I began going out with my father on these road-working expeditions as soon as I was old enough to wield the implements. It was a wonderful experience, a sort of a jubilee, or get-together, for the men. Money or station in life meant nothing, as everyone, rich or poor, turned out. The men would fill in the deep holes and wagon ruts with straw, brush, or sod, then scrape over the surface and cover it with fresh dirt. After working a while the men would stop to eat and rest, and they would start swapping stories. I would sit quietly and listen, soaking up the yarns I heard the men tell. It was on occasions such as these, and also at barbecues and political gatherings, that I heard many of the old Kentucky stories which I still use when I address a gathering. A good story is like a fine Kentucky bourbon; it improves with age and, if you don't use it too much, it will never hurt anyone.

I also used to get a chance to absorb stories from my father when I would accompany him on a wagon trip into Paducah or Mayfield. About twice a year we would take our crops into town for sale, and come back with a load of goods that would last us through the winter or summer season. These trips were made in the two-horse wagon, which was our all-purpose vehicle: in it we did our hauling, rode to church, and did what little visiting was in order. Whenever we went into town, if it was too late to return home we would spend the night at a wagon yard, which was an old-fashioned institution, somewhat on the order of a livery stable but with crude rooms where the farmers and teamsters could put up overnight. Father would sit up with the other men, chewing tobacco—his only "vice"—and spinning yarns, and I would be allowed to listen, so long as I stayed in the background and kept quiet.

I tried Father's chewing tobacco once—only once—by the way. It was a brand called "Peach Pie." He would keep huge plugs of it in a bureau drawer, and it was all doctored up with liquids and sweetening that gave it a delicious odor. One time my brother, Clarence, and I—Clarence died of typhoid at the age of twenty—sneaked a plug of Pop's tobacco and took it out behind the smokehouse to try it. It made me sick as a horse, and, after I crawled back into the house, I made a resolution never to try it again. This resolution I have religiously observed.

A growing boy in Kentucky had to know how to use his fists. I had my share of fights. One that I remember with particular satisfaction involved the community bully, a fellow named Tom Hurd. I was walking home from school when Tom, who was fetching a horse collar from the livery stable, caught me and began taunting and cuffing me. I endured it until he threw the horse collar over my neck, poked me in the rear, and yelled, "Giddap!" I remember turning on him and yelling, "Nobody's gonna treat me like a durned mule!" I fought him in the road and in my father's tobacco field. We tore down at least a quarter of an acre of tobacco, but in my righteous anger I finally was able to make him yell, "Uncle!" That was the last bullying he did around Lowes.

There were other altercations which did not turn out so well. Once Father sent me riding on Old Selum to get a sack of corn ground at Harlan's Mill, which was in the creek bottom on Wilson's Creek below the community of Lowes. There was a gang of Harlan's Mill boys, four or five of them, and they made a practice of jumping us Lowes boys, especially when they could get one of us at a time. They caught me this day as I approached the mill with a sack of corn, and told me to get off my horse as they wanted to have words with me. This was an understatement. "Well," I said with resignation, for I knew I was in for it, "let me hitch my horse." I managed to bloody a couple of noses, but the odds were too much for me and, after battering me up to their satisfaction, they started to throw me in the creek. At this point the miller, Arthur Lowe, came up and intervened, and I was very grateful to him, for at this time I had not yet learned to swim.

When I got home, Father took one look at my face, which was a mess and demanded, "What in the world happened to you?" I knew I was in for it again, for he had promised to larrup me good if I got into any fights. I had had enough punishment for that day, so I told a story—one of the few untruths I ever told my parents, by the way. "Well," I said, "as I was passing Old Man Rust's farm, he was plowing up an old fence row. Just as I rode past, his plow hit a bumblebee's nest, and they swarmed over and lit on my face." I do not think Father fully believed that story, but he accepted it, and I received no punishment.

I must have been a pretty fair physical specimen, for in later years, after I had entered public life, various of my boyhood friends gave out newspaper interviews testifying to my athletic prowess. One old schoolmate, Charles Howell, for instance, is on record as saying, "Alben could really jump! Why, when my brother, Elza, and I thought we were doing well at six feet, here'd come Alben and jump eight feet or ten feet. And wrestle! Fast as my brother and I would get up, Alben'd throw us down again."

I remember one near-altercation that had something of a moral to it. This one occurred after I had moved to Clinton. I was playing football with a schoolmate named Dick Hayes, who was one of my best friends. He was also a powerful athlete who probably could have licked the tar out of me.

The kind of football we played in those days was rather peculiar. We had no uniforms, of course, and under the rules anything was allowed—kicking the ball down the field, grabbing each other in any fashion, tripping, and so forth. Anyway, in the scrimmage, Dick grabbed me by the pocket of my good jacket, which I had no business wearing at play, and tore it right off. It made me so mad that I lit into him and called him every vile name a country boy could lay his tongue to. Dick, who really was afraid of nothing, looked at me and said very quietly:

"Do you mean what you're saying?"

I answered, "I certainly do!"

"Well," he said, "you know I don't take any foolishness from anybody, but, as long as you mean it, it's all right!"

While I still ponder sometimes on the subtle logic of Dick's reasoning, I do know that it avoided what would have been a terrible fight, and we remained friends.

Perhaps, in what we two youngsters did that day, there lies a lesson for nations: If a nation really means something, let it stand up and say so; the sniping and the double talk are what frequently bring on the misunderstandings and the incidents that lead to real shooting wars. Think what a fine world it would be if Russia would say to the United States, just as Dick Hayes said to me, "We don't take any foolishness from anybody, but if you really mean what you say, then let's agree and not fight."

Fire used to play an important role—both as friend and foe in our life in the country. I have already mentioned how, as the oldest boy, I had the hated chore of getting up and making the fire on cold winter mornings when Father would yell, "Ah-ben!" We had no sulphur matches in our house, so, if the fire went out, I would have to run a mile to the nearest neighbor's house to borrow a shovelful of smoldering coals. Fire was also responsible for the loss of a set of luxurious whiskers which Father wore as a young man. He bent too close in poking the logs one day and his whiskers were singed right off; he was so disgusted he never grew another set.

Another time, when I was nine years old, our rented house burned down, and we lost every earthly possession we owned, with the exception of one feather mattress which Mamma had outside for an airing. Father and I were working in the fields, and by the time we ran home it was too late to save anything. Father was a strong man, but he leaned against a tree and wept. It was the first time I ever saw him give way to emotion, and to me that was more upsetting than the fire. I wept too.

But the neighbors, in the custom of those days, came to our aid. They found us an empty house and made it ours, and they all brought us, from their own meager possessions, food, utensils, and furnishings with which to resume housekeeping. When my father saw the generosity of the neighbors, he leaned against the same tree on which he had wept, and cried out in a strong voice, "Thank Thee, dear Lord—they have given Your servant more than he ever had!"

CHAPTER 4

College Days—or "Barkley Swept Here"

O NE of my pet theories—based on my personal experiences in nearly
half a century of public life—is that sooner or later everything one learns
in early years turns out to be useful. For instance, there was the time in
1936 when I found myself in St. Cloud, Minnesota, on a brutally hot day,
campaigning for Franklin D. Roosevelt's re-election.

Despite the fact that I was wearing a thin white linen suit I was sweating profusely. As I spoke, I noticed that my audience was beginning to
snicker, and it worried me because I was not trying to say anything
funny at the time. I sneaked a quick glance downward and saw to my
horror that the perspiration was trickling through my ice-cream trousers. I was about to lose my audience and become a laughingstock to boot.

"Ladies and gentlemen," I said quickly, "I notice you are amused by
the fact that my trousers are becoming somewhat damp. Let me explain that. Four years ago this could not have happened. Under the
Hoover administration, all I could afford was thick cotton underwear
which would have absorbed the perspiration. But after four years of
Democratic prosperity, I am wearing silk underwear, and, as all of you
good people know, silk is just no good at all for soaking up sweat!"

That humorous switch saved the day for me. But the device I had
used in enlisting the audience's sympathy and getting it to laugh with
me instead of at me was one which I had learned as a young man in the
now-vanished Marvin College in Clinton, Kentucky.

I had entered the annual Oratorical Contest, determined to win the
gold medal. I think I wanted to impress some young lady. I was dressed
to the teeth for the event—hair slicked back, black suit, and new striped
shirt with the latest snap-on celluloid cuffs. I was doing fine until, right

at the climax, I thrust my right arm forward in a forceful gesture, and the celluloid cuff became unsnapped. As the cuff snapped, so did my memory, and I completely forgot the rest of my oration. Had I faltered, the audience would have become nervous and all would have been lost. Instinctively, however, I made a sweeping gesture that captured its attention, and slowly and deliberately adjusted my errant cuff as if this sort of thing was all part of the day's work. While fiddling with the snaps I concentrated desperately and managed to remember my lines. I finished the speech and won the medal. The judges later told me they gave me extra points for presence of mind.

The Clinton oratorical triumph, by the way, was a happier occasion for me than an earlier debacle which occurred at Lowes, when I was on the program to "orate" at the annual Children's Day celebration at the local Presbyterian church. I had wanted to do my best, not only because my father was an elder of the church, but because I had a crush at the time on the pastor's daughter, Sadie Ward, who had pretty auburn hair. The day before the event, Mr. Joe Dunn, who operated the farm next to my father's, saw me, and said, "Boy, I'll bet you're going to forget your speech tomorrow." When I got up to speak, I saw Joe Dunn sitting there in the middle of the front row, grinning at me. Immediately everything I had memorized went out of my mind. I was so mortified that I could not even face Sadie when the box lunches were opened.

I was fourteen when Father moved the family from Lowes to Clinton. It was only a distance of some twenty-five miles, but, in those days of poor dirt roads, it seemed formidable. Years later, as a county official, I campaigned for improvement of rural roads; then, when I went to Washington, I took keen personal pleasure in battling for legislation which would provide federal aid for state and county highways.

I hated to leave Lowes. All my boyhood associations were centered there, and I was overwhelmed at the thought of leaving them. "How dear to my heart," indeed, were the scenes where I had first gone to school; where I had finally learned how to paddle dog-fashion in the creek— "goin' in washin'," we country boys used to call it; where I had first discovered that awesome phenomenon known as "puppy love." How could I live if I was never again to see the pretty little girl who lived up the road, whose books I carried home from school?

It was in Lowes, too, that I learned the fine art, which every country boy must acquire, of "swappin'." (Some of this lore served me well in later years when I became incurably addicted to antique-collecting.) Every boy had a Barlow knife, and we developed a custom of trading them among one another, sight unseen; usually we would try to swap off a knife that had seen better days, but there was an unwritten code that no boy would swindle a buddy too outrageously by introducing a piece of junk into the market.

We played strenuous variations of baseball in those days. One was called "town ball"—the pitcher was on the side of the batter and tried to throw the ball so the batter could hit it, but the other side could "cross out" the runner by throwing the ball in front of him as he ran the bases. Then there was "cap ball," in which a ball (fortunately not a hard one) was thrown into a cap or hat, and the boy in the center would grab it and try to throw it so as to bean the fellow who had dropped it in the cap or hat.

We also used to play marbles for keeps, and it was a deadly serious undertaking. We had one particular maneuver wherein, if an opponent sought to take advantage of a rule permitting him to move his shooting taw to a more favorable position, we could block him from doing so by quickly yelling, "Venture Roundance!" I do not know exactly where this term sprang from, but it sounds definitely Elizabethan in origin. In any event, when I became Vice President many years later and some youngsters who were on their way to participate in a national marble tournament called upon me, I was able to discourse intelligently with them on their specialty; I was even able to assume a reasonably authentic shooting stance when we posed for pictures.

Though I did not fully appreciate the significance of it at the time, another fine point in my development that commenced at Lowes was the beginning of my education in practical politics. As a boy, I began to notice that when a Republican administration came in, Mr. Rodam Peck, who ran the village blacksmith shop and one of the two general stores, became postmaster. When the Democrats returned, Mr. John Lowe, of the family which ran the other general store, automatically recaptured the job. It was as regular, as inexorable as the changing of the seasons. It may be of some interest to report that, on the mercantile front, at least, a bipartisan spirit has descended upon Lowes's crossroads. Peck's store is no more, but Emil Peck, son of Rodam, now works for Roy Lowe, greatgrandson of Levi, at Lowe's store.

I also recall the jubilant celebration which Rodam Peck arranged when Benjamin Harrison defeated Grover Cleveland in 1888. There was no cannon in Lowes, so Mr. Peck put two anvils together, poured a charge of gunpowder in between and touched it off, producing an awesome and clangorous detonation. Coming from a respectable Democratic family,

I could not, of course, attend this demonstration in person, but I heard the explosion from afar.

I even experienced my first cyclone at Lowes. We were living in the little frame house—the only one Father ever owned when I was growing up—and I was convalescing from an attack of pneumonia. The cyclone hit our house, lifted it off its foundation, and moved it back about fifteen feet. We walked a quarter of a mile through the rain, wind, and mud to Joe Dunn's house, and, even though it was the first time I had been out since recovering from my illness, it did not bother me. For almost a year after, however, the sound of wind or the sight of a black cloud in the sky would make me nervous.

At that, though, I fared better than the Gupton girls, who lived on a nearby farm. They were asleep when the cyclone hit, and the wind picked up their bed and carried it, with them in it, to a nearby cornfield. The Gupton girls were mortified.

Father, by the way, never bothered to move our house back to where it had been. He figured he would just leave it where the cyclone had put it, so he jacked it up, put a new foundation under it, and that is where it stayed. He did take advantage of the disruption, however, to add an extra room and a fireplace he had always been wanting. That house is still standing at Lowes, and so is the original smokehouse, though subsequent owners have covered the log exterior with composition shingles.

My first impression of Clinton was not enhanced by the humiliating circumstances of the Barkley family's physical entrance into the town. We and all our possessions were driven over to Clinton in three open wagons in a driving rainstorm. The other two wagons were provided by neighboring farmers, who volunteered to drive. There was no compensation involved, of course; it was simply one of those things that neighbors did for one another in those days.

Among other things we had a Jersey cow that had to be transported. In order to get her to travel under her own power, my father put her newborn calf in the rear wagon, and the mother cow dutifully plodded behind, mooing anxiously. All went well until we reached Clinton after dark. The rain was pouring down; few lights were on, and there was not a soul in sight. The cow chose that time to get excited, and she began charging around the deserted, rain-swept town square. Her bell was clanging madly and the cow herself let out anguished bellows as if she were being led to slaughter. Popsy jumped down from the lead wagon and began chasing her, yelling, "Head that cow!" In my adolescent embarrassment it seemed to me that the whole town turned out to gape at the ruckus.

As it turned out, the move to Clinton was the best thing that could have happened to me at this period, for it gave me the opportunity to enlarge my education by attending Marvin College. Marvin was a Methodist institution named after a bishop of what was then the Methodist Episcopal Church, South. It was one of two colleges in the town, the other being Clinton College, under Baptist auspices. While not a full-fledged college by today's standards, Marvin was a thorough, well-run institution that granted Bachelor of Arts and Bachelor of Science degrees. Its cornerstone had been laid in 1883, and, as my parents had been visiting relatives in Clinton at the time, I had been taken to the ceremony. This first visit to my future alma mater must have made an impression on me, for I have remembered it through all the years, though I was only five years old at the time.

There was no money in our family for providing me with a higher education; indeed, Father was having a harder time than usual, because of the problem of getting settled after the move from Lowes to Clinton, which, among other things, involved a change from tobacco growing to corn and wheat farming. However, I had acquired—probably because of the constant encouragement given me by my early teachers—an almost fanatical urge to go further with my education, and I was willing to do anything to accomplish it. Father agreed that, if I could arrange to work my way through school, and at the same time keep up with my home and farm chores, it would be all right. I approached the joint presidents of Marvin, two gentlemen named Speight and Dean, and began working on them to give me a job as janitor at Marvin.

After much maneuvering and negotiating I finally persuaded Mr. J. C. Speight to bestow upon me the coveted janitor's job. Years later I was pleased to award his son, Edmund Speight, one of my first Congressional appointments to Annapolis, and he made a fine record as a naval officer.

So, at the age of fourteen, I entered what became the graduating class of 1897 at Marvin. As an illustration of the struggle which such small institutions went through in those days, my class consisted of one girl and three other young men—and one of the boys, Charles West, was also on a janitorial scholarship. Until just a few years ago, when Charlie West was killed in an automobile accident, all five of us alumni of Marvin, '97, were alive, and it gave us a good deal of pleasure keeping in touch with one another. The other alumni are Ernest Hilliard, a farmer, whose wife became postmistress at Clinton; Thomas E. Kennedy, who became a contractor and builder in Texas, California, New York, and Chicago, and "Miss Lillie" Foster, a retired telephone operator at Clinton, who never married.

I picked up a nickname at Marvin, as my schoolmates often remind me when they see me. They called me "Monk," because, they claim, I was always up to some sort of monkeyshines. As a matter of fact, I did not mind the nickname at all, having come from a family where much less attractive nicknames were freely bestowed. In our family I was known as "Doo," which was short for—I will have to spell it phonetically—"Dooee-coflycut." Do not ask me to explain that: it was bestowed upon me by little sister Ada at a period when she could not talk plainly. Ada, who died in 1915, was "Toshie." My late brother, Clarence, was "Cut." John Andrew, now living at Paducah, was "Shander." I forget what we called Harry, now deceased; George, a retired railroad conductor who lives in Indiana, or my sisters, Ima (Mrs. Edgar Brown), of Tuscumbia, Alabama, and Bernice (Mrs. William Theillman), of Paducah. But Popsy was "Soonk" and Momsy "Teetut"—though we did not call them that to their faces.

As co-janitor of Marvin College, which is no more, I fully lived up to the sign which is now on the only remaining building of the institution, saying, "BARKLEY SWEPT HERE." Not only did I sweep, but I also rang the bell in the morning, dusted the benches, made the fires, carried the water, and did dozens of other chores. I was handicapped somewhat in my studies by the fact that it was necessary for me to miss almost a month of school at both the beginning and end of the scholastic term so I could help my father with the crops. I still had to keep up my janitorial duties during these periods in order to qualify for my scholarship, and I did my best through homework and off-hour contacts with teachers and students so as not to fall behind in my subjects.

I decided to pursue a classical course and a Bachelor of Arts degree at Marvin. I learned to read Latin at sight, and even today I can give the Greek derivations of almost any English word with a Greek base. In addition to these classical languages I learned something about mathematics, physics, and other subjects, and I also advanced my oratorical experience. I became a practically inextinguishable light of the Periclean Debating Society. Its imposing name could never perish from my memory. I became a real stump speaker, for I used to go into the woods and in thundering tones rehearse my orations to the helpless trees and stumps. In so doing I was borrowing a leaf from what I had read about the great

Kentuckian, Henry Clay, who would practice his speeches to the pigs in the barnyard. The pigs couldn't talk back either.

Once I was nominated to take the negative—and highly unpopular—side of a debate on the question: "Resolved, that the United States Should Recognize the Independence of Cuba." I did not like it, as my sympathies were all for the struggling Cubans. I read in a newspaper, however, that Senator Eugene Hale of Maine had made a ripsnorting speech against Cuban recognition. Secretly, without even telling my partner, I wrote our local congressman—he was Charles K. Wheeler, for whom I later worked in Paducah and whose seat I eventually filled in Congress—and asked him to send me a copy of the Congressional Record containing Senator Hale's speech. That was my first experience in using a congressman as an errand boy—a practice with which I later acquired extensive experience on the receiving end. Anyhow I overwhelmed the opposition with rhetoric and our side won the debate. My partner, Jack Ward—he later became principal of the high school at Barlow and frequently invited me to come down and punish his graduating classes by speaking to them—could not understand how I did it, until, some time after the debate, I confessed all.

It was during Clinton days that I saw my first bicycle; it was the old-fashioned type with a big, high wheel in front and a little wheel behind. I never attempted to ride one of those; in fact, I could never understand how anyone could ride such an awkward contraption. Later, as a young man in Paducah, I acquired a bicycle—one with regular wheels—of my own.

It was in Clinton also that, at the age of seventeen, I used a telephone for the first time. Actually, I had heard a good deal about this contraption from the time I was twelve or thirteen, and I had even seen one—but not used it—on a trip to Paducah with my father. We were in a dry-goods store, making our purchases after disposing of a load of wheat, and, while seated near the old drumhead heating stove, sucking on the stick of candy which the storekeeper had given me, I noticed a man talking into some queer-looking black instrument with a little crank that was hanging on the wall. "That's called a telephone," my father elucidated. He told me what it was supposed to do, but frankly I did not wholly believe it.

In fact, I was like the man in the story we used to tell about the telephone agent who was trying to persuade a skeptic to install one of Mr. Bell's devices. A demonstration was finally arranged, whereby the skeptic's wife was to talk to him via an instrument located some ten miles away. The bell rang, and the husband put the instrument to his ear, shouting, "Is that you, Nancy?" Before she could say anything, a sudden storm blew up and lightning struck the wire and knocked the husband to the floor, completely unconscious. When he revived, his first words were: "There must be something to it—that was Nancy, all right!"

When I was living in Clinton, though, a telephone system finally was installed, and I decided to try it out. A young lady whom I was courting at the time lived three or four miles out in the country, and her parents had installed one of these devices. One night I took my guitar—as a would-be dashing young blade, I had taught myself to play the guitar—and walked into the telephone exchange. I got my young lady on the phone—the way I was yelling, I suspect she could have heard me without benefit of the instrument—and asked her to hang on a minute. Then I stood up on a chair so I could get my guitar near to the mouthpiece, and plucked away as I sang her a song. I remember the title of the song, "Sweet Bunch of Daisies", and I think the words went like this:

> Sweet bunch of daisies,
> Brought from the dell,
> Tell me, do you love me?
> Daisies won't tell!

Incidentally, in addition to playing the guitar, I was a pretty fair hand in those days with the harmonica; in fact, I had what we country boys used to call "mouthitivity." I was not so good with that other weird little instrument called the "French harp" or "jew's-harp"—a piece of metal through which you hummed while twanging away at another piece of flexible wire with your right index finger. I did not like the way the wire banged on my front teeth. I have forgotten all the chords on the guitar, but I still can coax some music out of a harmonica.

At one time I even considered learning the fiddle—and I mean "fiddle," not violin. Ben Camp, the barber in Clinton, was always after me to become a fiddler. But I observed the fiddlers around town and it did not seem to me they had much of a career; they were just fiddlers. So I turned to law.

And speaking of music, it is well known that "Wagon Wheels" is my favorite song, and I have sung it on many occasions. Actually, to me it is more than just a song. It reminds me of my boyhood days when the two-horse wagon was the only vehicle we had. As I have related, we used it on the farm to haul, we took our crops to market in it, and on Sunday we went to church in it. Frequently, in the dry summer weather, the wooden spokes and the rims of the wheels of this wagon would get dry and shrivel up, and the steel tires would roll off the rims. So we would push the wagon into the pond overnight so that the wood would swell and the tires would not come off. Those are some of the things I think of when I sing "Wagon Wheels."

Hay rides, square dances, and occasional swimming parties were our diversions in those days. I remember once when about twenty of us young couples organized a chaperoned trip to a place on the Mississippi River near the town of Columbus, Kentucky. Columbus, by the way, has a rather interesting history. It was blockaded by Union forces during the Civil War, and at one time it was the seat of Hickman County until the Illinois Central Railroad came to Clinton, bringing about a change of the county seat to Clinton. The Mississippi is very treacherous at Columbus, and it was eating into the bank, gradually threatening to engulf the entire town. In 1927, as a United States senator, I enlisted the aid of the American Red Cross and the Army in moving Columbus from its original site on the lowlands along the riverbank to a safe location on the bluff overlooking the river. Our efforts evoked considerable opposition from some of the older residents who did not see why—river or no river—they should have to move from their homes. However, Columbus now is on high, safe ground, and what was once the business center of the town is practically in the midstream of the Mississippi.

In the old days when our crowd from Clinton used to go to Columbus for outings, there was a big, one-room sort of clubhouse on the riverbank. The young ladies slept in the house, and the young men slept out under the wagons. The only one among us young men who actually owned a bathing suit was a boy named Scott Birdsong. While the girls stayed at the clubhouse, some of us boys went about a mile up-river for a swim. The current was so strong that it carried us downstream below the camp. Since we were swimming *au naturel*, we could not, without violating the decencies, get back to get our clothes. So we sent Scott Birdsong, who had the only bathing suit, to get a skiff and row us back to where we had left our clothes.

I was the first to roll into the skiff, stretching out flat for purposes of concealment. I did not know that the bottom of the skiff had been covered with a fresh coat of tar. When I got out, I was literally covered with tar. I stood in the sun for a while to let it soften, and my friends helpfully "assisted" me by rubbing me with gravel and sand. After they got through with me, I was sore for weeks. Anyhow, it toughened up my hide for politics.

My political education also was advanced in Clinton days, particularly during the torrid presidential campaign of 1896. Democratic voters in Kentucky—as well as elsewhere in the nation—were split over the gold-versus-silver coinage issue, the latter espoused by the magnetic William Jennings Bryan, who favored free and unlimited coinage of silver at a ratio of 16 to 1. Though I was not old enough to vote, I became an ardent "gold Democrat," largely due to the influence of my Marvin College mentor, President Speight, who ran for the state legislature and was elected on an anti-silver platform. In those days, United States senators were elected by the state legislatures, and Speight became highly unpopular in his home district because he refused to vote for the incumbent Democrat, Senator Joseph C. S. Blackburn, a free-silver man, thus helping to pave the way for the election of Kentucky's first Republican United States senator, William J. Defoe. In our part of Kentucky most people thought it was humiliating to be represented up in Washington by a Republican. When Bryan was defeated by McKinley, for instance, my uncle Bob Cook, who was married to my father's sister, Aunt Betty, was so sick at heart that he took to his bed and did not get up for a week.

Professor Speight stuck by his principles, though, and, in the national election, supported the "gold standard" Democratic candidates, Palmer and Buckner, who split the Democratic vote, contributing to the defeat of the regular Democratic nominees, Bryan and Sewall, by McKinley and Hobart. Eventually Mr. Speight drifted into the Republican party, losing a race for Congress, but becoming postmaster at Mayfield under President Taft.

Such political defection was not taken lightly in those days. In fact, some people used to say that Professor Speight reminded them of the young fellow who wrote a letter to the "Advice to the Lovelorn" editor, saying, "I am in love with a beautiful girl of fine character and want to marry her. She knows about my sister who is a prostitute, my brother in the penitentiary and my uncle in the insane asylum, but she doesn't know I have two cousins who are Republicans. Shall I tell her?" However, still grateful to my old prexy for the janitor's job, I remained his staunch friend, personally if not politically.

I remember the first time I ever heard the name of William Jennings Bryan mentioned. It was after the Democratic convention in Chicago in 1896, which nominated him for the first time. I was working in the field on a hot day, breaking ground for a wheat crop. The weeds were almost as high as the horses, and I had to stop frequently to unchoke my plow; it was very disagreeable work. While I was doing this, a neighbor named Burnett Johnson, who owned the farm which my father rented, rode into the field on his slick black horse, and said, "Well, the Democrats have nominated William Jennings Bryan." Knocking another clump of weeds loose with my foot, I grunted, "Who's William Jennings Bryan?" Mr. Johnson replied, "I dunno. Never heard of him either." Our ignorance was an apt commentary on the limited means of mass communications and dissemination of information in those days, for this man we had "never heard of" was the "Great Commoner," who was to become the only man in United States history to run for President three times unsuccessfully as the nominee of a major party. In today's society, with its universal press, radio, and expanding television systems, citizens of even the remotest areas are familiar with the names and faces of every public figure of consequence.

Many years later, when Mr. Bryan and I became good friends, I told him this story. I also told him about the night of the political rally at the courthouse in Clinton, and how a fist fight broke out when someone stuck a Bryan banner into the face of Senator William Lindsay. Senator Lindsay was an interesting Kentucky political figure. The story goes that he was working on a strawstack one hot July day, sweating like a mule and just about to cave in with the heat, when he suddenly put down his pitchfork and said, "The devil with this—there must be an easier way to make a living!" He left the farm, went to Clinton, and took up the study of law, and eventually went on to the United States Senate. I could sympathize with Senator Lindsay thoroughly, for many a time in the fields I felt exactly the same way.

Senator Lindsay, though a Democrat, was a gold-standard man and thus out of sympathy with Bryan, his party's nominee. While he was making his gold speech, young Eugene Brooks, a Bryan enthusiast, also too young to vote, sneaked up front with a Bryan banner and thrust it in front of the senator's face. A fracas broke out and, in the course of it, Charlie West, my co-janitor, got poked in the eye. I was there but managed to escape with no scars.

I also regaled Mr. Bryan with the story of the inspired coup staged by Senator Lindsay's forces one Saturday afternoon a couple of weeks before the election. They lined up twelve beautiful golden-haired girls, dressed them in yellow frocks, mounted them on twelve more or less yellow horses, and paraded them around Courthouse Square. Next Saturday, however, the pro-Bryan free-silverites retaliated with a parade of twelve silvery-colored horses ridden by twelve brunettes in gleaming white dresses. We anti-silverites taunted them for not playing it fair and using silver-haired ladies, but I suppose they figured this would not have been good showmanship.

Mr. Bryan, who, despite his fundamentalist leanings, was a man of considerable humor, enjoyed these stories. I remember a story he told me on himself. After one of his defeats for the presidency, Bryan, one of the most celebrated orators of the age, was touring the country, making speeches at Chautauqua meetings. In one small town, where Bryan was to speak in a tent, the local director came up and said, "Now let's see, Mr. Byron—do you speak or yodel?"

I graduated from Marvin College with my Bachelor of Arts degree. Speaking of degrees, I have received a number of honorary degrees since then, but the closest thing to a Ph.D. degree I ever received was the one granted me in 1952, when I was still the "Veep," by the Circus Saints and Sinners Club, a fun-loving organization in New York City. They conferred upon me the initials, "P.H.D.," for "Poor Honest Democrat."

In making speeches around the country I often joke about degrees and scholastic honors. I once told a convention of bankers my definition of an economist—"a financier with no money, who wears a Phi Beta Kappa key at one end of his watch chain, and no watch at the other end."

After leaving Marvin I wanted to continue my education. I had my eye on attending Emory College at Oxford, Georgia, now part of Emory University at Atlanta. Again there were no funds. So I tried to raise the money by becoming a "traveling representative"—i.e., peddler—of an Ohio firm which manufactured cooking crockery guaranteed not to crack under heat. I was given the south end of Graves County as my territory, and I pitched my headquarters in a conveniently located small railroad town called Water Valley. Hiring a handsome black horse, I rode through the countryside, calling on farmers' wives. I carried my samples in a saddlebag which resembled a doctor's satchel and I came to acquire the nickname of "young Doc" Barkley. I was a persuasive salesman, and I thought for a while I had earned the money for college. When I rode the circuit the second time, however, I was greeted by irate housewives who were sure I had swindled them because half the "guaranteed" crockery had cracked. I made all the losses good out of my own pocket, and wound up with a deficit approximating the cost of renting the saddle horse.

This financially ruinous venture paid off for me later, however, for, when I campaigned through that area in my first race for Congress, the ladies remembered me as "that honest young fellow who kept his word," and they got their husbands to vote for me.

I then managed to borrow $200 from a local judge, Nathaniel P. Moss, to finance my studies at Emory. Judge Moss had confidence in me, but at the same time he required me to get the signatures of seven of the town's leading citizens on my note. He also charged me 10 per cent interest.

I remained at Emory for one year. The president of the college at that time was Dr. Warren A. Candler, a brother of Asa Candler, the Coca-Cola millionaire. Dr. Candler, who later became a bishop, was one of the greatest preachers I have ever heard, and I counted him as one of my good friends and a source of inspiration to me until his death. There were other outstanding teachers at Emory, and the year I spent there was a major factor in shaping my thinking.

When I returned to Clinton after my year at Emory, I fully intended to return and continue my studies. But the financial strain was too great and I was forced to abandon my plans. Thus ended my academic preparations for the study of law.

I was determined to go on with my education, however, so, as a temporary measure, I took a position as a teacher in the intermediate department at Marvin College. It paid me $25 per month. I held out only until Christmas, however. In the first place, I had no great affinity for teaching, and I was anxious to start reading law. In the second place, I just could not seem to maintain discipline among the boys with whom I had sky-larked and the young ladies whom I had courted; they remembered all too well my nickname of "Monk"! So I submitted my resignation.

Meanwhile, my father, for the first time in his life, had given up farming, and had followed one of his brothers to Paducah to take employment in a cotton cordage mill. I had stayed behind in Clinton while pursuing my short-lived career as a pedagogue. I decided to follow the family to Paducah. It was a move which I undertook with a feeling of considerable excitement, for Paducah was by far the largest city in which any of us had lived up till then.

So shortly after my twenty-first birthday in 1898, I arrived in Paducah to begin the reading of law. Aside from a small suitcase containing a few extra shirts, some linen, and a couple of spare collars my sole assets when I arrived in Paducah consisted of 50 cents in my pocket and a letter of introduction to Lawyer Charles K. Wheeler, then a member of Congress.

CHAPTER 5

Paducah Days; I Become a Lawyer and Family Man

I DO NOT suppose I ever worked harder and earned less than I did during my first few years in Paducah when I was learning the law. Though I was young, vigorous, and full of ambition, there were times, I must admit, when I felt somewhat like an old fellow I sometimes tell about who was attending a revival meeting.

He was a gnarled and bent old man, all crippled up with rheumatism and other ailments, and he sat silently in the back of the revival tent while the evangelist called on members of the flock to stand up and tell what the Lord had done for them. One by one they rose and "testified." Finally the preacher spied the old fellow sitting in the back of the tent.

"Brother Jones—oh, Brother Jones!" the preacher sang out. "I see you back there! Won't you rise and tell us what the Lord has done for you?"

Old Brother Jones stood up painfully, leaned on his crutch, and quavered:

"All I can say is—He mighty near ruint me!"

Those early years in Paducah "mighty near ruint me," but I survived. As a matter of fact, a little hardship never hurt anyone. Among other things it forced me into learning one accomplishment which, when I later went to the House of Representatives, caused President Woodrow Wilson to take notice of me as a person rather than just another freshman congressman.

The incident occurred at one of my first conferences with President Wilson, who, as I will relate in a later chapter, became my lifelong political ideal. As we talked, I noticed that he was taking notes of our conversation. I peered closer and saw that the notes were in shorthand

—Isaac Pitman system. "Mr. President, may I see that?" I remarked, leaning forward rather brashly and taking the notes from him. I thereupon proceeded to read them back to him.

"Where did you learn that, Congressman Barkley?" the President asked.

"Oh," I replied, "I learned shorthand back in Paducah, when I was practically starving to death trying to become a lawyer and had to take up something to bring in a little extra money."

Wilson was delighted to find a fellow Ike Pitman man, and he kept me with him for an extra fifteen minutes, discussing shorthand lore. He told me he had used shorthand for twenty-five years: as a professor at Princeton, he used to deliver his lectures from shorthand notes, and, as President, he found himself automatically taking notes on conversations so there could be no later confusion as to what had been said.

In the days when I went to Paducah it was still possible to gain admission to the bar by reading law privately in an attorney's office and then passing the bar examinations. My letter of introduction was to Mr. Wheeler, who in 1896 had run on the free-silver Democratic ticket and defeated Colonel John K. Hendrick, a "gold Democrat." Colonel Hendrick himself only two years earlier had displaced old Captain W. J. Stone, a one-legged Confederate veteran.

Congressman Wheeler received me affably if somewhat absent-mindedly, and allowed that it would be all right for me to work as a clerk in his office and read his law books when I was not busy. My salary was to be exactly nothing per month. I agreed to this arrangement, and for several months all the spending money I had was what I could earn by clerking at odd jobs in shoe stores and such on Saturdays. In desperation I made an arrangement to study shorthand in the evenings with Congressman Wheeler's secretary, Miss Lulu Flowers. I was so tired when I had finished a day of clerking and reading that I could hardly stay awake over the pothooks, but the pressure of sheer necessity sharpened my powers of concentration and in about eight weeks I was able to earn some income by taking depositions for lawyers. Eventually a friendly judge appointed me official reporter for the McCracken County Circuit Court.

During the first phase of my career as a law clerk and student I saw very little of Mr. Wheeler, as he was away most of the time, attending to his Congressional duties. Once during a House recess he came home and found me reading one of Charles Dickens' novels. "Young man," he admonished, "you will never become a lawyer by reading that book." I explained to him that I had taken it up only momentarily, having been exhausted by Blackstone, Kent, and other legal treatises. However, I put down the Dickens and went back to my cases.

Finding my financial arrangements with Congressman Wheeler something less than satisfactory, I arranged to shift my clerking and law reading to the office of Judge William Sutton Bishop and former Congressman Hendrick, who had a law partnership. They were willing to pay me $12 per month. Judge Bishop, one of the greatest legal minds and rarest personalities I have ever known, was the actual living prototype for the famous "Judge Priest" stories by the world-renowned Paducah author, the late Irvin S. Cobb, who also was a friend of mine. We used to say of Irvin, who began his literary career as a newspaper reporter in Paducah, that all he did in writing his stories was to demote the judge from a bishop to a priest.

Judge Bishop had a head of thick, wavy white hair, a mustache and a little white goatee, and penetrating eyes. Cobb, in his biography *Exit Laughing,* describes "the high bald forehead, the pudgy shape, the little white paintbrush of a chinwhisker, the strident high-pitched voice which, issuing from that globular tenement, made a grotesque contrast, as though a South American tapir had swallowed a tomtit alive and was letting the tomtit do the talking for him." The judge was a careless dresser, addicted to old-fashioned string ties and black suits, usually unpressed. Both he and his law office on Fourth Street, which was Paducah's now-vanished old "Legal Row," could have come straight from the pages of Dickens. I can still close my eyes and conjure up the musty, dusty, leathery aroma of that office.

Except in the field of law, where his mind was incredibly keen, the judge was probably the world's most absent-minded man. Once he held court in a county seat so small that he had to share a hotel room with three or four visiting lawyers. He was an early riser, and, when they awoke, they found the judge and all their vests gone. As they later learned from his well-padded appearance in court, he was concentrating on some legal problems when he dressed, so he absent-mindedly put on all the vests in the room and squeezed his own coat over them.

I remember once seeing Judge Bishop walking on Broadway, Paducah's main street, with a $5.00 bill clutched in his hand. It seems that Mrs. Bishop had sent him to Joe Wolf's jewelry store to pay a bill. He put the money in his left-hand pocket, sauntered down to the store, thinking, probably, of everything but his errand, and, reaching in his right-hand pocket when he arrived at the store, concluded he had lost the money.

He walked back home, casually stuck his hand in his other pocket to take out his key, and found the money. Then he walked back to Wolf's to pay the bill, but decided he had better hold the money in his hand so he would not forget again.

The judge had a favorite story he told on himself about the time he held court in the quaint little town of Smithland, the seat of Livingston County. Again the only hotel was crowded, and the judge was put into a room with an Irishman who had not been in this country long. While they were dressing, Judge Bishop said to the Irishman, "Mike, you would have lived in the old country a long time before you would have slept with a judge." "Yes, your honor," Mike replied, "and *you* would have lived in the old country even longer before you would have been a judge." Judge Bishop said he never again made the mistake of bantering an Irishman about anything.

Still, despite his peculiarities, Judge Bishop was one of the squarest, most brilliant jurists I have ever known, and he fully deserved his reputation of being able to look "straight as a gun barrel" at the law, the facts, and the justice of every case that came before him. I cherish the association which I, as a young man, was privileged to have with him. One of the favorite items in my large gavel collection, which includes a specimen made from a tree that grew on Abraham Lincoln's birthplace, is a gavel made from a piece of walnut taken from Judge Bishop's old home place, now torn down.

Paducah was—as it still is—a town with a distinct flavor. It was—and is—a good place, and an interesting place, in which to live. A great part of its personality was derived from such colorful citizens as Judge Bishop, Irvin Cobb, and others. It is, of course, a river town, located at a point where the Ohio and Tennessee rivers come together, not far from the Cumberland and the Mississippi. Though, like a lively young man just coming into maturity, Paducah was beginning to tame down when I came to live there, it retained much of the zest and vigor that is traditional with river towns. Steamboat traffic was still important; in fact, our Irvin Cobb, the pride of Paducah, got his start as a reporter—he had worked previously as a helper on an ice wagon—by chronicling the daily comings and goings at the steamboat wharf. In my own day I can remember when the landing was choked with vessels—side-wheelers, stern-wheelers, tugs, and ferryboats—and the docks were heavy with cargoes of tobacco, cotton, peanuts, and whiskey.

The town derived its name from Chief Paduke, a noble red man, who was head of a small tribe of Indians, known as Paducahs and related to the Chickasaws, who used to live in the region. An excellent history of the town was written by my old friend, the late Fred G. Neuman, *The Story of Paducah,* published in 1927. Mr. Neuman quoted Cobb, who had made an extensive study of the subject, on the derivation of the word "Paducah." According to Irvin, it was originally *"Pakutukah,"* or, as pronounced by the Indians, *"Pak'tuka,"* and it was a compound word in the Chickasaw language, meaning "wild grapes hanging," or "place where the grapes hang down." There are a lot of wild grapevines in the woods around Paducah.

Among its other claims to immortality Paducah has had the distinction of having a town in Texas named after it. Not only does Paducah, Texas, admit it is smaller than Paducah, Kentucky, but it also acknowledges that our town came first; this, coming from any place, individual, or animal in Texas, is practically phenomenal.

Anyhow the original Paducah was founded and christened by General William Clark, of Lewis and Clark expeditionary fame, who came to the area in 1827. General Clark found a primitive settlement, known as Pekin, existing on the riverbank, but, in the process of laying out a new town, he changed its name to Paducah in honor of the chief. The general's claim to the land was by virtue of a grant made by the government to his late brother, General George Rogers Clark, the noted soldier and explorer, who had opened up much of this territory and had preceded him to the Paducah area in 1778, bringing an expedition of riflemen on their way to fight the British at Vincennes. In between the grant and the younger Clark's arrival the white men's title to the land had been formalized by the so-called "Jackson Purchase" in 1819, whereby the Chickasaws ceded much of what is now West Kentucky and West Tennessee to the palefaces.

Whatever may be said of our early treatment of the Indians, old records show that Chief Paduke was treated with respect. This has been commendably continued into the present day, for a heroic statue of the chief, executed by sculptor Lorado Taft, was commissioned and presented to the city in 1909 by the local chapter of the Daughters of the American Revolution. In addition to being handsome, imposing, and a favorite subject for postcards, the statue in earlier days, before it was moved from a downtown to a residential location, had a fountain in its base which gushed fresh, clear Kentucky water for all who would quaff. Many a time I have refreshed myself at the feet of old Paduke, recalling, as I drank, the majestic opening line of the poem, composed by a local lady in honor of the statue and read at the unveiling. It began "The paleface daughters set his image here . . ."

Paducah had already experienced much colorful frontier history before General Clark, the younger, laid out and platted the town in 1827. Its incorporation came four years later. It had a rough but not disastrous time during the Civil War. Although Kentucky remained officially neutral, the sympathies of many Paducahans leaned toward the South. There was a strong pro-Southern colony in the city which bore the unofficial title of "Little Charleston."

But Ulysses S. Grant—then a brigadier general—seized the town in September 1861, and it remained in Union hands throughout the war. Grant, when he came, issued a firm but temperate proclamation, stating, in effect, that anyone who minded his business and gave the Union soldiers no trouble had nothing to fear. He had no illusions about the temper of the town, however, for Paducah even had its own Barbara Frietchie, a rather redoubtable lady named Mrs. Emily ("Aunt Em") Jarrett, whose exploits were more valid than the questionable act of the Northern heroine of Whittier's poem. It is a matter of record that our Aunt Em actually drove to Third and Broadway, where a homemade Confederate flag (made from silk dresses and petticoats contributed by the patriotic ladies of Paducah) was being fired on by Federal gunboats. While the Yankee shells were whizzing overhead, she had her nine-year-old colored servant, who was scared stiff, shinny up the pole to rescue the flag. All during the occupation she resolutely refused to surrender the Stars and Bars to the Union soldiers, and, though they searched her premises several times, they never found it. There is a strong suspicion that Aunt Em wore it under her own petticoats.

One of the Union generals who for a time commanded the forces occupying Paducah was General Lew Wallace, who later wrote *Ben-Hur*. The strongest Southern assault upon Paducah came in March 1864, when that dashing Confederate cavalryman, General Nathan Bedford Forrest, managed to penetrate the city itself in a daring raid. However, the Federal stronghold, Fort Anderson, could not be breached, and after a bloody battle Forrest's raiders withdrew from Paducah.

By the time I came to Paducah, the pastime of rhetorically refighting the Civil War was beginning to take on an academic rather than a vitriolic flavor. To a young man from the country it was a lively, and even exciting, place in which to live. For amusement we young blades used to go to Fisher Gardens—later called LaBelle Park, and then Wallace

Park, not after the Yankee general but after the local streetcar magnate—to dance the waltz, the two-step, and the schottische.

Then there were the visits of the circuses and the river showboats with their wonderful, earsplitting calliopes, and the original "Buffalo Bill" show; also such fiery "pyrotechnical extravaganzas" as "The Last Days of Pompeii" and "The Destruction of Rome," which sometimes frightened the wits out of the local citizenry.

There also were hot-air balloon ascensions, and in 1910 there was the memorable day when a barnstorming aviator came to Paducah in the first heavier-than-air flying machine ever seen in those parts. On this occasion Colonel Ben Weille, a prominent citizen and merchant, with whom I later campaigned all over the state for good roads, became the first Paducahan in history to fly in an airplane. As a later-day flying enthusiast, I have always rather envied the colonel this distinction.

As I have already indicated, Paducah took a great pride in the career of our home-grown humorist, Irvin S. Cobb. Though he has passed on, we are still pretty proud of Irvin in Paducah, and a number of things have been named after him, including a cigar, a hotel, a bridge, and a mint julep concocted according to his special recipe.

Cobb's Paducah career has been carefully retraced by historian Neuman. His first day's work on a newspaper, after he left the ice truck, was done on the old Paducah *Daily News* in 1893; he was sixteen years old, and his first bit of reporting, in its entirety, was as follows:

> Cal Evitts, the efficient and popular market master, says there were more rabbits brought to the local market this week than any week this winter. Molly Cottontails sold for ten cents dressed or five cents undressed.

I must admit there was little in the above item to presage the talent of the later-day humorist!

Practically everyone in Paducah can tell you "a story I heard Irvin tell." One favorite concerns the time he returned on a visit, and stopped to chat on Broadway with an old newspaper colleague, a rather opinionated and garrulous woman who was decidedly not noted for personal tidiness. At one point in her peroration she stopped and, in a rare burst of self-deprecation, said, "Irvin, I guess I'm just a wishy-washy old woman." "You may be wishy," said Cobb, "but you're not washy."

As every student of humor knows, a good story can be told again and again, with variations to suit the occasion. Cobb himself uses the "wishy-washy" story in his biography, but credits it to his own Aunt Laura, who is supposed to have uttered the devastating criticism about a local spin-ster who was more taken with good deeds than with soap and water.

Once I was asked to introduce the humorist at a big civic reception given in his honor in Paducah. I warmed up to my assignment with a series of rhetorical questions. "Who is Irvin Cobb?" I thundered. "I re-member when he was a reporter on the wharf . . . Who is Irvin Cobb? I remember when he went to the big city . . . Who is Irvin Cobb . . . ? I thought I was building it up pretty well, but, about the tenth time I asked the question, some old fellow in the back of the hall jumped up and yelled, "Barkley, I'll bite—who the hell is he?"

Some time later Cobb returned the compliment, so to speak, by writing a piece about me in his nationally syndicated column. It was in 1940, one of the convention years when I was being mentioned, as usual, as a pos-sible nominee for President. Irvin wrote:

> . . . It's high time we had somebody from Paducah for President. For a hundred and fifty-odd years this republic has followed along without one of our local boys sitting up there in the White House, writing messages to Congress condemning the use of sugar in corn bread and proclaiming that, if any traitor dares to pull down fried catfish, shoot him on the spot.
>
> With Alben on the job, we'll not only have homegrown states-manship in job lots, but silver-throated oratory which, by compar-ison, would make Patrick Henry seem like a tongue-tied man suffering from chapped lips. For Al can talk an hour and never use the same word twice or the letter "r" once.
>
> Nominate Barkley and that night there won't be a dry throat in McCracken County. Elect Barkley and—well, I always did think I'd make a middling-fair Secretary of the Interior; certainly nobody could botch up the Indian Bureau worse than it is.

Now I do not go along with everything Irvin said in that column, but I will say he made a lot of sense about that corn bread and catfish. I might have been willing to give him to the Indians at that.

After two years of reading law I was admitted to the bar. I hung out my shingle in 1901. Although today, in the sidewalk in front of 510 Broadway, on Paducah's main street, there is a bronze marker which reads, "HERE U.S. SENATOR ALBEN W. BARKLEY HAD HIS LAW OFFICE (1904)," I must relate in all truthfulness that there was no mad stam-pede of clients to my door. Therefore, in order to make a living, I con-tinued my duties as court reporter for several years. Between the law practice and the court reporting I was able to earn enough money to pay off the debts I had acquired during the lean years since leaving Marvin College. By frugal living I was even able to save a little, and this enabled me, in the summer of 1902, to advance my legal background by going to the University of Virginia law school at Charlottesville to take special courses under Raleigh C. Minor, Minor W. Lyle, and other outstanding teachers.

While at Charlottesville I used to hike almost every Saturday to Monticello, just to walk on the grounds of Thomas Jefferson's home, which had not then been restored and made into a public shrine. I used to sit there near the old house, drawing on my imagination and picturing in my mind how Jefferson would walk about the grounds, pondering the many problems that occupied his fertile mind. All my life I have had a deep reverence for American historical shrines, and I have driven many hundreds of miles in order to visit most of these places.

Brief as was my stay at the University of Virginia, I felt I left there with a more profound understanding of the law. As it developed, my career turned rather quickly into political channels and I did not devote many years to private practice. As a matter of fact, my early friends in Paducah used to banter me about my qualifications as a lawyer. I was quite a joiner in Paducah, and one of the many fraternal organizations of which I became a member was the Benevolent and Protective Order of Elks. At one election a friend, who had not informed me of his intentions to do so, nominated me for the office of Exalted Ruler of the lodge. He made quite a speech in my favor, and I swelled up with pride as I listened to it.

Then another man got on his feet. "I've got nothing against Barkley," he said. "But he's a lawyer, and the lawyers are getting everything in this town. Why, look at them—they hold almost all the offices of the city and county, and now they're taking over our fraternal organizations. I'm against Barkley because he's a lawyer."

As I sat there uncomfortably, my sponsor arose again. "I've listened to what my friend said," he began. "There may be something in what he says, for it's true that the lawyers are getting right prominent in our affairs. But, in the case of Brother Barkley, don't let it worry you, because he ain't much of a lawyer!"

That was an election, incidentally, that I did not win.

In 1903, at the age of twenty-five, I was married to Miss Dorothy Brower. She was a lovely girl, five years my junior, who had grown up in Paducah. She had gone to live in Tiptonville, Tennessee, where her father had purchased a hardware store. I kept corresponding with her and visiting her whenever I could. When I had begun to establish myself in the legal profession and had saved up about $800, I proposed to her and was accepted.

Our marriage was a happy partnership which lasted until her death in 1947. During the last few years of her life she was ill with a heart ailment that made her an invalid. It was during this period that I began accepting speaking engagements in all parts of the country to earn the money necessary to provide the treatment and the special nursing care which she needed. I never kept up my law practice after I went to Congress, and I had little income outside of my salary as a senator. In 1948, when I was given the Collier's award for my services in the Senate, I gave the $10,000 check which accompanied the award to the University of Louisville medical college to carry on heart research as a memorial to my first wife.

If I needed any additional incentive to try to get ahead in life, my marriage as a young man provided it. Most of my $800 went into the down payment on a modest four-room cottage, which was our first home. With my own background of having lived most of my life in rented homes I took an almost fierce pride in having made the start toward owning my own home. It was a little white frame house, lit by gas illumination. In the evening, when dusk was settling and the lamps were lit, I used to go out of the house, walk across the street, and just stand there looking at it, taking sheer joy in saying, "This is my own."

My wife was a wonderful homemaker, and over the years we owned and furnished several homes. Together we developed an interest in collecting antiques—not only early-American pieces, but lovely furniture, china, pictures, and so forth from all parts of the world.

This interest actually began in New Hampshire, one summer when our two girls were at camp there. Marian, the older, developed an acute sinus infection which required an immediate operation. I was campaigning in Kentucky at the time and my wife was with me. I could not be reached immediately, so Wahwee, our youngest daughter, Laura Louise, as the nearest available "next of kin," had to give permission for the operation to be performed.

I left the campaign at once, of course, and we hastened to New Hampshire. While staying there during the period of Marian's convalescence, we began visiting old homes and antique shops in that historic countryside. It depressed me to see lovely homes going to ruin and family heirlooms being auctioned off. We bought a number of fine pieces and had them shipped to Washington.

In one hotel where we stayed I admired a walnut settee and offered to buy it, but was told that it had once belonged to Franklin Pierce, the fourteenth President of the United States, and that it was not for sale. About a month after we returned to Washington, however, the owner of the hotel sent us that settee as a gift—let no one try to tell me that New Englanders are not generous.

As we traveled around the United States and later to other countries, my wife developed an almost psychic instinct for recognizing worthwhile antiques, however decrepit they might be. She could almost see through six coats of disfiguring paint and varnish and recognize what was underneath. Once in a farmyard she saw a horse eating out of a queer-looking trough. She offered the farmer three dollars for it, and he almost died laughing as he took her money for this piece of "junk." When she had it restored, it turned out to be a priceless old cherry chest.

On my trips abroad I became an inveterate visitor to the famous "Flea Market" in Paris, and to other places where unusual objects could be acquired. In Russia I bought a silver coffeepot that once belonged to Czar Paul; several Gobelin tapestries, and some interesting samovars. In Berlin, after World War II, General Lucius D. Clay personally took me to the barter market, a place which had been established for the mutual benefit of our soldiers, who wanted to acquire various objects, and the people of the bombed-out city, who were willing to trade their possessions for clothing and food. I acquired a large collection of beautiful Meissen figurines. When I saw them, I almost took the coat off my back to trade for them, as you couldn't buy anything for money at this barter market. General Clay made me keep my coat, so I sent over 450 pounds of coffee in exchange for the figurines.

My antiques came to mean a great deal to me. In fact, they tell a story on me about them. During World War II, when an overseas relief group had a benefit auction sale of antiques, I was asked to contribute an item to the sale. According to the story, I was supposed to have told my wife, "I can't bear to give up any of our antiques—go out and buy a new antique and donate it to the sale."

In 1937 my wife and I acquired Angles, my present home in Paducah. It was a fine old pre-Civil War residence that I had admired and dreamed about owning since I was a young man. It originally was the home of Colonel Quintus Quintellus Quigley, one of Paducah's pioneer lawyers. It took its name from the fact that the ground on which the home sat consisted of three tracts of land, some forty-five acres in all, which came together at sharp angles.

I like to claim that I live in what I call "the original ranch house" in our section of the country, for Angles is a large structure, originally containing eleven rooms all built on one floor. Though it has brick walls some fourteen or fifteen inches thick, the house was in deplorable condition when we bought it, as it had not been used as a regular residence for at least twenty-five years. It had no electricity or plumbing, and few closets or anything like that. The water supply was a large, enclosed cistern on the porch. But the old place was built soundly, and gradually we made it into a lovely and immensely livable home. It is furnished almost entirely with antiques, but you do not have to be afraid to sit on any of the chairs or sleep in any of the beds, for, although old, they are solid.

One thing you will not find at Angles is any sign saying, "PRIVATE PROPERTY" or "KEEP OFF." Nor is there any gate barring my driveway. If my neighbors, or visitors from anywhere, want to drop in and see my place, they are always welcome. If I happen to be out in the yard, pruning the trees, or up in the pasture by the red barn, looking at my herd of cows, I will be glad to greet any callers. That has always been a rule at Angles.

In the early days of our married life, thanks to our three wonderful and lively children, the Barkley home life was never dull. Our first-born was a son, David Murrell, nicknamed "Bud." He became an army pilot, and flew the mail back in the days when that service was taken over briefly by the Air Corps. He resigned from the service, but returned to serve as an Air Corps major during World War II.

It was Bud who once gave me one of the most hair-raising airplane flights of my life. I had gone to visit him, shortly after he earned his wings, at a field at which he was stationed. His commanding officer suggested that Bud take me for a flight, and I agreed. Before we went up, however, the colonel, who did not want the wits scared out of any visiting senator, regardless of his relationship to the pilot, took Bud aside and told him that nothing less than a court-martial was in store for him if he did any tricks. "Yes, sir!" said Bud, dutifully saluting. Then he took me up and gave me a complete course in aerial acrobatics. He still insists that it was a gentle, low-level sight-seeing hop, but, to me, he flew like a fugitive from "Hell's Angels"—I have never experienced such close acquaintance with so many treetops in my whole life!

Our second-born, Marian, known as "Sis," is now Mrs. Max O'Rell Truitt, of Washington. She was my official hostess when I was Vice President, during the period between the first Mrs. Barkley's death and my second marriage. Sis claims that, in social matters, I am the world's worst procrastinator, and she insists she once had to conspire with my secretary to smuggle her into my office incognito one morning so she could make me say "yes" or "no" to a foot-high stack of invitations.

Then came "Wahwee." This is not an Indian name derived from any descendants of old Chief Paduke or anything like that: it is simply a typical Barkley family phonetic adaptation of the way she pronounced her name when she was a baby and could not speak plainly. Wahwee— the nickname has stuck all her life—is the wife of General Douglas MacArthur's nephew, Douglas MacArthur II, a career diplomat and Foreign Service officer, who, at time of this writing, is Counselor to the State Department. They and their daughter, Mimi, have lived in foreign capitals in various parts of the world. Douglas was assigned to our embassy in Vichy, France, when the Germans captured Paris during World War II, and he was interned by the Germans at Baden-Baden. Wahwee and Mimi got out of France about two jumps ahead of the Germans.

Wahwee claims she was the only member of the family with sufficient stamina ever to wear me down in a family debate. I do not know about that, but she was energetic enough to chauffeur me around Kentucky in grueling political campaigns when we would cover 400 miles and better in a day. This was in the period when I acquired the political nickname of "Iron Man" by delivering as many as sixteen speeches a day. Wahwee was as good a chauffeur as any man, if not better. She would wrap me up in a blanket for warmth, wind a scarf around my throat to protect my voice, and off we would whiz through the country-side. She would argue like an opposition congressman when I proposed taking a turn at driving, for she contends—I plead *nolo contendere* to the charge—that when I drove I would start to fall asleep at the wheel. She developed a device for waking me up, however. She would simply yell the name of my political opponent in my ear, and I would snap out of it and (according to Wahwee) automatically start delivering a speech.

Now there are seven grandchildren and one great-grandchild, and I have had a lot of pleasure from them all. I also acquired two lovely daughters when I married Mrs. Carleton S. Hadley, a widow, in November 1949. They call me "Dad," and I regard them as if they were my own.

No matter how busy I became in Washington, I managed to spend time with the children. Personally, I think it is a great tragedy for any father to become a stranger to his children, no matter what demands a career makes upon his time. I saw to it that we had picnics and Sunday drives together—first in the old-fashioned surrey I owned in Paducah, and then in our first automobile, a touring car with a collapsible top and isinglass curtains. On at least two out of three of such outings it would invariably rain, and I would have to get out and struggle with the curtains, passionately denouncing the man who had invented such contraptions.

We also had many vacation trips together. Often they were long auto tours to the scenic and historic places of America. In a family photo album somewhere there is a picture of me bending over a tire which had blown out before we had gone ten miles on the road, and scrawled across a strategic portion of my anatomy in Bud's schoolboy handwriting is the legend: "The Broad Expanse of a Sturdy Seat."

On another vacation trip, when Congress was in adjournment, we took the girls to Panama with us, and the Air Corps gave Mrs. Barkley, the girls, and me a flight across the isthmus in two open-cockpit observation planes. I remember insisting at the last minute that my wife and I fly in different planes, each taking one of the girls with us, so that, in case of accident, our remaining two children would have at least one parent left.

When the children were very young, they remained in Paducah with their mother. I chafed at the separation. When I finally came home after one long session of Congress and Wahwee acted as if she did not know me, I decided that this had to end. So when Congress met again, I took the family to Washington. We visited Paducah at every opportunity, however, and, as a practical politician, I had to caution the youngsters to say, when questioned in Kentucky, that Paducah was really home to them. Once, as we neared the state line while driving back to Washington, Marian piped up, "Daddy, can I tell the truth now?"

To this day my children will regale, and even overwhelm, anyone who will listen with stories on Life With Father in Politics. They even insist that I used to fine them 25 cents every time they forgot the name of a Kentucky voter. Whenever they bring up this subject, I maintain a dignified silence.

From time to time one hears that modern kids are being raised "too soft," and that the modern generation is "going to hell." In my own adult life, covering more than half a century, I have heard this so many times that I almost start to believe it myself every now and then. But then I see how youth stands up under such cruel and arduous tests as two World Wars and the Korean conflict, and I am convinced that this talk of "soft" youth is a lot of bunk. What I say goes for the girls as well as the boys, for many a time I have heard lamentations and wailings over the reckless course of the "flapper" and the "jazz baby" and whatever they call them today; yet American girls are making intelligent and devoted wives and mothers.

No, I have a great deal of faith in the so-called "modern generation"—and I have seen quite a few of these "modern generations" go by. Whatever the peculiarities of the times are, they usually work out their own problems according to the needs of their generation.

When I was a boy, of course, I had to go out, as I have related, and turn in a man's work—at least, what you might call a poor man's work—from the age of ten on, working in the fields and on the roads. It was good for me, for it strengthened my muscles and my body, and to these experiences I attribute much of my present good health, strength, and vigor at seventy-six. In general I think it is a good thing for a boy to do some hard work, though I realize, of course, that it can be overdone.

Going back to my own experiences as a father of young children, I tried to do my best not to spoil the youngsters, but I think I was a lenient father. I know we had a lot of fun together. I remember one of the first Christmases when we had a heavy snow in Paducah. In order to preserve the Santa Claus legend, I climbed out on the roof of the broad porch of our home, and made tracks in the snow leading to and from the chimney. When the kids saw the footprints, they were sure Old Santa had called.

There were some spankings, but not many. Once I tried to punish Bud for some misdeed. When I turned him over my knee he looked up at me, laughed, and said, "Daddy, are you playing?" "No, I'm not playing!" I answered gruffly, and lifted my hand. "Daddy, are you playing?" he repeated.

I had to laugh too, and that ended that spanking.

CHAPTER 6

I Ride into Politics on Horse (Not Mule) Back

THERE is a die-hard rumor, still extant after all these years, that, when I took my first plunge into politics as a candidate for prosecuting attorney in 1905, I rode a mule around McCracken County looking for votes. This story is a base canard, and, here and now, I wish to spike it for all time. It was not a mule—it was a horse.

The deal came about in this manner: I sorely needed some means of transportation, and my uncle Andrew Barkley had a spare mule by the name of Jude. I arranged to swap Jude for a one-eyed horse named Dick; I had to pay $25 to boot to Dick's owner, a neighboring farmer known as "Brother" Rudolph. Dick was a good horse. His only defects were that one bad eye and a tendency to slip the bridle. He was quite smart about slipping the bridle; you would tie him, securely, you thought, to a hitching post, and when you came back he would be half a mile down the road.

Anyway, it was this one-eyed horse that I rode around the county during my first campaign, not a mule. After the race was over and I had won, I returned Dick to Uncle Andrew. He got a horse, and I got an office.

My entrance into politics was inevitable. I was a Kentuckian and a lawyer, and I had, in those days, a natural inclination to stop whatever I was doing and start making a speech any time I saw as many as six persons assembled together. Back in those early Paducah days I once even made a speech to a local sportsmen's organization on the assigned subject of "Cracklin' Bread and Sweet Milk." It is a source of regret to me that a copy of this address has not been preserved for the archives, for I am sure that it must have been most illuminating.

Furthermore, I had politics in my blood, for, as I related in an earlier chapter, I had family links, through my paternal grandmother, with Adlai E. Stevenson, who had been Vice President under Cleveland, and Congressman "Quinine Jim" McKenzie, the noted Democratic orator.

When I first began considering the race for prosecuting attorney, a friend asked me if I had sufficient money for the campaign. He was a seasoned and somewhat cynical politician. I told him I did not have very much. He urged me not to run, assuring me it would be impossible for me to be elected without a large campaign fund. This advice annoyed me. I told him that, if I had to buy the office, I did not want it, but that I had more confidence in the people than he apparently had. I went on to make that campaign, and to win it, on a total expenditure of $250.

I have always retained my confidence in the people, and I have a deep respect for public opinion.

Political campaigning, as it was practiced in those days, was a fine art. Some of the subtler nuances, I am afraid, are becoming dulled today. To be a successful politician, a man had to be a cross between a statesman, a work horse, a cracker-barrel humorist and philosopher, a diplomat, and, though we hardly knew the word then, a psychiatrist. It also helped to have a stomach like a cast-iron furnace, for the demands made upon the gastronomical system were both prodigious and all-important. I was fortunate in the latter department, for I have always been able to eat and digest anything, and in ample quantities.

I have eaten my way through barbecues, burgoos, picnics, and church suppers from one end of the state to the other—"from the Big Sandy to the Mississippi," as an old Kentucky political saying has it. As a candidate for public office, I have subsidized the purchase of sufficient sheep and pigs as offerings for the barbecue pits to stock a fair-sized farm.

Of all the political eating I have indulged in, however, the most memorable are the church suppers. The good ladies of the communities would band together and give a public supper to raise money for the church— or maybe it was the school or some other worthy cause. Every one of the ladies would prepare delicious viands: fried chicken, stewed chicken, baked chicken; country hams, boiled, baked, and sliced; roast beef, poundcakes, layer cakes, devil's food and coconut cakes; pies of all kinds: apple, cherry, pumpkin, custard, strawberry, and gooseberry; then the vegetables in great profusion, and the pickles, and the hot breads, biscuits, rolls, and preserves. They would spread starched tablecloths right on the ground, and there, stretching for a hundred feet or more, were these gleaming white corridors laden with victuals, past which the candidate, who had bought a ticket, or as many tickets as his campaign budget would allow, would march, eating, complimenting, eating, smiling, eating, and handshaking. And woe unto the would-be office-seeker who passed up so much as a single pickle, if that item happened to be the homemade specialty of the wife of an important committeeman!

I always measured up manfully to my duties in the politico-gastronomical department, for eating has always been one of my long suits. In fact, there is suspicion in certain quarters that I am the original party about whom that old phrase, "He can eat a keg of nails," was coined. During my first race for the Senate one of the Kentucky newspapers wrote an article about me, quoting a number of my friends of early days, including Ernest Hilliard, of Clinton, who, with his brother, Calvin, operated a wheat-threshing enterprise for which I worked. "He could eat more Irish potatoes than any man I ever saw," Ernest recalled. "He used to amaze us all when he got to the cook-wagon."

But eating was not the only physical requirement. Like a soldier, one had to be able to bivouac wherever nightfall found him. In my first campaign, when I rode old one-eyed Dick around McCracken County, I slept in wagons, in barns, and sometimes on the ground. Once when it was too cold to sleep outside, I even shared the only heated (by fireplace) bedroom of a cottage with a farmer, his wife, and his daughter. The ladies retired first, while the farmer and I diplomatically removed ourselves to the front porch; then we came inside and the farmer deployed me strategically on a pallet against a far wall.

I have also pitched hay, threshed wheat, sawed logs, and dampened my head with a bucket of well water while speaking. For speaking in courthouse squares on hot summer days I advocate exterior sprinkling of the head rather than internal consumption of water; if you drink too much water while speaking, it does your voice no good. If one must quaff, however, there are communities where the tin dipper—or, better still, the gourd—is the approved vessel. There are also communities where a candidate with any perception can tell how he is doing simply by observing whether corn is served him on a plate or in a jug. I preferred the plate.

I won that first race, and, on the first Monday in January 1906, assumed the office of prosecuting attorney of the county to which I had moved as a young man only seven years before. The prosecuting attorney in Kentucky not only handles criminal cases but serves as legal advisor for the county government. One of my first duties—not a pleasant one —was to send an old friend of mine, an embezzling county official who had been elected on the same ticket with me, to prison. Before the sheriff took him away, I made a point of seeing the man I had convicted. I shook his hand and wished him well. He later rehabilitated himself and remained my good friend; he told me my gesture of friendliness had meant a good deal to him when he was down. I have always remembered that incident and have tried not to judge people too harshly. It helped me in later years to understand what Dean Acheson, Secretary of State in the Truman administration, really meant when he said he would not turn his back on Alger Hiss; he was not condoning Hiss's obnoxious crime, but was merely expressing a sentiment of Christian charity.

Dean Acheson, to digress momentarily, is one of the most delightful men I have ever known in public life. He has the rare gift of being able to jest, however wryly, at his own discomfiture. I remember asking him, when the anti-Acheson anvil chorus was in full crescendo, how he was bearing up.

"Well," Acheson answered, "I feel like the drunk who was tossed out of the saloon for the third time. As he lay there in the gutter, bruised and battered, he raised his head slightly, looked up at the bouncer, who was still standing over him, and said, 'You, sir, are a lousy — — — — and you have other faults, too!' "

During my term as prosecuting attorney I prosecuted other faithless public officials and compelled them to restore thousands of dollars of misappropriated funds to the county treasury.

At the next election I was nominated and elected to the office of county judge. The title is somewhat of a misnomer, for the judgeship is more of an administrative than a judicial post. I functioned, in effect, as the general business manager of the county. In this position I was able on the county level, to begin my lifelong efforts to improve rural roads. I later continued these efforts on a national scale when I went to Congress. I am still proud of what I was able to do in McCracken County, for we developed a system whereby farmers agreed to work with their teams on improvement of the primitive dirt and gravel roads of that day. The county did not ask them to work for nothing, as was the custom in my grandfather's and father's day, but it paid them half the usual wage. As the work was undertaken after crops had been brought in, both the farmers and the county benefited. It was a splendid demonstration of how citizens are willing to work for their communities.

On the very day on which I was sworn in as county judge I came in for a bit of good-natured hazing. A county judge is authorized to perform marriage ceremonies, and, immediately after I took my oath, the county clerk informed me that a couple was waiting to be married. I had never performed such a ceremony before. When I stepped into the court-room, I found not only the young couple but a crowd of more than one hundred persons, including my immediate predecessor, Judge Richard T. Lightfoot, and all the other county officials, waiting on me. The audience had been rounded up by County Clerk Gus G. Singleton, a prankish sort of fellow, and the presence of such a crowd made me nervous. I was especially conscious of Judge Lightfoot, who had per-formed hundreds of marriage ceremonies and was, in fact, noted, as the saying went, for tying a nice knot. I began to choke up so I could hardly speak the words of the ceremony. I grunted, sneezed, coughed, swallowed, bit my lips, blew my nose, wiped my eyes, rubbed my brow, and shook at the knees.

Finally I undertook to lecture the hapless wedding couple on the seriousness of the step they were taking. I got all bogged down in a wordy and windy sermon. It is still something of a wonder to me that I did not scare them completely out of the notion of wedlock.

At last, in desperation, I stopped short, blurted out, "You're married!" and fled, pausing only to collect my three-dollar fee.

Forty years later, when I was delivering a political speech in behalf of Senator Scott Lucas in Illinois, I received a note from this same couple, who happened to be in the audience. They brought with them their marriage certificate, the first I had ever signed. I interrupted my talk to bring them to the platform, where I told the story, sparing no details, to the crowd. I was glad to learn after all the years that I had not botched the job.

This Gus Singleton, by the way, who was sworn in as clerk on the same day on which I became judge, was an amusing fellow. Three times he had run unsuccessfully for the office. Finally he made a fourth and successful race in which his main campaign issue was the fact that he had tried so hard and so often and really would like to have the office for just one term. Actually Gus had become so popular by this time that the people were going to elect him anyhow.

He made a good clerk, and, when his four-year term had rolled by, he announced his candidacy for a second term. At a political rally one day he was making his speech when someone in the crowd yelled, "Hey, Gus, didn't you promise us four years ago that you only wanted the job for one term?"

"Well," said Singleton, making a really masterful recovery, "I may have said that, but I was laboring under a little misapprehension. At the time I made that statement, I thought this was a lifetime job."

In 1912, not quite thirty-five years old, I made my first race for the House, announcing myself as a candidate to represent the First Congressional District. The district, comprising thirteen counties, was then represented by a veteran legislator, Ollie M. James, who was vacating his seat in order to run for the Senate. James was a huge man, both physically and from the standpoint of his political and oratorical reputation. I remember introducing myself to a country storekeeper during the campaign one day and announcing, "I'm running to fill Ollie James's place." He looked me up and down, as if taking careful note that I was at least 150 pounds lighter than Ollie, and replied, "Son, you'll never make it."

In addition to his bulk Ollie James was one of Kentucky's most colorful political figures, and he was nationally known as an orator, ranking close to William Jennings Bryan. In those days, prior to enactment and ratification of the Seventeenth Amendment, United States Senators were elected by state legislatures rather than by direct popular vote of the people. When James went after the Senate seat, the incumbent, Senator Thomas H. Paynter, prudently withdrew, and James was named senator practically without opposition.

Kentucky politics in those days was still being influenced by an event that had taken place twelve years earlier—the assassination of William Goebel. The Goebel affair was the strangest chapter in the entire history of state politics; indeed, one of the strangest episodes in nationwide political history. I shall relate the highlights briefly to give an idea of the ruggedness of the political arena into which I was plunging.

Goebel was a highly controversial figure, in many ways a ruthless man. He had once killed a political enemy in a pistol duel on the streets of Covington. There seemed to be no middle ground in the reactions of those who knew him: he inspired either fanatical hatred or equally fanatical admiration. Some have compared him to such dictators as Hitler and Mussolini, while others praise his memory to the heavens. He has even been the subject of one adulatory biography titled *The First New Dealer*, which seeks to portray him as a pioneer of social reform.

In any event, Goebel was an aggressive, ambitious leader in the state Senate in the days when the Louisville & Nashville Railroad practically dominated Kentucky politics. Under the direction of Milton H. Smith, also a ruthlessly ambitious man who had risen from telegrapher to president of the railroad, the L. & N., by making liberal use of railroad funds (and also scattering passes like peanuts among legislators and politicians), had a virtual strangle hold on state politics. Its influence extended from county to federal offices.

In 1899, Goebel, who was opposed to the railroad machine, entered a three-cornered race for governor. This was in the days before Kentucky's present compulsory primary law, and gubernatorial nominees were selected by a convention called together by the state committee. Goebel was low man in the number of delegates pledged to him, but, by joining forces with the second-strongest candidate, he managed to outmaneuver and defeat the candidate having the largest number of delegates.

There was much talk, not entirely without justification, of chicanery in the method by which Goebel secured his nomination. For years the term "Music Hall Convention"—a name derived from the hall at Louisville where Goebel was nominated—was regarded by some in Kentucky as a synonym for political trickery. Dissident Democratic factions put up a rival candidate, and, as a result, in the bitter election that followed, a Republican, William S. Taylor, was declared elected by a close margin as governor of Kentucky.

Taylor, a decidedly weak man, was sworn in and took office. The state legislature, however, was Democratic, and Goebel challenged the election by filing a contest before the legislature. While the contest was in progress, the pro-Goebel forces charged the opposition with bringing 1200 armed mountaineers—a lawless army—into Frankfort, the state capital.

One day, as Goebel was about to enter the state capitol, he was shot from ambush. The shot came from the window of the office of Caleb Powers, the Secretary of State who had been sworn in on the ticket with Governor Taylor. But Powers was not in his office at the time: he was on an L. & N. train between Louisville and Lexington, carrying on his person a pardon issued in advance of the shooting by Governor Taylor! It was never determined beyond question who actually fired the shot that killed Goebel.

The legislature promptly named the wounded Goebel as the legally elected Governor of Kentucky. But he died a few days later, and young Lieutenant Governor J. C. W. Beckham, his running mate on the "Music Hall" ticket, was sworn in. Secretary of State Powers was arrested, and the ousted Governor Taylor fled to Indiana, which refused to extradite him.

The Goebel affair produced an aftermath of bitterness and vengefulness that lasted for years. It made and broke many political figures.

Caleb Powers was tried four times, and was sentenced twice to life imprisonment and once to hanging. However, at the fourth trial, a jury disagreed, and the ex-Secretary of State languished in jail until another Republican governor, Augustus Wilson was elected in 1907 and pardoned him and others implicated in the assassination. Powers then became a candidate for Congress, campaigning on the slogan that "the Republicans ought to keep me in Congress as long as the Democrats kept me in jail." They did!

I had come of age and cast my first vote for a gubernatorial candidate the year all this took place. As a Democrat, I voted for Goebel. Nearly thirteen years later, when I first went to Congress, the Goebel affair was still a topic of political discussion in Kentucky.

Although senators were chosen by the legislature, aspirants for the House had to stand for popular election. That year—1912—was the first year of the compulsory primary law in Kentucky, and I found myself facing a stiff campaign in the hot summer months, quite different from the winter campaign I had made in 1905, when I rode old Dick around the county in my quest for the prosecuting attorneyship.

When I entered the race, I pitted myself against an able and outstanding citizen, Judge Joseph E. Robbins of Mayfield, who had already announced. At an early stage of the campaign Judge Robbins sent word to me he had decided to withdraw in my favor, and that he would make an announcement to that effect whenever I desired. In my political inexperience I reasoned incorrectly that, if the popular Judge Robbins withdrew in my favor at this stage, it would scare off all potential opposition. I asked him to make the announcement at once. This was a mistake, as it immediately brought three other formidable candidates into the race.

One was Jacob Corbett, a well-known lawyer from a nearby county. Corbett, an excellent and entertaining speaker, kept the audiences interested and amused, but he was somewhat like William J. Bryan, who once told me, "Barkley, I draw greater crowds, get more applause, and fewer votes than any man who ever ran for public office."

Another candidate was Denny P. Smith, the district commonwealth's attorney, who not only was a good campaigner but had the support of the state administration with all its patronage. The third opponent was my old law preceptor, former Congressman Hendrick, who, by the way, had been one of the prosecutors who attempted to convict the parties accused of assassinating Goebel. I had worked first for Colonel Hendrick when he was the junior partner of Judge Bishop, and I later continued my law studies under him when he became senior partner in the firm of Hendrick and Miller. As I have already indicated, the colonel was annoyed at the presumption of his onetime law clerk in seeking to stand up against him for Congress, although I had announced long in advance of his own candidacy.

In fact, Colonel Hendrick once denounced me before a crowd as a dangerously ambitious young man. "Why, if you elect him," he warned, "next thing you know he'll be asking you to send him to the Senate!" In reply I admitted frankly that if I ever saw a senatorship lying around loose that looked as easy to win as this House seat, I certainly would reach out after it.

I also made a point of tossing the "ambition" charge right back at the colonel, who was well known for his eagerness to run for office. I used to tell our audiences, "The good colonel will run for anything not nailed down or locked up. He'll run for anything he can see, and we can be glad his eyesight is no better. Why, when the Pope died some years ago, nobody would tell Hendrick, for fear he would declare for that office!"

The crowds used to roar at these jibes, and the colonel hastily dropped this line of attack. He did, however, take after me on the grounds of being "socialistic" because I advocated federal aid for roads. This did not bother me, as I remembered, and pointed out to our listeners, that Grover Cleveland also had been denounced as a "socialist" because he established rural free mail delivery. Midway in the campaign the Democratic national convention which nominated Woodrow Wilson adopted a plank in its platform advocating federal aid to highway construction. The colonel then had to backwater or be in the position of opposing his party's platform, so overnight I ceased to be a "socialist."

All in all, the colonel kept himself in such a state of self-annoyance that his political judgment was warped. It is a good idea for any candidate, whether he be running for constable or President, to keep his sense of humor, for once you begin stewing over petty things you usually are in the soup. In this 1912 race, for instance, the colonel became enraged because the Woodmen of the World, a fraternal order of which I was a member, would call on me regularly to deliver memorial orations for departed brethren. He finally made a speech bitterly attacking the Woodmen of the World, and that alienated some 5000 members of the lodge in our Congressional district.

On another occasion Colonel Hendrick became so enraged when speaking about a political enemy before a mixed audience that he used the same term of opprobrium that got President Truman in hot water when he applied it to a well-known columnist. It was one of those phrases one is not supposed to use without smiling, and the outburst did not help the mercurial colonel one bit.

Occasionally, however, the colonel could muster up some wry humor at his own expense. I remember once when all four of us candidates were sitting under an oak tree waiting for a crowd to assemble. A man came up, tapped Denny Smith—he was the candidate with the state patronage to dispense—and drew him aside for an earnest conference. Then someone tapped me and took me off for a private talk. That left Colonel Hendrick and Jake Corbett sitting there by themselves. "Jake," said Hendrick to Corbett, "did you see that ragged-looking fellow take Denny Smith off? He was after some little old two-bit job with the state, which Denny probably will give him. And did you see that dirty-faced clodhopper approach Barkley? He was asking him to come out here next Sunday and preach over some Woodsman's tombstone. Here you and I sit with not a damned thing but brains, and nobody wants 'em!"

We four candidates covered the district together, participating in joint debates. To keep down expenses, we agreed to ride together, sharing the cost of two buggies, and sometimes automobiles. I always felt that Colonel Hendrick, in consenting to travel with us upstarts who were presuming to challenge his right to return to Congress, was somewhat in the position of the bereaved husband who was asked by the undertaker to ride to the cemetery with his mother-in-law. "All right, I'll do it," he told the undertaker, "but, dang bust it, it'll ruin my whole day!"

As we rode around the district to the various meetings, we would switch around between the two buggies. When I rode with Hendrick, he would say to me, "Alben, did you ever see two worse demagogues than those fellows, Smith and Corbett?" Next day, when I rode with Corbett, he would say, "Did you ever see two worse demagogues than Hendrick and Smith?" And when I rode with Smith he would ask if I had ever seen a worse pair of demagogues than Corbett and Hendrick! I was perfectly willing to agree with them all.

As I think back upon that campaign and recall how an opponent sought to tag me as a socialist—a radical, if you please!—because I advocated federal aid to roads and other new and progressive legislation, my mind is naturally and almost automatically focused on a serious problem of our own times. I refer to the use and abuse of the powers of Congressional investigations through its standing or special committees, coupled with the almost epidemic use of what has come to be called the "big smear" technique.

I do not like the word "smear" as it has come to be used. Not every investigation or accusation is a "smear." Unsupported or unjustified innuendoes may constitute an attack upon one's character or reputation. On the contrary, guilty persons may seek to divert attention from their derelictions by crying "smear!" In my opinion neither the use of the "smear" technique nor the use of the word as a cloak behind which to hide is legitimate. But neither is it legitimate for ambitious men to use the investigative power to gain publicity or notoriety to advance their personal or political fortunes. Such procedure or purpose is despicable.

If a person in public life, incidentally, is the victim of a real smear—an unjust and false accusation—the best way to handle it is to go to the people and tell them the truth. Truth, in my opinion, is still an all-powerful weapon.

Investigations of public questions by committees of both Houses can be, and frequently are, necessary and valuable legislative instruments, theoretically conducted for the purpose of obtaining information pertinent to the enactment of needed legislation.

I have given a great deal of thought over a good many years to the subject of Congressional investigations. In fact, in 1947, when the short-lived, Republican-controlled Eightieth Congress came in, I wrote an article, entitled "Advice to the Republican Party," in which I had something to say concerning probes. What I wrote then seems just as timely today; I said:

> A prominent Republican member of the House of Representatives was recently quoted as saying they would open every day's session with a prayer and end it with a probe.
>
> This may have been an enthusiastic outburst of specious alliteration, but, if literally adopted, it might cheapen both the prayer and the probe.
>
> There are beyond question some things connected with the war and the expenditure of public moneys which are legitimate subjects of investigation, including the misconduct of public officers, legislative or executive. But there are too many vital problems on the Congressional doorstep to justify the consumption of the entire time of Congress for the next two years in conducting inquisitions only, especially if inspired by partisanship or a desire to make hay for the next presidential election.
>
> I believe that the public interest frequently requires the most searching and pitiless inquiries into wrongdoing wherever it may be

found. This is necessary to punish criminal guilt and to warn others of the fate which awaits faithless public servants. Such investigations should have the support of the minority and will have it.

What should be avoided is any tinge of witch-hunting obsession, looking to some political advantage for a party or a candidate. I have observed and participated in a number of investigations in the last thirty years. I have never seen one that either elected or defeated a political party or a candidate for President, including the Teapot Dome investigation in the Harding and Coolidge administrations.

The plain fact of the business is that Congress is a lawmaking body. It is not a police agency, a grand jury, or a trial court. It cannot try or convict anybody for a violation of any law. It is true that one cannot always foretell whether legislation will result from investigations. I myself have participated in and presided over many hearings which led to the enactment of new or amended laws affecting many subjects such as communications, currency, banking, taxes, stock market practices, employment, commerce, and others.

It seems, however, that some of the more recent, much-heralded hearings have been projected into purely political fields wherein there may be no legislative cure.

Any sensible person will applaud, rather than condemn, Congressional hearings, when they are properly conducted for a legitimate purpose. But it would be an intolerable thing for the investigative power of Congress to be prostituted for the purpose of promoting the personal or political ambitions of a group or of an individual. It is beyond the purpose of legitimate inquiries for any member of Congress to use such investigations, either to exploit himself as a hero or to do injustice to individuals who may be the innocent subjects of ruthless procedures. My long experience has taught me that there are no indispensable men who have been anointed exclusively as the "saviors" of our inherited political and social institutions.

I would be less than frank if I did not state that many investigations which may not have led to legislation have been wholesome and beneficial. For instance, the disclosure of the "Teapot Dome" and other scandals during the Harding administration, while it did not defeat the Republicans, did throw the spotlight on many men unworthy to hold public office. The investigation into the Pearl Harbor disaster, over which I presided, while it may not have resulted in specific legislation, was useful in clarifying a confused public opinion, and fixing some degree of responsibility for the disaster. There have been others of equal public benefit.

It is true that some unsavory characters, who were, and are, unquestionably enemies of this country and who should be rooted from public life, have been exposed through the inquisitorial type of Congressional investigations. At the same time it is a serious matter when the innocent can be made to suffer along with the guilty, without the protection of what we have always cherished as "due process of law." It is deplorable when individuals, and even whole classes or groups of people, religious, educational, or economic, are condemned by such procedures, often without the opportunity of replying or defending themselves.

I suppose it is natural in times of hysteria or fear for these injustices to be expected. But it is surely not in harmony with our process of government, which provides legitimate methods of dealing with violations of law or breaches of public trust, for any official group to blast the reputation of innocent men or worthy institutions by procedures which would not be tolerated in any court of law.

Out of it all has grown what seems to me an urgent and obvious need for a Congressional code of procedure, defining the areas in which investigative committees can move and establishing rules for the protection of witnesses. Both Houses of Congress have the power to correct abuses by any of their committees. They owe a responsibility to the public to do so. I think that public confidence in our great legislative institution would be effectively and wholesomely enhanced if Congress itself would enact a sensible code of procedure to achieve these aims.

Some observers have suggested that part of the remedy would be to amend the Constitution so as to remove the immunity from the charge of libel which members of Congress are afforded when they speak on the floor or in committee. I do not agree. The immunity clause was put into the Constitution for a good purpose—to protect members from being intimidated by threats of lawsuits or other prosecution, so they shall be free to speak what they consider to be the truth. There is no doubt that the immunity clause has been abused; there are some men who will abuse any worth-while privilege. However, the original aim of the provision was wholesome, and I seriously doubt whether Congress should— or ever would—submit an amendment which, if ratified, would change that provision of the Constitution.

One rule which I certainly would like to see adopted by Congressional committees is the right of any witness to be advised by counsel, and, within reasonable limitations, to ask questions of his accusers. Many

Congressional committees already follow this procedure, which is as it should be, but sometimes the right to have counsel is circumscribed. It is a principle of law in this country that a man accused in any court of a crime shall have counsel to defend him; and if he cannot employ counsel, the court will appoint one to represent him without fee.

Sometimes before Congressional committees, however, a witness will be hauled in, interrogated, occasionally abused, exposed to the eye of television and the ear of radio and the press. He is almost helpless. He is like the boy who was being whipped mercilessly by his father, who said, "Son, I hate to do this to you—I'm only doing it because I love you." The boy replied: "I sure wish I were big enough to return your affection!"

However, returning to my personal story, I won my first Congressional race against my three opponents. I became a member of the Sixty-Third Congress on the same day on which Woodrow Wilson was inaugurated. Wilson, a man of great idealism and vision, one of the truly great Presidents of the United States, became my political idol. My political philosophy, the liberalism which I have always espoused, was nurtured by my association with him. For the next eight years I worked eagerly to do my part in bringing about the lasting accomplishments of the Wilson era, a momentous period of American history.

CHAPTER 7

I Go to Congress: The Wilson Era

WOODROW WILSON was inaugurated on March 4, 1913, the same day on which I was sworn in as a freshman congressman. I came to revere him as the greatest statesman and greatest President under whom I ever served. It was said of President Wilson that he loved humanity en masse but not individually. This was no more true of Wilson than it was of Franklin D. Roosevelt, about whom the same slur was repeated twenty years later. Though Wilson, the intellectual, was no extrovert, he had a deep and abiding love for people as individuals, and he displayed his warm humanity in many homey little ways.

President Wilson revealed his own true nature in a remark I once heard him make in talking about men who enter public life. "Some men grow; others swell," he said. Wilson grew but did not swell. With the weight of the country—and later of the world—on his shoulders, he never became too big to listen sympathetically to the problems of those in lesser positions.

I recall the first interview which I, as a young, unknown newcomer to the House, sought with him, and was granted. I had patronage problems. My complaint was startlingly similar to one of the laments raised by the Republicans who came in under President Eisenhower in 1953 —all of which goes to prove there is really nothing very new in politics.

It seemed that the outgoing Republican President, William Howard Taft, had issued an Executive order blanketing all fourth-class postmasters into Civil Service without examination. Since the rural free-delivery system had not been extended all over the nation at this time, this meant that thousands of small-town and village postmasterships were frozen for the G.O.P., and we "deserving Democrats," as William Jennings Bryan used to say, were suffering. I had just won a hard race for Congress and was being besieged by my supporters to produce some patronage.

President Wilson listened to me patiently. He said he was aware of the problem and planned to do something about putting these postmaster-ships on a competitive-examination basis, which he later did. I recall vividly how Wilson, in commenting to me on the large number of new congressmen who were carried into office with him in the Democratic landslide, said to me, "I look upon you younger members of Congress much as I looked upon my students at Princeton. You have had no ex-perience yet in legislative matters, but you will learn." He went on to say that he too had lacked experience when he became president of Princeton and later Governor of New Jersey, and that he now looked forward to learning, along with the newcomers in the House and Senate, more about the machinery of government. The sincerity and humility of his manner won me completely.

There was another occasion when President Wilson took the trouble to write a detailed letter which rescued me from a ticklish local situation. The postmastership at Mayfield, Kentucky, was open and no Democrat had held the job for twelve years. I had ten applications for the post, all from able citizens who had been my staunch supporters. One day Mr. Wilson sent for me and explained he had a personal interest in the May-field appointment. One of his Princeton professors had married a May-field girl, and her brother, a man named W. Lindsay Hale, who was an outstanding local citizen and a personal friend of mine, was one of those who sought the job. "I would like to appoint this gentleman," Wilson told me, "but I do not want to deprive you or any congressman of his right to recommend appointments. How do you feel about it?"

I promptly answered that I would not dream of standing in the way of any personal appointment which the President of the United States de-sired to make, but that I would certainly appreciate it if he would write a letter which I could use at home to square myself with the other appli-cants. He wrote such a letter, so courteously and diplomatically worded that when it was published in Mayfield all the disappointed applicants accepted the President's intervention in good grace. As a matter of fact, had it not been for the President's friend's brother-in-law, I probably would have lost nine friends or made nine lukewarm supporters!

Though an intellectual, Wilson was no ethereal cloud dweller. He loved vaudeville, and, since I was a devotee myself, I often saw the Presi-dent and Mrs. Wilson in their box at what was then Chase's Theater—now Keith's—in Washington, enjoying a Saturday matinee. He particularly relished the slapstick comedy acts, and his deep-throated laughter could be heard halfway across the theater. He had a deft turn of his own with the humorous phrase. His Vice President, Thomas R. Marshall, once came to him with one of Wilson's scholarly volumes on American history, and Wilson unhesitatingly inscribed it: "To My Favorite Vice."

He also poked fun at what he insisted was his personal lack of beauty. I have heard him recite a Limerick which, as I remember it, went something like this:

As a beauty I'm not a great star.
Others are handsomer far
But my face—I don't mind it
Because I'm behind it
It's the folks out in front that I jar.

The President had the nation's sympathy when the first Mrs. Wilson died. Likewise, the public took a great romantic interest in his remarriage to the charming widow, Mrs. Edith Bolling Galt. Later in life I myself went through a similar experience of bereavement and remarriage.

Woodrow Wilson's entrance into the White House was a breath of fresh air in the then stale atmosphere of American politics. He succeeded President Taft, an amiable but indecisive Chief Executive, though a great lawyer and later an outstanding Chief Justice. Taft's qualities were best summed up in a remark passed by my predecessor in the House, Senator Ollie James. "Mr. Taft," said James, "is a well-meaning man who was born with two left feet."

One thing which I always admired about the massive and rotund Mr. Taft, however, was his ability to retain his sense of humor in the face of unpleasant developments. His one-term administration as President came to grief, among other things, over the unfortunate tariff policy which he was forced by his party to accept, and he was resoundingly defeated in the election of 1912. In fact, he received fewer popular and electoral votes than Theodore Roosevelt, who had been his predecessor in the White House and who, because of his dissatisfaction with Taft's policies, split the Republican vote by running independently as the "Bull Moose" Progressive candidate. Taft actually captured only eight electoral votes—four from Utah and four from Vermont—and this inspired a widely repeated Washington anecdote. A Republican leader, conferring with President Taft after the debacle, happened to look out the window and saw Senator Reed Smoot of Utah coming up the White House steps.

"Look, Mr. President," he said, "here comes that old Mormon from Utah with half your votes in his vest pocket!"

There was a Minnesota congressman named Adam Bede, who was quite a joker and who once took the liberty of patting President Taft on his enormous stomach and asking, "Mr. President, what are you going to name it?" Instead of being offended, the good-natured Taft chuckled and replied, "If it's a boy, I'll name it Theodore, and, if it's a girl, Theodora. But if it's what I think it is—plain wind—I am going to call it Adam Bede after you!"

As I write this, the tragedy of the death of Senator Robert A. Taft, son of President Taft, is still fresh. I would like to digress for a personal tribute to this outstanding Republican leader, whose own ambition to go to the White House was never realized. While I disagreed frequently with Bob Taft's political ideas, he was a man of great ability, integrity, and patriotism whose personal friendship I valued.

Sometimes Bob Taft was criticized for shifting his position so frequently on important issues in the face of new developments. But even that showed a great deal of courage, a willingness to admit that new facts can alter one's previous judgment. He reminded me in that respect of a statement that my old colleague, Senator Henry Ashurst, of Arizona, one of the most eloquent men in the Senate in his time, once made about himself. After quoting Emerson's lines, " 'A foolish consistency is the hobgoblin of little minds, adored by little statesmen and philosophers and divines,' " Senator Ashurst declared, "I am proud of my consistency in my inconsistency."

Bob Taft well deserved his title of "Mr. Republican," and nothing was more indicative of his devotion to his party and his country than the course he followed after he lost the nomination to General Eisenhower. Not only did he campaign for the election of the man who had captured the prize he himself had ardently sought for so many years, but, as majority leader of the Senate before his tragic death in 1953, he became the Administration's loyal and most effective lieutenant on Capitol Hill. When I stepped down as "Veep" in January 1953, I was doubly proud that it was Robert A. Taft who introduced the resolution commending my services as presiding officer of the Senate, and who said of me, "In all times, he has been fair in the decisions he has been called upon to render."

The decisiveness of the Democratic landslide in 1912, with overwhelming majorities elected to both House and Senate, indicated conclusively that President Taft could not have been re-elected even if former President Theodore Roosevelt had not split the Republican party with his Bull Moose movement. However, Woodrow Wilson's own nomination that year came after a bitter convention fight in which Champ Clark of Missouri, the powerful Speaker of the House of Representatives, held a majority of votes for several ballots. At that time it was necessary for the nominee to receive a two-thirds majority, but it also had been an unwritten custom for the convention to swing to the man who received a simple majority. In this case a dramatic switch from Clark to Wilson by the eloquent William Jennings Bryan threw the nomination to Wilson—and once again the course of history was changed from what it might have been.

Speaker Clark never fully recovered from his bitter disappointment. When I first went to the House, Clark, himself a former Kentuckian, went out of his way to guide and assist me, and I enjoyed a close relationship with him. Nevertheless, when this country was drawn into war, I was shocked by the extremity of his opposition to the draft law recommended by President Wilson. He left the rostrum to take the floor—an unusual action for a Speaker—and scathingly denounce the President's request. The line he used that I never could approve was a statement to the effect that "in Missouri, conscripts and convicts are synonymous."

I was among those who fired back and helped to pass the draft bill over Speaker Clark's opposition. "We are invited to play a coward's part beneath the Stars and Stripes," I declared. "I will play no such ignoble part. . . . Those [who] have set themselves against the just request and recommendation of the President unconsciously appeal to what they believe is the cowardice of those whom they attempt to represent.

"It would be worse than criminal folly," I continued, "for us to delude ourselves as to the character or the extent of the task which has been forced upon this nation by the German government." I went on to say that I voted for the declaration of war because an undeclared war already had been forced upon us in actuality by the German Empire, and that "there was no other honorable course left for this nation to pursue."

Twice in my lifetime I have had the distasteful duty of voting to draft the young manhood of our country for the defense of democracy. Twice I have seen the published pictures, melancholy in their sameness, of our Secretaries of War—Newton D. Baker in World War I; Henry L. Stimson in the next one—drawing the numbers from the goldfish bowl that sent the young men off to battle. Conscription is never a pleasant dosage, but the time comes when a democracy must take bitter medicine, or perish. Pray God there will never be another goldfish bowl—that the old dream of Woodrow Wilson for real peace in the world will someday come true.

Woodrow Wilson's reputation as a liberal scholar was established during his days as professor of political economy and later as president of Princeton University, and his renown as a political liberal began with the progressive program he inaugurated during his term as Governor of New Jersey, prior to his election as President. Among other things, during his short time as governor, he recommended and secured passage of a series of bills known as the "Seven Sisters"—so called because there were seven related acts—which set up rigid and much-needed regulation of trusts and monopolies. The pattern he followed in the state House presaged the course his administration would take when he moved into the White House.

One of the most revealing early personal experiences I had with President Wilson occurred when I went to the White House with the Kentucky Congressional delegation to urge the appointment of a Kentucky man, Judge James M. Benton, of Winchester, to fill a vacancy on the Supreme Court. Judge Benton was an outstanding jurist and would have made a great justice. Wilson listened patiently to everything we had to say; then, when we had all finished, he asked but one question, "Gentlemen, does your candidate believe that the law *grows,* or does he take the legalistic view that it is finished?"

Shortly after that Wilson filled that vacancy by nominating Justice Louis Dembitz Brandeis, also a native Kentuckian, who, throughout his entire long and distinguished career on the bench, demonstrated by his decisions his belief that the law is a living, growing thing.

The late Justice Brandeis, incidentally, was one of the great jurists and great citizens of our times. I came to know him rather well, and often used to visit the Justice and Mrs. Brandeis at their modest apartment in Washington. It was Justice Brandeis who largely fired my zeal for Zionism and my interest, long before the state of Israel was set up, in seeing that the homeland of the Jewish people was restored. When I first visited the Jewish homeland, then called Palestine, in 1934, I drove over the desert and could not visualize how such a wasted and denuded land ever could have been a land of milk and honey, or ever could be again. On trips over the same terrain since the Jewish people have developed Israel, I have been filled with amazement bordering upon awe at the magnificent gains they have accomplished.

The social significance of the Wilson era was overshadowed—and, indeed, the scope of its accomplishments was circumscribed—by the out-

Dorothy Brower in 1900. When Dorothy's family moved from Paducah to Tennessee, Barkley continued to court her by letter and visits, whenever possible.

Dorothy Brower at the time of her graduation, in 1900.

Mrs. Barkley in 1910. Barkley's marriage to Dorothy, in 1903, had provided him with an additional incentive to get ahead.

With three children, the Barkleys' home life was never dull. David, Marian, and Laura Louise are shown with their mother in 1918.

Mrs. Barkley in 1936. The marriage of Alben Barkley and Dorothy Brower was a happy partnership, which lasted until her death in 1947.

No matter how busy Congressman Barkley was in Washington, he managed to spend time with his family. Here he is, in 1916, with Mrs. Barkley, David, Laura Louise (left), and Marian (right).

The Barkley family vacations were usually spent seeing the scenic and historic places of America. Congressman Barkley took his three children to Independence Hall in 1920.

Marian Barkley (Sis) at twenty. She is now Mrs. Max O'Rell Truitt of Washington.

David Murrell Barkley (Bud) at twenty. David is now a farmer and businessman in Paducah.

Laura Louise Barkley (Wahwee) at fourteen. She is now the wife of Douglas MacArthur II, nephew of General MacArthur.

Mimi MacArthur, Barkley's granddaughter.

Dorothy Anne and Alben William Barkley II, children of the David Barkleys, are shown at their grandfather Barkley's desk in the Senate, Inauguration Day, January 20, 1949.

Wide World

Max O'Rell Truitt

William Barkley Truitt

Thomas Hulen Truitt

Stephen McKenzie Truitt

The four Truitt grandsons. It was Stephen who originated that Barkley-inspired word "Veep."

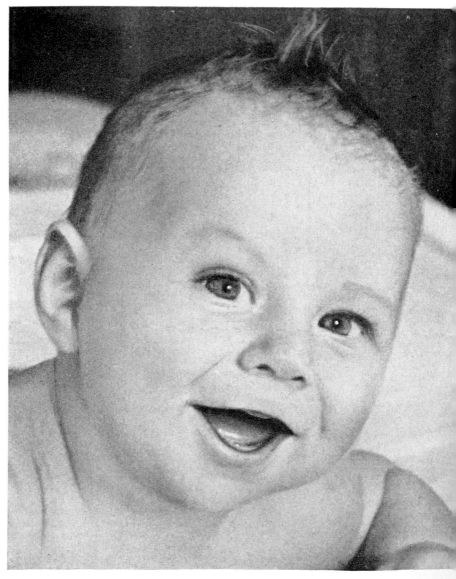

The Veep's first great-grandchild. Peter Tyson Truitt, son of Mr. and Mrs. Max O'Rell Truitt, was born in Honolulu, April 10, 1954.

break of World War I. However, in the years before the United States was drawn into that conflict, the Wilson administration gave the country the most far-reaching social and economic reforms of any administration in our history up to that time. The broad vision of Woodrow Wilson was not equaled again until the early days of Franklin D. Roosevelt's New Deal, when once again a leader with courage and imagination took far-seeing and bold measures to deal with the demanding realities of the day.

To me, as a new congressman, those were exciting years. The Wilson landslide had swept out a number of important figures and had brought a lot of new young faces into Congress, mine included. There were strong and colorful personalities operating in both the House and the Senate, and, for a young man fresh out of Paducah, it was a stimulating experience just to be there among them.

For instance, one of the men who was a tradition during my early years in the House was Joseph G. Cannon of Illinois. "Uncle Joe" had lost his Speakership when the Democrats captured control of the House during the latter days of the Taft administration, and, indeed, he was out of Congress entirely during my first two years in Washington, having been one of the casualties of the Wilson landslide, but he came back later. Even while he was gone, he was a favorite source of House legends. He was one of the most authoritative Speakers who ever presided over the House—a real "czar," ranking along with Thomas B. Reed of Maine, whom I shall discuss later.

In Cannon's day the Speaker had authority to appoint committee members, not only of his party, but of the opposition party, and Cannon wielded that power with such absolute ruthlessness that even his own Republicans finally revolted against him and voted to strip the Speaker of his appointive and many other powers.

I remember an anecdote about the chin-whiskered, cigar-smoking Uncle Joe which illustrates his salty type of humor. During the debate over the declaration of war against Germany in 1917, Uncle Joe, who was back in Congress by then but no longer Speaker, was taking issue with a lady member of the House. He rose and asked, "Will the lady yield?"

She replied graciously, "The lady will be delighted to yield to the gentleman from Illinois."

Uncle Joe, then in his eighties, thereupon leaned over to the representative sitting next to him, and, in a ferocious stage whisper which could be heard for several benches away, said, "My God! Now that she has yielded, what can I do about it?"

There was a great deal of good comradeship in the House in those days. I remember once succumbing to a small touch of self-importance when the newspapers saw fit to report that, on the adjournment of a session of Congress, Representative A. W. Barkley (D., Ky.) led his colleagues in singing "My Old Kentucky Home" on the floor of the House. My assistant song leader on that sentimental occasion was Representative James Mann, then the Republican minority leader of the House.

Ironically enough, Jim Mann is remembered today principally for his sponsorship of the Mann ("white slavery") Act, prohibiting transportation of women across state lines for immoral purposes. In his day, however, he was one of the ablest members of the House, but he was relentless in fighting to block action on any bill, whether it was introduced by Republican or Democrat, if he thought it was a bad bill or one that would raid the Treasury. He made so many enemies among his own party that, when the Republicans captured control of the House in 1919, they passed him over and chose another member, Representative Gillett, of Massachusetts, to serve as Speaker. Jim Mann had more sympathy on the Democratic side of the aisle, where we felt he had earned the Speakership by his vigorous leadership, than he did among his fellow Republicans. I had many talks with him, and I know that he felt a bitter disappointment that remained with him for the rest of his life.

All of which impels me to say that a man who has not worked out a personal philosophy for living with his disappointments, large or small, should not enter public life. I have had my share of disappointments, as I will relate later, but I have tried to take them as part of the game, just as if I had lost a match to a worthy opponent on the athletic field.

I do not wish to call names, but I have seen far too many men in public life—many of them good friends of mine—reduce themselves in stature by their conduct after they have fallen out with a former friend; they devote the rest of their lives to backbiting and petty vilification, and the result is not attractive. There are several melancholy examples of this among the ranks of former New Dealers who became members of the "Hate Roosevelt" club. Hate is an ugly thing which hurts the hater as much as it does the recipient of his ill-will, if not more; it usually breeds nothing but hate in return.

I like to see a man behave like a good sport in defeat. The public may love a winner, but it also admires a good loser in politics, just as it does in athletics. An admirable example of good sportsmanship in defeat is the case of my old friend and colleague, former Senator Kenneth D. McKellar of Tennessee. I have had many spats with "K.D.," but I have an affection for him and admire the way he took his upset by a younger man in the 1952 election. Everyone thought that the former dean of the Senate, who had served longer than any living senator, would wither on the vine after the first defeat of his incredibly long political career. Instead, he took it in good grace, congratulated the man who defeated him, and, as this is being written, is busily at work setting down for history his recollections of public life.

When I went to Congress, I had hoped, because of the vital interest of my home district, which has many navigable streams, to be assigned to the Rivers and Harbors Committee. I put in my request for assignment to that committee, but, on advice of Judge W. C. Adamson, then chairman of the Interstate and Foreign Commerce Committee, I listed the latter committee as my second choice. He told me he would like to have me on it if I was "willing to work." Actually, this appointment was extremely fortunate for me. Because of the volume and importance of its work, Interstate and Foreign Commerce was one of the twelve so-called "exclusive" committees of the House, whose members were not permitted to split their time by serving on any other committee. As a member of such a key committee, I was in the foreground, rather than on the side lines, in developing much of the Wilson administration's important legislation, and this was rather unusual for a freshman congressman.

Another new member of the same committee was Sam Rayburn of Texas, who became my lifelong personal and political friend. He remained in the House, where, at the time of this writing, he still serves, and "Mister Sam" later served as Speaker of the House for longer than any man in history. He is widely respected and admired by both Democrats and Republicans.

Under Congressional protocol there has to be seniority for members, and, although we both came to the House at the same time, I "ranked" Congressman Rayburn on our committee, either because my name came earlier in the alphabet than his or because Kentucky was admitted to the Union earlier than Texas. Sam and I have always had a private joke between us that I left the House and went to the Senate to clear the way for him to become Speaker.

When I consider Sam Rayburn's tenure in the House and think how valuable his long, unbroken experience is to the country, it makes me realize how, in one respect, British Parliamentary customs have been superior to ours. I have always felt the British had the best of it in keeping their good men in Parliament for long periods—Gladstone, Lloyd George, and Churchill, to mention a few examples—instead of replacing them every few years as we do in many cases.

One of the earliest bills which I helped to pass as a member of the Wilson team was the Underwood Tariff Act. One of Wilson's campaign pledges called for repeal of the incredibly prohibitive Payne-Aldrich Tariff Act, which was limiting our opportunities in certain areas of foreign trade, and which, in fact, was one of the rocks on which the Taft administration was wrecked. Traditionally the Republican party has followed the Alexander Hamilton doctrine of favoring higher-tariff taxation. This is on the theory that you can tax the shirts off the backs of the people if they don't realize it, for high tariff is really a sort of hidden tax. It is collected at the customs house, but is paid for in actuality by the people who buy the imported goods. The Democratic party throughout the years has stood for lower tariffs, largely for revenue purposes.

I made my maiden speech in the House of Representatives on April 24, 1913, in behalf of the Underwood Tariff Act. This bill, in general, provided lower tariffs in line with the Democratic party's traditional policies, and it was described by many impartial observers as the most fair and honest tariff bill ever enacted. Later, in further implementation of the Wilson program, Congress created the forerunner of the present-day bipartisan Tariff Commission to deal with questions of import duties on an economic rather than a political basis.

The sponsor of the bill was Representative—later Senator—Oscar Underwood of Alabama, who was his home state's "favorite son" at the famous deadlocked Democratic convention of 1924. Thanks to coverage of this convention by the then infant radio industry, the nation—or that part of it which had radio receivers—could hear the chairman of the Alabama delegation drawl, "Twenty-four votes for Underwood" right up to the 103rd, and final, ballot, and his name became a household word.

It was Representative Underwood who paid me the honor of asking me to speak in behalf of his tariff measures. As I began to talk, I noticed my predecessor, Senator Ollie James, come onto the House floor and settle his huge bulk into a seat: he had come over from the Senate to attend my oratorical debut. Though the presence of the imposing Senator James, himself a superlative orator, made me slightly nervous, I did not blow up on my lines as I did in the early incident at Marvin College which I have already recounted.

For a freshman congressman I was a positive, and not exactly unpartisan, speaker in those days. In refreshing my recollection of that maiden speech in 1913 I leafed through a reprint of my address from the Congressional Record, and I noticed that I was interrupted frequently by what the record shows as "[Applause on the Democratic side]." I started right off by banging the Republicans between the eyes in these words:

It is futile to seek to harmonize the differences between the Democratic and Republican parties upon the subject of tariff taxation. Those differences are fundamental. The conflict which has for many years been waged between them upon this subject is as irrepressible now as when the difference was first emphasized by the respective followers of Hamilton and Jefferson. It is not a conflict merely between two theories as such. It is not a dogmatic clinging to a fetish on the one hand, or a fine-spun, visionary policy upon the other. It is, and has always been, a clear-cut fight between right and wrong, between justice and injustice, between the rights of the people and the demands of their despoilers.

I went on to get a little sarcastic about the Republican party's tariff ideas, saying:

In the past, Mr. Chairman, when the people have called upon the Republican party for relief from the burdens of unjust taxation they have acted as if they were of those who, having ears, hear not, and having eyes, see not. When the people have asked for free lumber in order that they might build humble homes in which to abide, the Republicans have responded by placing acorns upon the free list. . . . When in the past the people have asked for cheaper meat upon which to feed themselves and their children, the Republicans have responded by placing bones upon the free list. When we have asked for cheaper shoes, they have given us free spunk. When we have asked for cheaper milk, they have responded with free dragon's blood. When we have implored them . . . for cheaper sugar, they have handed us untaxed ipecac. . . . And so on, from bad to worse, the shameful story runs ad infinitum. . . .

I even had a little anecdote and poem with which to close my speech. I told of the young man who married a rich man's daughter "down in Christian County in the good old State of Kentucky," but found, as his family continued to grow, he could not make a living for them all. Finally he borrowed $200 and a team of mules from his father-in-law, and set out to become a farmer in the West. After failures in Colorado and Kansas he despondently loaded his family into the wagon and started the trek back to Kentucky. Just before rounding the hill for home he stopped, picked a bunch of pokeberries, mashed them into ink, and, across the side of his wagon, wrote the following jingle:

Colorado irrigation,
Kansas winds and conflagration,
High tariff and taxation,
Bill Taft's administration,
Roosevelt's vociferation,
Hell-fire and damnation
Bring me back to my wife's relations.

This, the Congressional Record shows, produced "[Laughter and applause]."

There was nothing lazy about a congressman's life in that era when I first came to Washington. Those were hectic years for those of us who took our inspiration from our great leader, Wilson, and who battled in Congress for his legislative reforms.

One epic accomplishment was the legislation liberalizing monetary standards and setting up the present-day Federal Reserve System. Again the cry of "socialism" was raised, and it was charged that the Government was attempting to take over the banks. Some of us who worked on monetary reforms, however, thought we were pretty conservative, for we had to beat down a number of eccentric proposals. Certain congressmen, for instance, wanted to overliberalize currency to the extent of basing it on agricultural crops; their proposals were ridiculed as the "ragweed" and "corntassel" amendments. It was generally agreed later that it would have been difficult for the United States to finance its participation in World War I without the Wilson monetary reforms.

During the Federal Reserve fight I went to Mr. Wilson, seeking his support for a Constitutional amendment I proposed to introduce, ending the then prevailing system of permitting "lame-duck" Congresses to continue until the fourth day of March after the national election. Even as a freshman congressman, I was dismayed by the filibustering and obstructive tactics carried on by defeated legislators, and I saw no reason why they should be permitted to gum up the legislative machinery by remaining so long in their jobs. President Wilson said he was extremely sympathetic to my proposal but that he did not wish to take on that additional major fight while his administration leaders were attempting to pass the monetary legislation. I introduced the anti-lame-duck resolution anyhow, but got nowhere with it.

Years later, during the Herbert Hoover administration, it was my pleasure to support a similar amendment, introduced by the late Senator George W. Norris, which was successful. Now lame-duck congressmen have their wings clipped on January 3.

The same era saw the modernizing of the antiquated anti-trust laws, and establishment of the Federal Trade Commission, a protective bulwark for American business. Into the new Clayton Anti-Trust Act was written a "charter of liberty" for labor and agriculture, which previously had been subject to unfair penalties under the old Sherman Anti-Trust Act.

Under the Wilson administration there was a sensible division of what had been the Department of Commerce and Labor into two separate departments. Important bills were passed affecting the fields of water-power development and the merchant marine. I took satisfaction in playing an active part in the passage of the Adamson Act, providing an eight-hour working day for railroad employees; this act helped avert what would have been a paralyzing threatened strike on the nation's railroads in 1916.

Congress also enacted safeguards against the then flagrant misbranding of products sold in interstate commerce. We set up a rural credit system for hard-pressed farmers, and passed legislation providing for federal aid to state and county highways. Even today I find it hard to believe that, until the Wilson administration, the United States, a leader among nations, was twenty years behind certain smaller European countries in rural credit programs, and that our roads system in many sections could have been so primitive. Up to that time, for instance, my home state of Kentucky did not even have a highway department.

It was under the Wilson administration that the public conception of Uncle Sam as a quaint sort of cartoon character, sitting astride the Capitol dome and not doing much of anything, began to change. Uncle Sam began to work for the people. I suppose it was the Wilson administration that laid the foundation for much of the later-day criticism about "bureaucrats," for we certainly created plenty of new bureaus. I have never felt it is particularly fair of politicians to complain about "bureaucrats," when Congress itself creates the bureaus. I had a little fun with this theme when, in delivering the keynote address at the 1948 Democratic convention, I defined a bureaucrat as "a Democrat who holds some office that a Republican wants."

I also recall our efforts—eventually successful—to give women the right to vote. Washington was besieged by marching, picketing, highly vocal suffragettes. I never had any trouble with the ladies, for I was on their side all the time. I remember the time, however, when they finally cornered one of their die-hard foes, Senator Boies Penrose, the political boss of Pennsylvania, in his office. "You might as well be for suffrage, because it's coming!" one of them angrily called to him.

"Yeah!" said Senator Penrose. "So is death, but I don't have to go out and meet it halfway!"

In 1919, Congress finally presented the Nineteenth Amendment, granting women the right to vote, to the various state legislatures for ratification. The ratification drive lagged, so one evening an informal delegation from the Senate and House, of which I was a member, called at the White House to ask President Wilson to issue a statement urging the legislatures to take speedier action. If the amendment was to be ratified, as we were confident it would be, we felt that women should have the right to cast their first vote in the presidential election of 1920.

President Wilson listened sympathetically to our appeal. He pulled a writing pad out of his pocket, took a lead pencil, and, resting the pad on his knee, there and then wrote out a crisp but eloquent and effective plea for action. Former Senator Ashurst of Arizona was in our group and, sensing the historic interest of the Wilson note, quickly said, "Mr. President, I would like to have that statement to put in my scrapbook." The President gave it to him. I often wish I had thought to ask for it first.

The forward drive of the Wilson administration was tragically interrupted by the outbreak of World War I, just as the Second World War a generation later disrupted the advance of the Roosevelt program. As World War I approached and the United States was finally drawn into it by a series of intolerable events, Congress found itself working on measures pertaining to the conflict. We passed bills such as war-risk insurance for merchant ships, and legislation providing for government operation of the railroads. Later, when it came time to restore railroads to private ownership, I took an active personal part in attempting to write in provisions protecting the rights of railway workers in case of labor disputes; this was but one of the many battles I have fought in behalf of guaranteeing fair play to organized labor and all branches of labor.

The attempt was not a success until some years later. Although I was a member of the conference committee of the two Houses, which was supposed to agree upon an acceptable bill, I had refused to vote for the Transportation Act of 1920 because it contained the provision for the creation of a Railroad Labor Board which was one-sided in its operation and administration. If an employee violated his agreement, the railroad could fire him. But if the railroad violated its agreement, the employee could not fire it.

Five years later I joined with Senator Howell of Nebraska in introducing the Howell-Barkley Bill, abolishing the Railroad Labor Board and creating a Board of Mediation and Conciliation. This legislation was enacted in 1926 and has been eminently successful.

The Wilson administration also saw the beginning of our historic encounter with the "noble experiment" of prohibition, as it came to be known under Herbert Hoover. Congress had passed a Wartime Prohibition Act, designed to conserve food, which took effect July 1, 1919. Meanwhile, the Eighteenth Amendment, making prohibition "permanent," had been adopted by Congress and ratified by the necessary three-quarters majority of the states, and it took effect in January 1920. The Volstead Act, designed to enforce provisions of the Eighteenth Amendment, also came along, and was passed by Congress in October 1919, over President Wilson's veto. I had supported the Eighteenth Amendment and, as I have already related, both voted dry and observed the law literally and strictly for its entire duration.

Years later, when it became apparent that the "noble experiment" was a failure and the American people wanted a change, I supported the Democratic platform plank calling for repeal of the Eighteenth Amendment. Like Senator Ashurst, I was proud at that time of "my consistency in my inconsistency," because it was consistent with the democratic theory that the people have a right to determine their course.

CHAPTER 8

World War I: An Era Ends

I SUPPOSE one of the saving graces of Americans is our ability to find something to laugh about, even in the midst of the most dire calamities. I cannot recall ever having seen a really convincing laugh pictured on the face of, say, the late Adolf Hitler, and the few allegedly smiling pictures I have seen of Mr. Josef Stalin always gave me an uneasy feeling, as if his glee were prompted by some new little atrocity he was concocting for the rest of the world.

I suppose I should qualify this by reporting that Secretary of State Dean Acheson, who always retained his own sense of humor in the face of outrageous insults heaped upon him by political enemies, once got the terrible Vishinsky to unbend in merriment by regaling him with some "Barkley jokes." It was interesting while it lasted, but it did no good in the end, as Vishinsky was just as ornery as ever when they settled down to business at the foreign ministers' conference in Paris.

This episode really started off at the Washington airport one day when I joined President Harry Truman in seeing Secretary Acheson off for Paris. President Truman, who can be a great kidder, was in high spirits that day, and he was teasing me for appearing in white flannel pants. He claimed he had not seen such pants since he used to sell haberdashery in Kansas City.

In any event, when I shook hands with the departing Mr. Acheson and wished him *"bon voyage,"* the President hooted, "Listen to the Veep trying to speak French! Let's check his accent. Where's old Bonnet?"

The President, of course, was referring to the dignified French Ambassador, Henri Bonnet. M. Bonnet thereupon stepped up and gravely listened to my pronunciation, which I repeated by request of the President, of *bon voyage*.

"*C'est merveilleux!*" the Ambassador decreed, a pronouncement which lucidly demonstrated why he is such a skillful diplomat, and that ended that.

When Acheson returned from the conference, he gave out an interview in which he cryptically expressed thanks to Vice President Barkley for assistance rendered in his dealings with Mr. Vishinsky. I was naturally mystified, since I had not been to Paris, and I asked Acheson to explain. He thereupon told me that he had been getting an extremely cold shoulder from the Soviet Foreign Minister, but finally was able to make not only Vishinsky but even the Russian interpreter roar by telling some of my stories. At the end of the recital Vishinsky put his arm around Secretary Acheson's shoulder and said, "I may not win anything negotiating with you, but it's a pleasure to visit with you."

The story Vishinsky particularly liked, according to Acheson, was one I frequently relate about an old constituent of mine who had supported me in every race I ever made. After each victory, he would come to me and say, "I want you to know I voted for you—I fought for you, sweated for you, and almost bled for you. I don't want a thing in return—all I want is for you to be a good official."

This went on through all my races for prosecuting attorney, county judge, congressman, and senator, and finally I was elected Vice President. Then he came to me and said, "Mr. Vice President, now I have a request. I want you to do something for me."

A little apprehensive, I asked what it was he wanted. He replied: "I want you to help me take out my citizenship papers."

What I started out to tell at the outset of this chapter, however, was not the Vishinsky story but the account of my airplane flight over London during the cheerless days of World War I. I have since flown many hundreds of thousands of miles—probably a million or more—including several crossings of the Atlantic and the Pacific, but this wartime flight in London was my first, and it provided one of the few lighter moments of the First World War period.

I had gone to Europe with a Congressional committee, and, while in London, I arranged to take a flight with an American Air Corps captain. In my innocence I told him I would like a sort of "lively" ride, and he took me at my word. He gave me the works: loops, spins, nose dives, wing-overs, and everything else in his repertoire. I thought for a while that the cloth-and-piano-wire biplane was going to come apart in the air.

When we landed, he asked me how I had liked it. I told him it reminded me of the story of the barnstorming aviator at a county fair in Kentucky, who was hauling sight-seers at ten dollars per head. One persistent fellow began nagging him to take up both his wife and himself for half price. Finally the pilot agreed, on condition that the pest would have to pay double if he so much as opened his mouth once during the flight. Loading the couple into the rear cockpit, he took off and practically shook his plane to pieces, just as this Air Corps captain had done with me. However, they landed without the passenger uttering a single word or sound.

When they touched ground, the pilot called back, "How in tarnation did you manage not to call out?"

"Well," the fellow said, "to tell you the truth, I almost spoke once."

"When was that?" asked the pilot.

The man answered, "When my wife fell out."

As the threat of our involvement in World War I became more ominous, President Woodrow Wilson began to draw criticism for some of his policies and public utterances. Just as his policy of "watchful waiting" drew fire from political snipers when border trouble with Mexico became tense in 1914, his cautious phrase, "There is such a thing as a man being too proud to fight," uttered at a time when Germany was unleashing submarine warfare, drew violent reaction. Wilson was accused of being a coward.

I had a private talk with him about the "too proud to fight" declaration. I told him I thought I understood what he had in mind, and certainly knew it was not cowardice that lay behind his utterance. He was in a self-searching, introspective mood, and he seemed anxious, rather than loath, to talk about it. He told me he realized his statement might have been bad politics, but said he had wanted to convey that we must maintain our national dignity in whatever crisis was shaping up, and that we must not rush into a conflict for which we were utterly unprepared.

Wilson's real attitude was summed up in another public statement which he made. He said, "We are not trying to keep out of trouble; we are trying to preserve the foundation upon which peace can be built."

In the early part of the Wilson administration I formed a friendship with William Jennings Bryan. The thrice-defeated Democratic presidential candidate, who had done so much to throw the nomination to Wilson at the 1912 convention, had gone into office as Wilson's first Secretary of State. Wilson and Bryan provided a fascinating contrast in personalities—Wilson, the profound thinker and intellectual, and Bryan, the fundamentalist and the master orator, who, in his prime, used his voice as a virtuoso uses a musical instrument to sway human emotions. Yet, despite their basic differences, I know, from my acquaintance with both Wilson and Bryan, that the two men had a mutual respect and liking for each other.

As the inevitability of our involvement in World War I became apparent, the deeply religious Bryan became more and more troubled. Finally, feeling he could not be part of an administration in power at a time when this country would have to take the plunge into war, Bryan resigned as Secretary of State. When war was declared, Bryan made the gesture of volunteering to serve as a private soldier; he was fifty-seven years old at the time and his offer, of course, was declined.

An odd facet of this paradoxical figure's background was the fact that, when the Spanish-American War broke out in 1898, Bryan raised a regiment of Nebraska volunteers and became their colonel. He went with his regiment to Florida, but his outfit never reached the battlefields in Cuba.

The last time I saw William Jennings Bryan was at a private gathering in Washington, celebrating his sixty-fifth birthday. It was a few months before his death. He had invited a group of his close friends, and he was in a wonderfully gracious and mellow mood. When the dinner was over, he called me aside and asked me if I had a car and would drive him to the train.

On the way to the station he confided to me that he had just made an important personal decision. At the time he was still much in demand as a speaker, and he had been pushing himself hard, traveling around the country to fill speaking engagements. Mrs. Bryan was an invalid and was unable to travel with him, and it was an unsatisfactory life for both of them. So he had decided to retire from public speaking, and settle down at home so he could complete his memoirs, covering the latter part of his career.

That was the last time I ever saw him; those final memoirs were never written. He became involved in the Scopes trial—the so-called "monkey case"—in Dayton, Tennessee, in which the right to teach the law of evolution became a *cause célèbre*. The trial was fought out in the stifling heat of midsummer in the close quarters of a small-town courtroom. Gradually it developed into a personal duel between the aging Bryan, as the champion of fundamentalism, and the aggressive and famous liberal lawyer, Clarence Darrow. The strain was too much for the weary old warrior. One Sunday afternoon Bryan lay down to rest on a couch and never woke up. A great figure in American history was gone.

In the 1916 presidential election "He kept us out of war" was the keynote of Woodrow Wilson's campaign for re-election, though the President himself was not responsible for the actual slogan. Although I was a novice in national politics, I was uneasy about the election, and, when President Wilson showed me the great honor of asking my counsel on the campaign, I told him what bothered me. First, I was worried by his plan, not to campaign for re-election, but to make his appeal through statements uttered in the conduct of his official duties. To this he replied that he had given the problem a great deal of thought and simply did not think it was dignified for a President in time of a threatening national crisis to go "barnstorming"—that was his word for it—through the country. There was a striking parallel in 1940 to Wilson's decision when President Roosevelt, on the eve of our involvement in another World War, attempted to campaign "from the White House" against Wendell Willkie. Roosevelt, however, altered his strategy out of what he thought was political necessity, and made a series of political addresses; Wilson held pretty close to his original decision.

As it turned out, Wilson almost lost the election to Charles Evans Hughes, who had criticized him strongly on his policies in relation to the European war. Mr. Hughes, who had resigned from the Supreme Court to make the race, went to bed thinking he had been elected President of the United States, but learned, on awakening next morning, that the California votes had defeated him. Hughes's loss of California was attributed to the fact that he had snubbed the late and then powerful Senator Hiram W. Johnson—a relatively small quirk of fate to have such an important effect on history.

Two years later I had occasion to give political counsel to President Wilson again on his request. In 1918 I told him, respectfully but frankly, that I thought he was making a mistake in appealing to the country for re-election of a Democratic Congress to support his policies. I thought he should have kept his appeal out of partisan channels by asking merely for a Congress sympathetic with the war efforts and the peace objectives. It can be risky, as Franklin Roosevelt learned when he attempted to conduct a series of "purges" in 1938, for the executive branch to try to handpick the legislative branch.

President Wilson's appeal for a Democratic Congress boomeranged on him. The Democrats lost their working majorities in both Houses, though it was close in the Senate, and it is possible that this factor played a role in the Senate's later failure to ratify the treaty of Versailles, containing the Covenant of the League of Nations. Not only was this the supreme tragedy of Wilson's entire career, but the failure of the United States to contribute its influence to the League may have been a factor that led to World War II and most of the problems that beset the world today. Yet, even with this somber example from the pages of history, there are isolationists today who deride our participation in the United Nations. They would have us withdraw into an unreal isolation—a *Götterdämmerung*, or "twilight of the gods"—leaving "the rest of the world" to burn. How blind must one be not to recognize these days that the flames of world conflagration leap high and far?

Whatever his idealistic political mistakes may have been, Wilson's war leadership, once we were drawn into the conflict, was magnificent. Early in his first administration Wilson had revived a practice, dormant since the John Adams administration, of addressing joint sessions of Congress. He was criticized for this too. The sharpest barb came from an ordinarily friendly Democratic senator, John Sharp Williams of Mississippi, who, in advance of the President's appearance, sarcastically derided it as "the speech from the throne."

But Wilson shamed most of the petty opposition when he stood before us for the first time on the rostrum of the House of Representatives. On this historic occasion President Wilson summed up the philosophy on which he based his decision to speak in person to the Congress in the following words:

> I am very glad, indeed, to have this opportunity to address the two Houses directly and to verify for myself the impression that the President of the United States is a person, not a mere department of the Government hailing Congress from some isolated island of jealous power, sending messages, not speaking naturally and with his own voice—that he is a human being trying to cooperate with other human beings in a common service.

The President continued his policy of addressing Congress on important occasions. So, when it became necessary on April 2, 1917, for him to request the declaration of war against Germany, he did it in person before the jointly assembled two Houses of Congress. I was present; I shall never forget the brooding solemnity of the occasion and the impressive nobility of the man as he took the awful but inevitable step.

The war brought many foreign delegations to this country. I remember being particularly impressed by the visit of René Viviani, a former

French Premier, who had the reputation of being one of the greatest of European orators. He came over with the French hero, Marshal Joffre, and was invited to address the House. Although Viviani spoke in French and most of us were unable to follow him, his eloquence and his gestures were so impressive that we knew instinctively when to applaud him. It was a marvelous demonstration of how a really superlative orator can transcend even the barriers of language.

Despite the crucial seriousness of those times the debates over Wilson's policies sometimes provided moments of fleeting humor. There was a Mississippi congressman named Percy Edwards Quin, whom we sometimes called "the corn-cob statesman." Percy was a sort of cracker-barrel philosopher who occasionally gave us a little much-needed amusement in the House. He was an ardent Wilsonian, and even when the President seemed to vacillate, Percy stayed with him. One day a Wisconsin representative, Henry Allen Cooper, a scholarly, distinguished-looking man with a handsome gray beard, arose to accuse Wilson of "inconsistencies."

" 'Stand by the President,' they tell us!" shouted Cooper. "I am willing to stand by him if he'll stay in one place long enough!"

At this point, Percy Quin from Mississippi jumped up and, without even waiting to be recognized by the chair, shouted, "By George, why don't you get yourself a pair of roller skates and keep up with him like I did!"

There was not much to laugh about in those days, however. In addition to our legislative responsibilities many of us had personal problems—after voting for war, we felt we should do our part and fight in it. I was almost forty and had three children, but I had a keen desire to enlist. I talked this over with both President Wilson and Secretary of War Baker. Just as he told young Franklin D. Roosevelt, then Assistant Secretary of the Navy, that his duty lay in Washington rather than in the field, and just as Roosevelt himself a generation later had to dissuade other congressmen from going off to war, Wilson told me firmly my job was at home. I would be of more value in Congress, he said, helping the Administration carry out its war policies, than as just another soldier or officer in the Army. Despite personal disappointment I accepted this as a directive from my Commander in Chief, and stayed in Washington.

Before the war was over, however, I made an extensive fact-finding trip to the fighting fronts as a member of a volunteer House committee. There were six of us: Representatives Marvin Jones of Texas, now Chief Judge of the United States Court of Claims, Aswell of Louisiana, Randall of California, Welling and Mays of Utah, and myself. We paid our own way, traveling over with soldiers on a troopship, and reported back to the House on our observations of the conduct of the war.

We had many memorable and exciting experiences, and our committee met many famous personages. We had audiences with King George V of England, King Albert of Belgium, King Victor Emmanuel of Italy, Lloyd George, Clemenceau, Orlando, Poincaré, and many other statesmen and military leaders.

I particularly recall our interview with Clemenceau, the white-haired old "Tiger of France." He was sitting at his desk, writing, when he received us, and I was startled to see that he was wearing gray suède gloves, which he never removed. Whether he had a germ complex or a skin ailment I do not know. Anyhow, after giving us the gloved handshake, he began inquiring about our home states. He was much interested when he learned that two of our group were from Utah. Turning to Representative Jim Henry Mays, the old Frenchman asked, "Are you a Mormon?"

"Nope, Mister Pree-meer," replied Jim Henry, who had a dry sense of humor. "I'm just a Gentile with Mormon inclinations!"

One of the American naval leaders I was especially glad to see in England was a Kentuckian, Admiral Hugh Rodman, a salty old sea dog. He commanded the American contingent with the Grand Fleet. I heard a story on my fellow Kentuckian when I visited a Scottish castle which once was the residence—and later the prison—of Mary, Queen of Scots. Mary was quite a gay girl, and she was gossiped about quite a bit before she—literally—lost her head. Anyway, the guide who showed me through the castle told me that Admiral Rodman had come to see the place and was escorted through it by a dignified and titled English lady.

When they came to the room where Mary had been imprisoned, she paused dramatically and announced, "And this is the room where Mary, Queen of Scots, was confined."

The admiral looked at her and said, "Whom did they suspect that time?"

On one trip to the front lines in the Ypres sector we went into the trenches about seventy-five feet from the German front lines. I was being guided by an American sergeant who was as whimsical as he was tough. He had me squatting and stooping as I plodded through the narrow, muddy excavation. Just for the hell of it I got him to stop while I took a rifle, stuck a helmet on it, and raised it above the trench level. Before I could snatch it back, the helmet was whanging around with eleven bullet holes through it. The sergeant looked at me and said, "Man, I wish the German Army knew there was a congressman within seventy-five feet of 'em—they'd just walk over here and surrender!"

Another time this same sergeant was escorting us on a motor trip into "no man's land." A German plane spotted us, notified the enemy artillery, and shells started dropping all around us. At one point the sergeant yelled, "Everybody out—hit the ditch!" and, following his lead, I sprawled flat on my face in a nice, muddy shell hole. It was lucky we did so, for a shell hit the rear wheel of our car and shattered it.

If it did nothing else, my visit into "no man's land" at least served to solidify my relations with one of my most important constituents back home—my ten-year-old son, David. In common with most American boys Bud was all wrapped up in things military. I went out on the battle-field, scene of a recent engagement. Scavenging through the debris of war—my friends, viewing my many collections of canes, gavels, shaving mugs, curios, china, and antiques, say I have the pack-rat instinct anyway —I picked up everything I could carry: German helmets, rifles, canteens, bayonets, etc., etc. I lugged it all back to the plush Crillon Hotel in Paris, where we were staying. Eyebrows were lifted when I entered the lobby, for I looked more like a peddler than a guest. But it was worth it, for, when I returned home with the souvenirs, Bud exclaimed, "Thank God, now I can hold my head up with the other boys—Daddy's been to war!"

Looking back on it, I realize it was a foolhardy and perhaps unnecessary thing that we congressmen did, but, at the time, it seemed the thing to do. Certainly none of us were heroes or had any particular desire to become corpses. However, it is a funny thing: when you are that close to danger, it all seems oddly impersonal. The over-all experience did give us an unforgettable firsthand realization of both the dangers and the physical discomforts our boys were facing, and this was of value to us as legislators.

After visiting the French and Belgian sectors we went to Italy and inspected an impressive Italian artillery installation, built around a mile-long tunnel carved into the top of Monte Grappa. The Italians obligingly allowed me to yank a lanyard which fired an artillery piece in the direction of Austrian troops along the Piave River. Years later I also fired an American gun in Korea, and I now have the casing as a souvenir. I had written my name on the business end of the projectile before firing it at the enemy lines, hoping that my aim was good.

As we were leaving Monte Grappa, we received word that King Victor Emmanuel of Italy, whose headquarters was five miles away, wanted us to come by and have dinner with him. We accepted with pleasure.

While we were standing in the modest reception room, waiting for the King to be announced, maybe with a flourish of trumpets, the door swung open and in walked this pleasant little man, wearing an outsized military hat. He was puffing on a cigarette and was completely unescorted.

We had an excellent meal and a lot of interesting conversation. The little King was well posted on America—he seemed to know something about each of our home states. I sat on his left, and he immediately brought up the subjects of Kentucky race horses and tobacco. Remembering that the Blue Grass State had sold a great deal of tobacco to Italy before the war, I put in a plug for a renewal of these trade relations as soon as the Germans were licked. I thought the home folks would be glad to know that, even while touring the battlefields of Europe, I had my constituents in mind. Once a congressman, always a congressman!

The part of the whole trip I shall never forget was a visit to a field hospital behind the front lines as a battle was taking place. When you see men brought in, raw and bleeding, with eyes shot out and arms and legs severed, you wonder if anyone ever wins a war, regardless of who is proclaimed victor on the piece of paper signed at the armistice table.

Another eloquent battlefield sermon was given us, through an interpreter, by a French general who was in charge of the sector in which the ruined cathedral at Rheims was located. One of the members of our Congressional party was so boiling-mad at seeing the wanton destruction of the beautiful cathedral that, when we reached the general's headquarters, he explosively said, "I hope, when you get into Germany, you give the Germans the same treatment that they have given France!"

When my colleague's remark was translated to him, the general, who, we had been told, had lost two sons of his own in the war, looked at the congressman reflectively and a little sadly.

"There is one thing we will never do," the general said. "We will not destroy their churches, as they have ours. For religion is not the blessing of any one nation but the boon of all mankind."

After all the grim and somber scenes which we witnessed I must confess I was glad to learn that the American soldier was keeping his sense of humor in World War I—even as he did a generation later in World War II and in Korea.

One night in St. Nazaire, for instance, we were walking behind a group of American Negro soldiers who came from Mississippi. They encountered some French native soldiers from Morocco, and tried to strike up a conversation.

"Where you from?" one of the Mississippians asked.

He got a reply in very fast and unintelligible French.

"I said, 'Where you from?' " the American repeated with emphasis, and once again came the torrent in French.

Finally the Mississippi boy said in disgust:

"You're a hell of a colored man—can't even speak your own language!"

We also heard a story which illustrates the indestructibility of humor, for it was resurrected in World War II, and probably had been told in the Civil War too. According to the World War I version the shells were dropping hot and heavy on the American sector, and one private got scared and started running to the rear. He ran so fast and so hard that his tongue hung out like that of a shepherd dog driving home the cows in the evening.

Finally he encountered an officer who shouted, "Halt! Why are you running?"

The soldier replied, "I'm running because I can't fly!"

"Disgraceful!" the officer said. "Do you realize who I am?"

"No, sir," said the soldier. "Who are you?"

"I," the officer grandly announced, "am a colonel."

"Oh," said the soldier. "I thought from those eagles on your shoulders that you must be a colonel, but, frankly, I didn't know I'd run that far back from the front!"

I told this story one night when invited to address a meeting of the Society of Kentucky Colonels in Louisville. The members seemed to enjoy it at the time, but I never got another invitation to address them.

We and our allies won our war in 1918, or so it said on the armistice papers, but the tragedy of our failure to win the peace was appalling. Woodrow Wilson was betrayed by shortsighted and puny men. He could not lead the required two-thirds majority of the United States Senate into seeing the wisdom, the overriding necessity, of backing up the promise he made at Versailles—that America would join the League of Nations and continue to fight at the council tables, as it had on the battlefields, to *keep* the world safe for democracy.

Many people, both Democrats and Republicans, felt at the time that President Wilson would have fared better on the Versailles Treaty when it came before the Senate if he had taken with him to Paris two or three outstanding Republicans such as Charles Evans Hughes and William Howard Taft, instead of those whom he chose to accompany him. President Taft had been sympathetic with the movement known as the League to Enforce Peace, and Mr. Hughes likewise was sympathetic with such a world organization. Taft had been President and Hughes had been his party's candidate for that office. The Republicans whom President Wilson appointed on the Peace Commission were honorable, able, and loyal Americans, but it was thought at the time that they did not represent the Republican party in the same outstanding degree as Mr. Hughes and Mr. Taft. This is, of course, speculative. No one knows whether it would have made any difference, but it might have given the opposition less ground for feeling that it had not really been represented at the peace conference.

The details of what happened are all too familiar: I traced most of them in a speech which I delivered on the floor of the House on June 2, 1920, shortly before the adjournment of the second session of the Republican-controlled Sixty-sixth Congress. "The Partisan Plot against the President," I called my talk, and in it I declared:

> If I may borrow an expression made famous by a very distinguished man now living, this Congress may be described as a "single-track" Congress. It has had but one consuming desire. It has been fired by but one enthusiasm. It has responded to but one call. It has enlisted in but one great crusade. All its burdensome efforts and its painful anxiety to serve the nation have merged into pitiful and fruitless wailings against the unmatched record of a great Democratic administration and the historic deeds wrought by him who has been the nation's leader during the past eight years.
>
> The Republican leadership in Congress has seemed to be obsessed with the belief that it could destroy the Democratic Party and undo its great record of service to the nation by destroying the influence and standing of the President of the United States, at home and throughout the world. And it has attempted to discredit the President, to undo his great work, to belittle his efforts to serve humanity, and to bedaub his escutcheon with the infamy of imputed wrong by methods more contemptible than any ever attempted by any similar organization of political buccaneers and freebooters in the history of the Republic.

As I reread these excerpts from a speech delivered after the close of the Wilson era, I am struck by the remarkable appropriateness of those words, spoken thirty-four years ago, to the present muddled political times. Even then there was a "great crusade" by an opposition party which deteriorated into an epic of mudslinging against the leadership and the accomplishments of the Democratic party.

In that long-ago speech I went on to say:

> Mr. Speaker, it is not my task to assign to Woodrow Wilson the

place which he will occupy among the great statesmen of America and the world. Impartial history will perform that duty. No word of mine can add to the fullness of his stature. No word or act of yours can detract from it. But if I may be permitted to indulge in a prophecy, it is not difficult to foresee that those who now snap at his heels like hungry jackals will take their places among the forgotten register of the nation's malcontents, while he will stand with Washington, Jefferson, Jackson, and Lincoln as one of the few great figures of this era.

Painfully familiar, too, are the details of how Woodrow Wilson died a broken and tragic figure—as much a casualty of the war as if he had been killed on the battlefield. He came back from Versailles, a soul dedicated to a great dream of peace, and he was thwarted cruelly by political partisans. Perhaps Woodrow Wilson could have saved some scraps from the peace table, had he been willing to compromise with the partisans. But he was too idealistic a figure to fail in any way to live up to the moral commitments he made at Versailles.

So he went out, a frail and physically worn partisan for peace, to sell the country on his ideals. He tried to rally the people behind him. He spoke to them such eloquent and moving words as, "The whole world is now in a state where you can fancy that there are hot tears upon every cheek, and those hot tears are tears of sorrow. They are also tears of hope."

But the times, and the politicians of mean intellect then in the saddle in Washington, were against him. Crushed by the Senate's rejection of his treaty aims, Wilson broke. The tired body could no longer keep pace with the noble spirit.

Wilson's physician and his friends had warned him of the physical dangers of making such an arduous speechmaking tour in his condition. When one of his friends protested, "But, Mr. President, you'll ruin your constitution," Wilson, in one of his last-remembered flashes of humor, quipped, "Then I'll live on my bylaws!"

The frightening sequel to the story is that one generation later the world drifted again into the same bloody chaos which Woodrow Wilson gave his life to prevent. And the frightening contemporary corollary is that today there are forces at work in this country which would have us walk blind, alone, friendless, and defenseless in the world. Should the will of these unseeing forces prevail, surely we shall drift into the third—and perhaps ultimate—Armageddon.

How well I remember the inaugural parade in 1921, after the Democrats had been defeated and Warren G. Harding came in as President. I can still see the terrible suffering that showed in the face of the stricken Wilson as he rode away from the White House in an open, horse-drawn carriage.

It was the last inaugural parade I ever watched, until I had to take part in one myself when I was sworn in as Vice President in 1949. I just did not want to see any more.

I remember walking to the Wilson home on S Street. My daughter, Marian—Sis—was with me. Hand in hand we stood among the throngs in the street, gathered to pay homage to the broken leader whom Fate had treated so cruelly. Painfully Wilson dragged himself to the window, once, twice, three times, to acknowledge the cheers.

Sis and I stood there with the people, joining in the homage, until Mrs. Wilson somehow saw me in the crowd and beckoned to me to come in. My daughter and I walked into his house, went upstairs; Sis stood in the background solemnly and silently, a young girl who somehow knew she was present at a tragic moment in history, while I groped to find a few words to say to the great wartime leader. That day was the end of an era.

CHAPTER 9

The Twelve Republican Years

I NEVER think of the "twelve long years" of Republican rule between Woodrow Wilson and Franklin Roosevelt without being reminded of the story of the illiterate deputy sheriff from a certain county in Kentucky.

Though this fellow was uneducated, and had many other shortcomings, he possessed qualities which made him quite a hero to some people. Finally, after he had managed to accomplish a feat that appealed to the popular imagination, the people of his county rewarded him by electing him sheriff.

On the day when he was to take his oath of office—a ceremony that has become known in certain sections as "qualifying" oneself—the sheriff-elect walked into the county judge's office and said, "Judge I want you to qualify me for the office of sheriff of this here county." "Well," said the judge, "I can swear you in, but all hell can't qualify you."

It is my opinion—and I freely admit it is a matter of record that I have been a lifelong Democrat—that history's verdict on those twelve years will be that, like the deputy sheriff, some of the Republican stewards of that period were sworn in, but "all hell couldn't qualify them!"

I had been a delegate-at-large from the state of Kentucky in 1920 to the Democratic convention in San Francisco, which nominated Governor James M. Cox of Ohio for President and Franklin D. Roosevelt as his running mate. I might add that I have been a delegate-at-large to every Democratic convention since then, and three times the keynoter. I campaigned in Tennessee and Kentucky with Governor Cox, who came out strongly for the Wilsonian principle of United States participation in the League of Nations. During the campaign I also enlarged my acquaintance with young Franklin Roosevelt, whom I had known in his official capacity as Assistant Secretary of the Navy under Josephus Daniels during World War I.

Governor Cox's Republican opponent, Senator Warren G. Harding, also of Ohio, had been chosen in the famous "smoke-filled room" in Chicago when the G.O.P. convention became deadlocked between Governor Frank Lowden of Illinois and General Leonard Wood. In conducting his campaign Harding shied away from taking any firm stands on almost anything that might be described as constructive in nature. He was particularly evasive on the all-important question of this nation's participation in world efforts to maintain peace by international co-operation. Harding opposed the League of Nations, but pledged himself, and, inferentially, the Republican party, in favor of some sort of "association of nations" without the controversial covenant by which a majority vote of the League could obligate all members to take action against an aggressor.

The country went overwhelmingly for Harding and his vice presidential running mate, a dry, laconic man named Calvin Coolidge, whom Fate later was to tap upon the shoulder. But Mr. Harding's cheery and vague promises of international co-operation with an "association of nations" came to remind me of the sharecropper farmer who owed the country storekeeper a long overdue bill. One day the farmer came into the store and said he was going to pay his account.

"That's fine," said the storekeeper. "Would you mind telling me how you plan to pay it?"

"Oh," said the farmer, "I'm going to raise me a crop of tobacco next year."

"Yes?" said the storekeeper. "What then?"

"Well," said the debtor, "when the crop matures, I'm going to sell it and use the money to buy me a mare. Then I'm going to breed that mare to a jack over in the next county and get a good mule. When the mule gets grown—maybe in a couple of years or so—I'm going to sell the mule, buy a cow, and breed her to a thoroughbred bull. After that, the first bull calf I get, I'm going to sell it and pay you what I owe you!"

So far as President Harding's talk about an "association of nations" was concerned, this country got just about as far as the storekeeper with the sharecropper.

President Harding was a personally likable man, a hail-fellow-well-met type, whose handsome countenance and silvery hair gave him the look of a statesman. He was not a deep man, however, and, coming after Woodrow Wilson, his intellectual limitations were starkly emphasized.

The real tragedy of Harding was his lamentable inability to say no to his cronies—and he was doubly cursed by probably the worst set of cronies ever assembled by any man who has risen to the Chief Executive's office. In politics even a strong-willed man can be embarrassed by his so-called friends; in the case of a weak-willed man, such as Harding, the results can be calamitous. What the members of the "Ohio gang" did to their chief and to their country with their wholesale spree of bribery and general corruption is one of the more sordid stories of American political history. Teapot Dome and other malodorous oil deals, and the wholesale irregularities and swindles in the Veterans' Bureau and the Alien Property Custodian's office, are scandals which will never be forgotten. Before it was over, one Cabinet officer and several bureau chiefs had been sentenced to prison; two other Cabinet members were forced to resign, and other lesser fry were ousted. There were even strange deaths, including one case written off as suicide which, in the opinion of some investigators of that era, was never satisfactorily explained.

Almost at the outset of the Harding administration I had a personal experience that was an ironic portent of what lay ahead. One of Harding's worst betrayers was former Senator Albert B. Fall, who became Secretary of the Interior under Harding and eventually was convicted of taking a $100,000 bribe from oilman Edward L. Doheny. This was the infamous "little black bag" case. Fall was fined $100,000 and sentenced to one year in prison.

I had held Fall in low regard ever since the contemptible thing he did on his visit to the bedroom of the stricken President Woodrow Wilson. Fall was one of the political vultures who professed to believe that Wilson was not really ill but was shamming in order to gain sympathy for his League of Nations fight; it was Fall who, as one of a committee of senators who called on Wilson, brazenly lifted the covers from the bedridden President's limbs to see whether he was really paralyzed.

Fall was a Kentuckian—a circumstance to which we do not point with pride—who took Mr. Greeley's advice and went West, where he eventually became a rich man and United States senator from New Mexico. But—perhaps as a forerunner of the massive thieveries ahead—it seems that he had departed from Morganfield, Kentucky, owing his landlady, a widow, a rather large board bill. After he had been sworn in as a Cabinet member, I received a letter one day from a Morganfield attorney who represented the widow. She wanted her money and figured a congressman ought to be able to do something about it.

I forwarded the letter to Secretary Fall without comment. He promptly paid the bill—with interest and elaborate apologies. In my forty years on Capitol Hill my constituents have asked me for a lot of things, ranging from free seeds to jobs, but this was the first—and last—time I was ever asked to collect a board bill!

Calvin Coolidge, the taciturn New Englander who succeeded to the presidency after Harding's sudden death while returning from a trip to Alaska, was an entirely different sort of man from his backslapping, congenial predecessor. He had come into national prominence because of the part he played, as Governor of Massachusetts, in settling a policemen's strike in Boston. Coolidge was a man of unimpeachable personal integrity, and he quickly got rid of any remaining officeholding scoundrels from the Harding administration.

"Silent Cal" fitted in conveniently to the situation then confronting the American people. The country had practically turned its back upon the results of World War I so far as any real formal co-operation with other nations was concerned. The Dawes and Young plans for refinancing German reparations had been worked out and were in process of partial consummation. While agriculture was unhappy and on the decline, the stock market was high, and the country as a whole thought it was prosperous. The people simply did not want to be bothered by government in any way, or by any new ventures in the fields of politics or economics. Mr. Coolidge accommodated them. As I had occasion to say in my 1932 Democratic convention keynote address, "For six years, profound silence was mistaken for profound wisdom." The people were satisfied to let it go at that.

My principal censure of the Coolidge administration is that it did nothing positive and even went so far as to accentuate the negative. As the hot air began to leak out of the Coolidge balloon of false prosperity, the President failed to take effective steps to stop the drift toward economic disaster. He merely camouflaged the situation—I doubt that he ever really knew what was coming—by starting a practice, continued by his successor, Herbert Hoover, of issuing reassuring statements, telling the public that all was well. Every time there was a drop in the stock market or some other ominous economic portent in that Coolidge-Hoover period, we could count on a comforting statement from either Secretary of the Treasury Andrew Mellon or one of the two Presidents. But no real remedies were offered until the country reached the dregs of depression, and Franklin Roosevelt came along.

As an individual, however, I liked Coolidge, and often enjoyed demonstrations of his peculiar form of dry wit. Mrs. Coolidge also was a charming woman, one of the most gracious First Ladies I have ever known.

There are many legends about Coolidge's famous verbal impecuniosity. Once, for instance, he was supposed to have been seated at some function next to a Washington society woman, who boldly said to him, "Mr. President, someone has bet me that I would not be able to get you to say more than two words all evening." Coolidge looked at her without a trace of expression, and opened his lips just wide enough to say, "You—lose."

Another time he finally granted a much-sought-after interview to an influential journalist. The correspondent asked him a wide gamut of questions, and Coolidge answered each one with a "no comment." Then, when the "interview" was over and the reporter was departing, Mr. Coolidge said to him, "By the way, don't quote me."

I was among those present on one occasion when a United States senator could not provoke even a "No comment" out of "Silent Cal." A group of some ten or twelve of us senators had been invited to the White House for one of Coolidge's periodic breakfasts. I will say this: he fed us well. That morning we had cantaloupe, Corn Flakes, scrambled eggs, sausage, toast, griddle cakes and syrup, and coffee. Coolidge had just returned from the Black Hills, where he spent his summers, and he had made his historic announcement that "I do not choose to run." There was a lot of speculation as to whether his disclaimer actually meant he would not take the nomination if it were offered to him. One of our group, the late Senator Thaddeus Horatius Caraway, Democrat, of Arkansas, who was always a great conversational gadfly, began needling Coolidge as to whom he favored for his successor. We all knew there was no love lost between Coolidge and Vice President Charles G. Dawes, so Caraway, hoping to get a rise out of Coolidge, began praising Dawes to the heavens.

We all sat there, waiting for Coolidge's reaction. He picked up his fork, loaded it with scrambled eggs and sausage, used his knife to maneuver an extra piece of griddle cake onto the tines, put it all into his mouth, and chewed down on it like a squirrel eating a nut. Not so much as by one word, or even a flicker of a facial muscle, did he indicate that he even knew Senator Caraway was there.

The Coolidge-Dawes coolness stemmed partly from their disagreement over various legislative matters—"Hell-and-Maria" Dawes favored a more liberal agricultural policy than Coolidge—but mainly from the fact that Vice President Dawes was not present in the Senate one day when Coolidge needed him. The Vice President had a habit of going to his room at the Willard Hotel, quite a distance from the Capitol, for a nap after lunch each day. One afternoon, while Dawes was napping, the nomination of Charles B. Warren, who was Coolidge's nominee for Attorney General, came up for confirmation in the Senate. The only time when the Vice President has a vote is when there is a tie. This vote was a tie and Mr. Dawes was not there to break it by casting his vote in favor of the President's nominee. Coolidge never quite forgave him.

It is risky business for the Vice President to stray too far from base when the Senate is in session. Vice President Henry A. Wallace also was embarrassed on one occasion because he was at lunch when an important Administration measure was being voted on, and he could not get back to the rostrum in time to cast the vote that would have broken the tie. During my four years as "Veep," I am happy to say, this never happened to me—though I sometimes had to cover the distance from my office to the Senate Chamber at a fast trot.

Even though I did not admire the political complexion of the twenties, it was a period of my life that was particularly rich in personal memories, both of family and of friends with whom I served in the House and Senate. As I reminisce of Coolidge, I think again of my mother, for it was during his administration that she paid us a visit. I took Mamma to the White House to meet the President, and he was most courteous. There was a vase of red roses on his desk, and he took one out and presented it to her. As we left the White House, Mamma said, "Alben, that Mr. Coolidge is a pretty nice man for a Republican."

As I related in an earlier chapter, covering my growing-up years in the country, Mamma was a firm believer in feather beds; when we had the disastrous fire that destroyed our home when I was a boy, the only household object saved was the feather bed which Mamma had taken outside for an airing. So, before she came to visit us, she packed up her own feather mattress in a wooden box and shipped it up to Washington—none of these inner-spring contraptions for her.

We had a wonderful visit, and Mamma used to go into the kitchen and bake me all the dishes which I had enjoyed as a boy, particularly her marvelous egg custard pie. She always said, however, that she could have done much better if we had had a wood-burning stove such as she was accustomed to at home.

Once while visiting us, my mother got a little homesick. So I drove her out to the nearby town of Rockville, Maryland, where a county fair was in progress. We toured all the exhibits, with Mamma casting a critical eye on the cooking and canning entries, and she felt much better for the remainder of her visit in Washington.

She was a wonderful lady, with lots of independence and stamina. When she was eighty-eight years old, she tended her own vegetable garden; one day a neighbor's hog got into the garden and, while irately chasing him out, she tripped over an old set of coil bedsprings someone had discarded on the lot, and sprained her ankle. She was up, walking around on a cane in two days, but the incident served to confirm her distrust of anything but a feather mattress. My mother died of double pneumonia in December 1945, just four months short of her ninetieth birthday. President Truman placed his plane, the Independence, at my disposal, in order that I might fly to her funeral.

My father, who, as I have related, was a farmer most of his years, came to Washington soon after I was elected to Congress, and served as a doorkeeper in the House of Representatives. It was the adventure of his life; he had many new experiences which he enjoyed thoroughly. Though he remained a faithful churchgoer, he did acquire one worldly vice in Washington—a passion for the movies. He used to get terribly excited when the bad men would close in on William S. Hart, and sometimes the ushers had to restrain Father when he would start shouting, "Shoot 'em, shoot 'em!"

Father was proud of his job as a House doorkeeper. Although he had originally desired that I enter the ministry, he was also proud of the fact that he had a son in Congress. Strangers visiting in the House gallery sometimes were startled when Father would tap them on the shoulder, point down to where I was sitting, and say, "That's my son." I do not think he could ever have been as tolerant of any Republican as Mamma was of Mr. Coolidge, for, when the Republicans came in, he lost his job in Washington and went back to Kentucky. He died in July 1932, at the age of seventy-eight.

I moved my family to Washington early in my Congressional career, for, as I have related earlier, I did not want to be separated from my three growing children. It was quite a problem finding a place to live—particularly on a congressman's salary—where three lively youngsters, which mine were, would be welcome. First we lived in Congress Hall, a now-vanished hotel building where rentals were made almost exclusively to members of Congress, but the combined Barkley children were a little too much for some of our staid fellow tenants.

The kids also used to play in the Capitol building while my wife was out house-hunting, and sometimes they would come onto the House floor and help Daddy with his papers while I was trying to listen to debate on legislation. I do not recommend to any new congressman that he attempt to combine his legislative duties with baby-sitting!

In those early days my wife had her hands full trying to be a mother, housekeeper, and hostess. One Saturday afternoon when the House was not in session she was entertaining a group of congressmen's wives, and, since we had no help, I asked if I could be of any assistance. "Yes," she said, "take the children out and let them wear off some of their energy, so they'll be willing to go to bed early when they come home."

This I agreed to do, so, rounding up Bud, Sis, and Wahwee, I took them to the Washington Monument, where I had the inspiration of walking them up and down the 898 steps of the towering shaft. When I got them home, they went straight to bed without even waiting for supper. "I told you to get them a little tired, not to kill them!" my wife exclaimed.

The most terrible moment of my whole life came one night in January 1922, when we were living in an uptown apartment house. It was on a snowy, icy Saturday evening. Our oldest child, Bud, then fifteen, had been given permission to go to a neighborhood movie. Later in the evening the switchboard operator rang our telephone. "Is any member of your family at the movie?" she asked. We told her yes, that Bud was, and she informed us in a choked voice that the roof of the theater had just fallen in. It was the Knickerbocker Theater disaster in which nearly a hundred persons lost their lives.

My wife and I left the two girls and ran down to the scene of the disaster. She stood in the snow, weeping, while I talked my way past the police lines and went inside to search in the rubble for Bud. I dug out several bodies, and finally saw the half-buried body of a young man with curly hair about the color of Bud's. Sick at heart, I dug the body out, but it was not my son. I kept up the search as long as I could. Finally, surrendering all hope of finding my son alive, I went outside, a crushed and broken man. When I stepped out onto the sidewalk, I heard a voice calling, "Dad! Dad!" It was Bud! He had actually bought his ticket and gone into the theater; then, realizing it was a picture he had previously seen, he left and stopped off to visit at the home of a school friend. On returning home and learning what had happened he ran to the scene of the disaster to find me.

After this I worked through the night, doing what I could to aid the rescue work. I helped carry out the body of a former congressman with whom I had served in the House. My wife also stayed up all night, making pots of coffee to send to the rescue workers.

With the exception of this incident and some of the normal alarms of parenthood ours was an extremely happy family life, until the later illness and death of my first wife. We always had a lot of fun together, and tried to do things as a family unit—vacations, games, and so forth. If a representative, senator, or any form of so-called "VIP" came to dinner at the Barkleys', he could count on being subjected to a peculiar form of inquisition known as the "Family Quiz Game"—questions-and-answers on all sorts of obscure historical, geographical, and other subjects—in which we all participated. The children would go to no end of research to find a question that would trip me up.

We also enjoyed spelling games around the family dinner table, and, thanks to the careful training I had had at Lowes school and Marvin College, the children came to regard their father as a spelling champ. Alas, one night I let them down under extremely humiliating circumstances. There was a spelling bee at the National Press Club in Washington, in which selected members of Congress were pitted against the geniuses of journalism. I was chosen as one of the Capitol Hill orthographic stalwarts. The whole family and some of the neighbors assembled around the radio at my home to listen to my anticipated triumph over the press. I went down on the third word given me, "optician," spelling it, "o-p-t-i-t-i-a-n." Thereafter, whenever spelling was mentioned, I got the silent treatment from my whole family.

On one of our family vacation trips—this was after I had been elected to the Senate—I picked up a nickname which my family has teased me about ever since. We took a cruise, and our ship stopped at Port au Prince in the Caribbean. One of the other passengers went ashore and imbibed not wisely but too well on the local specialty known as Planter's Punch, which is roughly the Jamaican equivalent of a Kentucky mint julep. When he came aboard, his tongue was a little thick, and he persisted in conducting a conversation with me in which he addressed me as "Sinister Barkley." Ever since then I have been known to my family as the "Sinister from Kentucky," and on occasions I have even signed personal notes to the children with that appellation.

In a downtown apartment building where the Barkley family lived for a while one of our neighbors was George Holden Tinkham, the colorful big-game hunter, blue blood, and millionaire, who at that time was a Republican congressman from Massachusetts. The black-bearded Mr. Tinkham fascinated my children in the apartment building, just as he sometimes fascinated me in the House. One day the gentleman from Massachusetts, who was not a particularly effective debater, undertook to take on the able Ben Johnson of Kentucky, and got much the worse of it. Late that afternoon I happened to be passing his office, at least three hours after the debate, and I heard Tinkham's voice rising in strident laughter.

Curiosity triumphing, I stepped inside and was surprised to find Mr. Tinkham all alone, holding his sides, throwing back his bearded chin, and cackling with glee.

"What's so funny?" I asked him.

Wiping the tears from his eyes, he gasped, "Remember over there in the House this afternoon, when I said such-and-such, and Ben Johnson answered me so-and-so? Well, I've just thought of what I could have said to him, and if I'd only have thought of it at the time and had said it, would it have floored him!"

Another colorful figure of those days was the late Senator J. Thomas Heflin of Alabama, whom I first knew in the House. He later became known as "Tom-tom" because of his bitter tirades in the Senate, particularly on the subject of Alfred E. Smith and the Catholic Church. I have often said that he literally talked himself out of the Senate.

Heflin had been a close personal friend of my own predecessor, Ollie James, and, when James graduated from the House to the Senate in 1913, Heflin naturally wanted to follow him there. But Alabama had two strong senators—Oscar Underwood and John Hollis Bankhead—so Heflin had to bide his time until death claimed Senator Bankhead in 1920.

One of the funniest things I have ever seen in either the House or Senate cloakrooms was a performance which Congressman Heflin staged just before his last race for the House. It was generally known that he was ambitious to run for the Senate; hence, it was important for him to retain his House seat as a springboard. There were rumors that a particularly strong man was considering running against him, and Heflin was frankly worried. About a week before the deadline for qualifying petitions to be filed he sent his administrative assistant down to Montgomery, the Alabama state capital, to "watch developments."

Came the fateful evening when, at midnight, the deadline would elapse, and Heflin was carrying on like an old horse with the heaves. The House had a night session in progress, but every half hour Heflin was in the cloakroom telephone booth, ringing up his assistant in Montgomery. His voice was as penetrating as a steamboat whistle, so those of us sitting in the cloakroom could hear his end of the conversation through the phone door. "That you, Jim?" he shouted. "Well, how is it down there? . . . Where are you? . . . Right in the Secretary's office, are you—right where you can see everything that goes on? . . . Well, has he filed? Has he filed against me? What! You say he has! . . . He hasn't! . . . Oh, he hasn't! . . . All right, old boy, thank you . . . Stay right there!"

This went on at intervals until one minute after midnight, Alabama time, when the deadline had elapsed. Congressman Heflin went in to place the crucial call. "Are you there, right there by the clock, Jim?" he said, this time in almost quavering tones. "You say it's one minute after twelve down there? . . . Are you sure—are you looking right at the clock? . . .

"Well . . . what did he do? Did he file? . . . What! He *filed!* You say he filed! He filed against me? . . . Oh—oh, you say he *didn't* file! He hasn't filed yet. Too late now, eh? It's after twelve, and he didn't file against me, and he can't file now! . . . Well, all right, old boy, thank you, thank you, good-by, see you later!"

Then Heflin came out of the phone booth. He filled his lungs with air, drew himself up like a pouter pigeon, and looked around at all of us, who knew perfectly well what was going on. "Damn his hide!" he boomed, with the old Heflin voice back in perfect form. "I wish he had filed. I'd have beat hell out of him!"

In 1923 I made the only unsuccessful race of my political career. Though I enjoyed my work in Congress and had no particular ambition to become Governor of Kentucky, I yielded to the urgings of many supporters and entered the Democratic primary for the gubernatorial nomination. At this time the state political picture was dominated by the racing interests, headed up by the powerful Kentucky Jockey Club. The Jockey Club then was virtually as powerful in politics as the Louisville & Nashville Railroad had been a quarter of a century earlier at the time of the Goebel assassination; its influence extended from the State House and the legislature down into the smaller country districts.

I have never been opposed to racing. Like most Kentuckians, I am proud of our state's tradition in the breeding of thoroughbred horses, and I get a thrill out of attending the Kentucky Derby. However, I felt strongly that the influence exerted at that time by the Kentucky Jockey Club was an unhealthy thing, and that it should be eradicated.

So I made the race on a campaign of vigorous opposition to the Kentucky Jockey Club's political influence, even coming out for abolition of the law which permitted legalized betting through pari-mutuel machines. The opposition poured terrific effort and a great deal of money into the campaign against me. Out of a total vote of around 241,000, I lost by approximately 9000 votes to Congressman J. Campbell Cantrill, a prominent tobacco grower, who had been a member of the Kentucky legislature and the national House of Representatives.

As a loyal Democrat, I immediately pledged my support to the man who defeated me. Congressman Cantrill, however, actually had been an ill man when he made the race, and he died before the general election. Since I had been the only other Democratic candidate in the primary and had run such a close race, I was urged to allow my name to be submitted to the state central committee, which was empowered to fill the vacancy. But I took the position that, despite certain peculiarities which were alleged to have taken place during the course of the campaign, the people had spoken, and I would not accept a nomination which did not come to me by choice of the electorate. So the committee chose another Democratic nominee, Congressman William J. Fields, who was victorious after a campaign in which I worked hard for his election.

Though this was my only political defeat, and naturally I did not relish it, I have never felt that this race was made in vain. I managed to focus the spotlight so glaringly on the then existing conditions that the hold of the Kentucky Jockey Club on state politics was broken to a large degree. Over the years the club itself reduced its political activities, and today it is an entirely different organization from the group I fought in 1923. So I always felt that, as Winston Churchill sometimes remarked about Britain, I had lost a battle but won my war.

In 1924, at the Madison Square Garden convention, which was deadlocked for 100 ballots between Governor Al Smith and William G. McAdoo, I had my first experience with that then new phenomenon known as the nationwide radio hookup.

The permanent chairman of the convention was Senator Thomas J. Walsh of Montana. He came into national prominence as the relentless senatorial investigator of the Harding scandals, and he would have been Attorney General in Franklin D. Roosevelt's first Cabinet except for his untimely death before President Roosevelt's inauguration. As the balloting in the deadlock between Smith and McAdoo dragged on, Chairman Walsh grew weary, and asked me to come up and preside for an hour while he caught a little rest. The "hour" stretched into two days, as Chairman Walsh did not return to the rostrum until just before the 103rd ballot, when John W. Davis was nominated.

Then, during the balloting for a vice presidential nominee, I was called on to preside again. At first, in the absence of any indication from nominee Davis as to whom he wanted in second place, the race was wide open, and there were enough "favorite sons" popping up to stock an orphan asylum. Then came word that Mr. Davis favored Charles W. Bryan, brother of William Jennings Bryan. There was a lot of confusion as the stampede to switch to Charlie Bryan began, and at one time there were at least eighteen delegations on their feet, all waving their standards in my face and clamoring for recognition. Losing my patience and forgetting for the moment that this new contraption, radio, was carrying our proceedings to the nation, I snapped, "Dammit, can't you wait!"

Next day I got a telegram from some listener in Texas, saying, "Watch your language, brother, you're on the air!"

I always felt that the Democrats practically threw away their chance to elect a President in 1924 when they allowed the party to be split by the bitter contest between Smith and McAdoo. Mr. Davis, the compromise candidate, was, and is, a distinguished public figure and a man of impressive bearing. When I entered the House in 1913, he was an outstanding representative from West Virginia, and later he served brilliantly as Solicitor General under Wilson, and as United States Ambassador to the Court of St. James. But the prolonged convention fight had so discouraged the Democrats and encouraged the Republicans that almost from the beginning the Democratic campaign was an uphill and, as it turned out, a futile contest.

In any event, as I have already indicated, the condition of the country was not good when Coolidge turned over the reins to Herbert Hoover in 1929. The so-called "Coolidge prosperity" was false—a sort of hectic flush on the cheeks of our economic system, like the flush on the cheek of a tubercular patient.

To me there were several paradoxical elements in the selection of Herbert Hoover as the Republican nominee. As was the case with General Eisenhower in 1952, there was a good deal of doubt originally as to whether Hoover was a Democrat or Republican. He had been a key figure in a Democratic administration, having served as wartime food administrator under Woodrow Wilson. His name was mentioned in connection with the Democratic nomination in 1920, and many people thought Hoover would have accepted it had it been offered him that year.

There was a discernible lack of enthusiasm on the part of President Coolidge for the man who was to succeed him. Though Hoover had been Commerce Secretary under both Harding and Coolidge, political observers of the time were convinced that Coolidge always felt that Hoover reached out too fast to grab the mantle after Coolidge made his "I do not choose to run" pronouncement. If Coolidge was trying to leave the door open for persuasion, Hoover certainly kicked it shut in a hurry.

The whole question of whether Coolidge really meant to withdraw from the race stirred up a lot of talk. His position was somewhat like that of the bashful country boy who had never had anything to do with girls. Finally he met one who appealed to him, and, after many weeks of mental travail, got up nerve enough one Saturday afternoon to write her a note, asking if he could call on her the next day. He sent the note over by another boy, who brought back her answer, which was "Yes." This so excited him that he immediately jumped on his horse, rode over to her house, called her out to the front gate, and stammered, "I got your note. Did you mean it?" In somewhat the same fashion the people got Mr. Coolidge's note, but wanted to know whether he meant it.

That phrase, "I do not choose," incidentally, is an old-fashioned expression which some people who have never lived in the country may not fully understand. When I was a boy and we had company for dinner, it was considered polite, when my mother passed the vegetables or meat or preserves for, say, the third or fourth time, for the guest to say, "No, I do not choose any more." He could be persuaded to take another helping if the hosts insisted. Some observers felt that Mr. Hoover snatched away the jam in an awful hurry after Mr. Coolidge politely said, "I do not choose."

In the last days of the Coolidge administration, persons who were close to the outgoing President told me that he used to refer to Mr. Hoover rather puckishly as the "wonder boy." I was told by Republicans that, when certain courses were recommended to the President, Mr. Coolidge dryly replied, "Let's let that go, and see how the 'wonder boy' handles it."

I had been elected to the Senate in 1926, defeating a Republican incumbent named Richard P. Ernst. Ernst, by the way, was the opponent whose name my daughter, Wahwee, says she used to shout in my ear to wake me up when I would start dozing at the steering wheel during our strenuous auto campaign trips. Two years after this victory there was a small boom for me to be nominated as the Democratic vice presidential candidate. This occurred at the 1928 convention in Houston, which chose Governor Alfred E. Smith as the presidential nominee. Without my permission my supporters plastered Houston hotel lobbies with banners proclaiming "Al and Al" and distributed cards carrying the same

slogan. Governor Smith's choice as his running mate, however, was Senator Joseph T. Robinson of Arkansas, who had earned the New Yorker's
gratitude for his spirited and effective reply on the Senate floor to an
unfortunate anti-Catholic outburst by Senator Heflin. As soon as the "Al
and Al" cards appeared, I made a special point of going to the hotel room
of Franklin D. Roosevelt, who was active in Smith's behalf, to assure
him I had nothing to do with their appearance and was not bucking
Senator Robinson. The convention, of course, followed Governor Smith's
wishes and nominated Senator Robinson.

Despite warnings from some of my cautious Kentucky political friends
that Smith's anti-prohibition stand and his religion would not be popular
in my home state, I made one of the seconding speeches in favor of his
nomination. I was asked after arriving at the convention to deliver the
speech, so I borrowed a typewriter, went off into my hotel bedroom,
and secluded myself for most of the day, typing out what I wanted to
say. I have always had supreme contempt for any form of religious intolerance, and in my speech I declared myself as follows:

> I believe that every part of the American Constitution is equally
> sacred; and we cannot with consistency or propriety emphasize one
> part and ignore another; and especially is it true that we who are
> followers of Thomas Jefferson, at whose instance it was placed in
> the Constitution, cannot afford to ignore the letter or the spirit of
> the Constitution which declares that no religious test shall ever be
> required as a qualification for office in the United States. Born
> and nurtured as I was in the lap of the Presbyterian Church, in
> which my father was an elder, educated as I was in a denominational
> college in the state of Georgia, presided over by one of the great
> bishops of the Southern Methodist Church, of which I am a mem-
> ber, I am not ashamed to lift my feeble voice in behalf of the
> nomination of one who is not of my faith, but who has as much
> right to his as I have to mine.

In the same speech I had a few words to say on both the shocking
political immorality of the Harding administration and the growing
doubt, as exemplified by Governor Smith's well-known views, as to the
wisdom of the Eighteenth Amendment. I said:

> In the past eight years we have witnessed in the United States
> of America a series of political crimes so nauseating and revolting as
> to make grand larceny sound like an announcement of a hymn or
> golden text at a Sunday school.
> Thieves and bootleggers, chiefs of Government bureaus and Cabi-

net members, have sat side by side in criminal courts of the country to answer to the charge of criminal conspiracy against the people and the laws of their country; and if every faithless and perfidious public servant who rose to the surface as a result of the Republican victory in 1920 were incarcerated in the prisons where they ought to be, the Congress would have to be called into extraordinary session to make another appropriation to enlarge the prisons of the United States.

Are we told that he [Smith] ought not be nominated because his views upon the wisdom of the Eighteenth Amendment and the laws passed for its enforcement may not coincide at every point with some of ours? I answer that neither did those of Woodrow Wilson.

Governor Smith sent me a telegram expressing his appreciation for the tone of my remarks. Later he asked me to take over his campaign in Kentucky. Again ignoring the warnings of my conservative friends that my association with the party's nominee might be "bad politics," I took the assignment. I even wore a brown derby in Kentucky!

The type of campaign waged against Smith constituted one of the most shameful chapters of American history. Every sort of appeal to prejudice and intolerance was indulged in, plus a liberal sprinkling of falsehoods and personal abuse. As a result Charles E. Hughes, Newton D. Baker, Rabbi Stephen S. Wise, Dr. S. Parks Cadman, and other prominent Americans organized the National Conference of Christians and Jews.

When Al Smith came to Kentucky to campaign, disgraceful rumors were circulated that he was in a state of chronic intoxication. This, of course, was a complete lie, and the "Happy Warrior" spiked it on one occasion by making a visit to the Lincoln shrine at Hodgenville and practically sprinting up and down the long flight of steps; no man even mildly "under the influence" could have managed such a physical feat.

On another occasion, when Governor Smith was speaking in the Louisville Armory on a sweltering night, someone turned on the furnace. I have heard of smoking out politicians, but this was the first time I had ever witnessed an attempt to sweat a candidate to death.

All in all, it was a year of dark reaction which could not be overcome. The Democratic party lost Kentucky—a normally Democratic state—by 177,000 votes. The party in Kentucky was split—underneath, if not on the surface—worse than an Oak Ridge atom. As Smith's campaign manager, my own personal popularity was such that, if I had been a candidate that year, I probably could not have been elected dogcatcher.

The bitterness was so extreme that some Democrats who had supported the national ticket wanted to expel those who had voted for Hoover, and forever bar them from Democratic primaries—a situation somewhat analogous to the more recent rows which have divided the party. I took a firm position against that: I preached that the election was over and the thing to do was to reunite the party instead of driving the dissidents forever into the opposition ranks. Over and over I hammered on this theme. In the presidential election four years later, when I myself was a candidate for re-election to the Senate, I had the solid satisfaction of seeing the state go Democratic by a plurality of 185,858.

My indictment of the Hoover administration is based on its indecisiveness and its lack of grasp of the realities of the time. The Harding and Coolidge administrations already had retarded the constructive measures taken during the Wilson administration when Congress passed the Underwood Tariff Act; the Hoover Congress set back our economy still further with the Smoot-Hawley Tariff law. How well I remember my unhappy feeling when the Republican Senate leader, the late Senator James E. Watson of Indiana—a good friend of mine personally—rose and declared with fervor and flamboyance that, sixty days after passage of the Smoot-Hawley law, every smokestack would be belching, employment would rise, and prosperity would cloak the land. It was pure political buncombe, and, of course, the exact reverse transpired.

Farm interests suffered under Mr. Hoover. In fact, they had already begun to slip under Mr. Coolidge, who had vetoed the McNary-Haugen bill dealing with agriculture. Hoover was not in sympathy with the remedies offered by his own Republican leaders. On his recommendation a Farm Board was created by act of Congress, and $500,000,000 was appropriated for its use. The money was dissipated ineffectively in trying to shore up the crumbling agricultural economy. The steps taken were too little and too late.

It was hard to find any humor in the situation, but the handling of the farm problem by the Hoover administration always reminded me of the country boy who rushed into a neighbor's house at mealtime. "My wagon just hit a rough place in the road and turned over with a big load of hay!" he gasped. "It's mealtime, son," said the neighbor. "Sit down and have a bite with us, and then we'll be glad to help you." "Thank you, but I'm afraid I better not," said the boy. "Pappy wouldn't like it." "Oh, sit down," said the neighbor. "Your pappy won't mind it—a few minutes delay won't hurt anything."

The boy continued to protest, but finally he was persuaded to sit down and eat. When the meal was over and they got up to see about the hay, the boy said, "I certainly do thank you for this meal, but I still think Pappy won't like it." "What makes you so sure," asked the neighbor, "that your pappy won't like it?" "Well," said the boy, "Pappy's under the hay!"

Under President Hoover, not only was agriculture "under the hay," but the entire nation was hit by the worst depression in our history. Banks were failing with such monotonous regularity that I was constantly being put in mind of the man in Mississippi who took a check to his bank to be cashed.

"We are not paying out any money today," the cashier told him.

"Why not?" the man asked. "This is a perfectly good check."

"To tell you the truth," the cashier said, "this bank is closed; we are busted!"

"Well!" said the depositor. "All my life I've heard about banks being busted, but this is the first time I ever had one bust right in my face!"

Whether President Hoover and his policies were wholly responsible, whether he was the victim of eight previous years of Republican mismanagement, or whether it all came about as a result of world conditions is still being debated. One thing that is certain, however, is that the Smoot-Hawley Tariff law, which provided the highest duties ever levied on imports into the United States, set the example for other nations to make for themselves watertight trade and economic compartments. The tragedy of it is that, in addition to all the other resulting miseries, it produced one which was the last thing in the world that Mr. Hoover desired: the mass hunger, deprivation, insecurity, hopelessness, and general hatred against society became fuel to feed the ugly fires of communism. We are still trying to bottle up the evil distillations that were brewed in that unfortunate era.

I like Mr. Hoover personally, though I find that I still disagree with some of his views as much as when I fought him politically in 1928 and 1932. In 1951, after he had made a strong isolationist speech, I delivered a reply in which, without mentioning the former President by name, I said:

There may be some who wish us to withdraw back into our shell—go into a storm cellar until conditions improve.

There are many others—and I happen to be one of them—who

believe the American people cannot avoid the leadership which destiny has placed at our door.

We have always realized that our liberties cannot be safe as long as liberty is endangered anywhere in the world.

That is what I have always believed, that is what I said in 1951, and it is just as true today as it was when I said it.

Mr. Hoover left office an embittered man. Partisan politics aside, it has been a source of personal satisfaction to me that, in recent years, thanks to the opportunities for public service given him by the Democratic administration of President Harry S. Truman, Mr. Hoover has enjoyed increased public esteem and the respect to which a former President of the United States is entitled.

He has also regained a cheerful outlook on life. A few years ago, when I was Vice President and we both were attending a ceremony at Princeton University, he made a witty little speech. I went over to him and said, "Mr. President, your talk displayed a quality which I never knew you had—a sense of humor."

"Oh," said Mr. Hoover, "I had that all along—only you Democrats took it away from me."

All of which is a far and happy cry from the Hoover story related to me some years ago by a Democratic leader in Charleston, West Virginia. It seems that, in the depths of the depression, President Hoover was dedicating some sort of memorial in Charleston. A huge crowd was assembled, and, as Mr. Hoover walked onto the platform, a nearby battery gave him the customary twenty-one-gun salute. As the cannonading died down, there was a moment of silence, and, back in the audience, an old fellow, shading his eyes and peering up to where Mr. Hoover was standing on the platform, was heard to exclaim with astonishment, "By gum, they missed him!"

CHAPTER 10

Franklin Roosevelt—Birth of the New Deal

In 1932 I campaigned for the first time with Franklin Delano Roosevelt, introducing him from the rear platform as his campaign train whistle-stopped through Kentucky. One day we pulled into Corbin, a sizable industrial town and railroad center. I was running for re-election to the Senate myself, and, as I pranced out on the rear platform, ready to make my little speech for Mr. Roosevelt, I saw to my delight that a huge crowd of many thousands was gathered. I felt that such an assemblage called for something special in the way of preliminary remarks.

"My friends," I began, "it has been four years since I spoke in Corbin, so naturally I cannot call every individual in this great crowd by name. But I can recognize that you are the same people I addressed here four years ago. The reason I know you are the same people is that, after four years of Hoover, you are all wearing the same clothes that you had on four years ago!"

The crowd roared, "Amen! That's the truth!" and F.D.R., who always loved a humorous dig, both in campaigning and in personal conversation, laughed with them. For years to come I often heard him refer to the Corbin incident as a choice example of pertinent political satire.

I have never been one to let a good gag die young, so, four years later, when I campaigned in Corbin again for Roosevelt's re-election, I gave it a different twist.

"Why!" I exclaimed, pretending bewilderment. "I hardly know you good people! After four years of a Democratic administration, you're all dressed up!"

As I have related, I first came to know young Franklin Roosevelt when he was Assistant Secretary of the Navy under Josephus Daniels during the Wilson administration, and our acquaintance grew during the 1920 presidential campaign, when he was the Democratic vice presidential nominee. Though, during the World War I period, he was a young man, and, to some degree, an impetuous and impatient one, he was by no means a figurehead in the Navy Department. Young Roosevelt knew and loved ships and the sea, and he carried a heavy load of responsibility for the administration of naval affairs. This I knew from my close friendship with his chief, Secretary Daniels. I also believe—notwithstanding contrary opinions held by some biographers—that Roosevelt's political maturity was developing rapidly in those days. I have never accepted the theory that he was a scintillating but shallow young man until his illness struck him.

I witnessed F.D.R.'s gallant appearances at the 1924 and 1928 conventions, after he had been stricken with polio. It was an overwhelming, almost painful experience, the sort of thing that grips your throat and makes you choke up, to watch the fine, tall figure standing there, propped on crutches but still courageous and smiling, as he placed in nomination the name of his old friend and political mentor, Governor Alfred E. Smith. That Franklin Roosevelt rose in adversity to greatness has always been, to me, a demonstration of the mysterious way in which the Almighty moves, His wonders to perform. But I am one of those who believe that F.D.R. would have been a great leader regardless of whether he had ever been stricken; the wheel chair was a circumstance, not a compelling factor.

I followed Roosevelt's career as a liberal and progressive governor of the state of New York, a post which, because of his physical disability, he was initially reluctant to seek. He finally did so on the urgings of Governor Smith, who, of course, wanted the popular Roosevelt to head the New York State ticket in 1928, the year when Smith made his presidential bid.

Though I fought hard for Governor Smith in 1928, I was not in sympathy with his bitterness over Roosevelt's nomination and his decision to "take a walk" any more than I was in sympathy with bitterness shown in later convention years by such good friends of mine as Jim Farley, Jimmy Byrnes and others. I felt, in 1932, that Roosevelt was the man who could lead the Democratic party to victory and the country back to a sound economic basis. In fact, I was a charter member of a small group of senators, called together by Cordell Hull, to work for Roosevelt's nomination, and I was proud to serve as temporary chairman and keynoter of the convention which nominated him.

I shall never forget that 1932 convention and that speech, which was my first major effort as a convention orator. At one point a forty-five minute demonstration broke out when I came out for the submission of an amendment to the Constitution repealing the Eighteenth Amendment. When Jim Farley criticized my speech as "too long," I told him I had not anticipated talking to such a vociferously thirsty crowd.

There were others who apparently thought my speech was on the lengthy side. Will Rogers, the famous humorist, was writing a syndicated newspaper column about the convention, and this is what he had to say about my maiden keynote effort:

> Now comes Senator Barkley with the "keynote." What do you mean, "note?" This is no note. This was in three volumes. Barkley leaves from here to go to the Olympic Games to run in the marathon. He will win it, too, for that race only lasts three or four hours.
>
> But it had to be a long speech for when you start enumerating the things that the Republicans have got away with in the last twelve years you have cut yourself out a job. . . . He had it all over the Republican keynoter, for [Barkley] was reading facts while the other fellow had to read "alibis."
>
> Barkley did a fine job of delivery, and, too, he was on his feet at the finish.

As I recall this delightful bit of Rogers' humor, I wish Will were here today. I would tell him that I learned something from his deft criticism, and I might go on to recite him a story about the time I read a prepared speech to the alumni association of my alma mater, Marvin College. I thought I had done a pretty good job, but when I asked the chairman what he thought of my talk, he replied:

"Well, I have three criticisms. In the first place, you read it. In the second place, you read it poorly. And in the third place, it was not worth reading."

To digress a bit further, the above story can be a risky one to tell. I once used it to close my extemporaneous remarks at some function at which I was sharing speaking honors with my good friend, Senator Theodore Green, then Governor of Rhode Island. As I sat down, with the audience still laughing at my sally about persons who read their speeches, Governor Green leaned over and hissed in my ear, "You——, you've ruined me!" Then he got up, faced the audience, and sheepishly pulled from his pocket a long, typewritten speech manuscript.

In preparing my speech I gave meticulous care to the wording of my declaration on the Eighteenth Amendment, not only as to intent, but as to style. I wanted it put in language so simple that there could be no misunderstanding as to its purpose, and no grounds for accusing the Democratic party of using weasel words in its prohibition plank, as the Republicans had done the same year at their convention which renominated Mr. Hoover.

Before the convention I went to Albany to confer with Governor Roosevelt. I had then tentatively drafted all of my speech with the exception of my remarks on prohibition, and I outlined it to him. "That's grand," he said, using one of his favorite expressions. "But what do you intend to say about the Eighteenth Amendment?"

I told him what I had in mind. "I think," Roosevelt suggested, "you ought to go further and come out flatfooted for repeal."

"Now, Governor," I replied, "I voted for the Eighteenth Amendment and for the laws to enforce it, and I have observed them in my own conduct ever since they were on the statute books. It seems to me that about all I can be asked to do is to advocate that an amendment be submitted to the people and allow the people to pass on the question of repeal."

"Well, all right," Governor Roosevelt agreed. "But I hope that the Democratic platform itself will come out in favor of outright repeal."

So, in my keynote address, I approached the question of repeal by pointing out that the Republican convention, in dealing with the Eighteenth Amendment, had promulgated something "it called a plank" but which was really a "promiscuous agglomeration of scrap lumber." It attempted, I declared, to promise both support of repeal for benefit of the wets and opposition to it for benefit of the drys in different sections of the country.

"Whatever may be the divergent views of men and women on the merits or demerits of the Eighteenth Amendment as a national policy," I went on to say, "it is inconceivable that this or any other part of the Constitution of the United States should ever apply to a part and not the whole of the American nation. . . .

"This convention owes it to the people of this nation to make its declaration upon this subject clear, understandable and unequivocal. There is no reason why a political declaration should look in every direction and see nothing."

I continued:

"In order, therefore, to obtain the present will of the American people on this subject of universal controversy, this convention should in the platform here to be adopted recommend the passage by Congress of a resolution repealing the Eighteenth Amendment. . . ."

At this point I was interrupted by a demonstration which I shall never forget. The convention organist started whooping it up with "Hail, Hail, the Gang's All Here," "Maine Stein Song," and "How Dry I Am" (played in fast time), and the delegates went wild. There were parades and snake dances all over the floor. There was even a little fist fight over whether the Texas standard, among others, should join the pro-repeal parade, and the Texas wets won. At one point a policeman rashly offered to arbitrate the Texas squabble, whereupon *both* sides turned on him, shouting, "You keep out of this! This is a private fight!"

I tried, of course, to restore order, but for forty-five minutes it was futile. At one point I almost precipitated a crisis by coming perilously close to smashing the radio microphones on the speaker's rostrum with my four-pound wooden gavel.

When a semblance of order finally was achieved, I went on to repeat that the convention should recommend passage by Congress of a resolution repealing the dry amendment, and submission of the question to the people of the states through conventions whose delegates should be chosen exclusively for that purpose.

"If the people are to pass again upon this question, which they have a right to do," I declared, "let them pass upon it in such bald, naked, unequivocal terms as to make their decision intelligent, certain and final. If their verdict shall be in favor of retaining the Eighteenth Amendment to the Constitution, then let every true citizen of the nation accept the decision and abide by it in letter and in spirit. If, on the contrary, the verdict shall be for the repeal of the Eighteenth Amendment, then let every branch of our Federal Government exercise all the powers they possess to protect the states in the observance and the enforcement of the laws which they themselves shall enact to control, regulate, or prohibit the manufacture of liquor."

My declaration on the Eighteenth Amendment was generally well received. Columnist Walter Lippmann, writing from the convention, observed:

> With equal directness Senator Barkley dealt with prohibition by proposing that the Democratic party return to the Jeffersonian tradition. He declared without weasel words of any kind that the convention should recommend to Congress the passage of a resolution repealing the Eighteenth Amendment and submitting it to con-

ventions elected by the people of the States. It is impossible to deal
more simply or more straightforwardly with the issue, and this
statement should please everyone who has been wondering whether
political parties would ever again be intellectually candid on controversial issues.

The Democratic convention responded to the repeal challenge with
admirable directness, as Governor Roosevelt had hoped it would. A majority report of the platform committee submitted a recommendation,
which was adopted, advocating repeal, subject to passage of a Constitutional amendment by Congress and ratification by a three-fourths majority of the states; also, immediate modification of the Volstead Act to
permit manufacture and sale of beer and other beverages of limited alcoholic content.

Of course, there were other portions of my speech dealing with the
shortcomings of the previous twelve years of Republican rule. Of these
passages the late George Creel, a distinguished editor and journalist,
wrote:

> When Barkley began to recite the crimes of the Republican
> party, even cold-blooded delegates from New England bayed them-
> selves into collapse, but, although prostrate, continued to blow froth
> and drum the floor with their heels.

Franklin Roosevelt was one of the most fascinating personalities I have
ever known. I have never regarded him as Woodrow Wilson's equal as a
profound thinker, but he had a deep and penetrating insight into both
the philosophy and the mechanics of government. No President has ever
surpassed him in personal knowledge of the details of every department.

In most instances he also had the instinct of a virtuoso for playing
practical politics—though, in the language of the late Fiorello LaGuar-
dia, when he did make a mistake it was a "beaut." He was an artist at
playing on people's emotions. "Mr. President," I said to him one day, "you
play with men like a cat plays with a mouse." He gave me a burst of the
famous Rooseveltian laughter, and chuckled, "Well, I don't devour them
in the end!"

As a political liberal long before I had even heard of Franklin Roosevelt, I was a natural supporter of most of his program. I had my disagree-
ments with him, some of them quite warm, as I shall relate later.
However, I had a great fondness for him as a person; I found him both
scintillating and stimulating. It was a pleasure to go fishing with him—
even though I usually am fonder of fishing in principle than in prac-

tice—and, toward the end of the day, enjoy some good conversation along with one of the libations for which he was celebrated. Some chroniclers have complained that F.D.R.'s old-fashioneds, into which he sometimes put everything but the kitchen sink, were too radical for enjoyment. My own considered judgment on F.D.R. as an amateur bartender is that, just as in politics, he was more liberal than radical.

In moments when we could relax F.D.R. and I used to compete in bringing stories to each other. I have already related the story I told him that made him whoop so loudly that the Secret Service guards almost came running to his bedroom. He enjoyed telling stories with a historical twist. For instance, I recall one that he dug out of some old book and passed on to me. It concerned a clandestine love affair reputedly being carried on during President Lincoln's administration by the ambassador of one powerful nation and the wife of another prominent diplomat.

The lovers would meet, of all places, opposite the White House in the little park which then was enclosed by an iron fence. One evening they were so absorbed in each other that they did not notice when the gates were locked at 6 P.M. It so happened that William H. Seward, Lincoln's shrewd Secretary of State, was walking by in the dusk, when, out of the bushes, he heard the ambassador's agitated voice: "Mr. Secretary, for heaven's sake, help me!" The startled Seward eased over to the fence, and got a briefing on the situation. In the interests of averting a diplomatic scandal he went over to the White House, looking first for a key to the gate, then for a ladder.

As F.D.R. told me the story, President Lincoln came upon his Secretary of State rummaging in the tool shed, and asked him what in the world was going on. On being acquainted with the delicate situation Lincoln, after choking down his mirth, helped Seward carry the ladder across the street and rescue the couple. Every time I think of this story—which may be apocryphal—I have a slightly irreverent feeling of thankfulness that it happened in Lincoln's time, and not ours, for I simply cannot imagine President Eisenhower and Secretary Dulles, estimable and accommodating gentlemen though they are, carrying a ladder across the White House lawn and Pennsylvania Avenue to relieve an embarrassing diplomatic situation. I hope I do them no injustice.

Another story about F.D.R. himself illustrates his uncanny knowledge of all sorts of little details about a myriad of persons. It concerns a certain American former diplomat who must remain unnamed. Years earlier this gentleman had served as our top envoy to a foreign country. He was a creditable diplomat, but, being a bachelor, he was also a sort of ladies' man. In fact, it was whispered that, when he entertained at his official residence, he was not above sneaking a gallant pinch, or even a daring pressure of the knee, under the table.

In any event, this gentleman had been out of the diplomatic service during the twelve Republican years. When Roosevelt came in, the former diplomat was desirous of returning to his old post. He was acquainted with me and with my then colleague from Kentucky, the late Senator M. M. Logan, and he prevailed upon us to call on the President in his behalf.

As we sat there, telling the President what a fine representative this gentleman had been and how we hoped he could be reappointed, I could see a quizzical look come over the President's face, and then an open smile. Before we finished, he threw up both hands and roared: "Oh, no! That's the man who pinched every leg in——!" —and here he named the country to which the former diplomat had been assigned.

I could not think of much to say, but, to my surprise, Senator Logan spoke up and said:

"Mr. President, I hope you won't hold that against him. All of our lives a lot of us have wanted to do the same thing and haven't had the nerve!"

Coming from Senator Logan, who was a lifelong Baptist, a deacon in the church, and for forty years a men's bible-class teacher, this was doubly amusing. F.D.R. whooped again, but he still would not give the man the appointment.

We were a sick nation when Franklin D. Roosevelt came into office. I shall never forget the thrill with which the nation responded to his inspiring inaugural declaration that "the only thing we have to fear is fear itself." After twelve years of numbing *laissez faire* it was a dynamic experience to serve in the Congress which, in the memorable "first hundred days" of the Roosevelt administration, began to bring the nation back to health.

I do not propose here to write a detailed history of the legislative record of the New Deal. That task has been undertaken by others, and it would be too monumental to include in these memoirs. As I write this, however, the country is experiencing a Republican administration, the first that has been in power since the beginning of the era which I am describing. From where I sit I see some of the same fumbling and indecision and uncertainty that marked the last Republican administration, which Franklin Roosevelt's New Deal set in order. In some respects the times seem even more grave now than they were then, because of reckless domestic passions that are being engendered by narrow partisan politics, and the dangerous and frightening spread of world communism, which can be contained and combatted only by a strong and united America.

In view of the current situation it may be useful to recall a few of the vitalizing measures which the Roosevelt administration swiftly took to strengthen the national economy. Bold, decisive steps were taken, and taken quickly, in every field wherein remedial action was needed. The devastating rash of bank failures was checked, and, through federal deposit insurance and other banking measures, the confidence of the people in our financial institutions was restored. Agriculture was given a sound aid program, so that desperate farmers again found it profitable to produce rather than burn their crops and dump their milk; in some areas farmers had been literally standing behind their shotguns to hold off sheriffs seeking to enforce mortgage claims. The needs of the unemployed, of the old people in our society, of harassed homeowners, of the residents of underdeveloped areas, where the great potential natural resources of America were going to waste, of labor, and of business—all were given appropriate treatments.

Looking today at the accomplishments of the New Deal, I venture to make this prediction: The contemporary partisans may criticize shrilly; they may yap and bark and snap at the heels of the giant figure of a new and stronger social system that came into being under twenty years of Democratic administration. However, I do not think that any administration or any political party will have the nerve to attempt to repeal the fundamental laws passed under Roosevelt and Truman which are now an inseparable part of our way of life.

Years after the beginning of the New Deal, in a Senate speech marking the third anniversary of President Roosevelt's third term, I summed up the pattern which had led to the administration's many accomplishments. I said:

> This condition did not come about by accident. We are where we are because we have had an administration, far-sighted and conscientious. . . .
> In the final analysis, the value of a political party to the nation is two-fold: It must propose a program and it must carry its program into action. . . .
> The stimulation of popular legislation beneficial to all the people, expounding the Jeffersonian theory of "the greatest good to the greatest number," has given to this nation renewed vitality, force

and defensive aggressiveness. Surely there is no one of rational thought, other than those politically prejudiced, who would ask for the repeal of Democratic national policy-making legislation. Such legislation has been the backbone of the country. . . .

Over the years I have also viewed with cynicism the howls of anguish that were raised, after our ailing agricultural economy began to mend, over what the New Deal did for the farmers. I have spoken on this subject many times, but I do not think I ever put it more succinctly than in these lines from my keynote address at the 1936 Democratic convention:

> They have wept over the slaughter of a few little pigs as if they had been tender human infants nestling at their mothers' breasts. They have shed these tears over the premature death of pigs as if they had been born, educated and destined for the ministry or for politics.
> But their bitterest tears are not shed over the fate of the little pigs. Their real grief comes from the slaughter of the fat hogs of privilege and plunder which they have fed on the people's substance.
> They are not weeping because we plowed under a few rows of cotton. Mr. Hoover started that. Their real sorrow springs from the fact that we have plowed under the sordid conceptions of Old Deal government and its chance ever to be restored to the control of American life.

It is particularly ironic to reflect on what the New Deal did for American business, and how certain segments of the business world later became the New Deal's most bitter detractors. As a member of the Senate Finance Committee, I took an active part in drafting the National Industrial Recovery Act. I have firsthand knowledge that a number of panicky industrial and business leaders came to President Roosevelt and begged him virtually to "take over" their factories and stores to save them from ruin. Roosevelt, the same man they later reviled as a "dictator" and as "King Franklin," would not do this, but his administration and the Congress which supported it did give business the NRA legislation which saved it from disaster.

I had many talks with the President on the subject of "dictatorship." He was a strong leader, but it is a grave injustice to picture him as desirous of dictatorial powers. He expressed repugnance for the idea and went further to assert very positively that no would-be dictator could ever establish himself in this country, because the people would not stand for it, for which he said, "Amen!"

We also frequently had philosophical discussions on the subject of ingratitude in connection with business and the NRA. F.D.R. said wryly that the attitude of some segments of business, once it began to recover, reminded him of the patient in the hospital who threw his crutches at the doctor who healed him. In other words, as Rabelais wrote, "The devil was sick, the devil a monk would be; the devil was well, the devil a monk was he!"

CHAPTER 11

That "Dear Alben" Letter

ON ONE occasion during the lifetime of President Franklin D. Roosevelt I was called upon to deliver a speech at the National Press Club in Washington. It was at a "Congressional Night" party, when new congressmen and senators, as well as some old ones, are exposed to the Fourth Estate, and I was asked to unburden myself on the general topic of "Advice to Newly Elected Senators."

After expounding a number of bits of advice, which I fondly hoped were both humorous and sage, I came to the meat of my topic. I said:

"If you get a letter from the White House calling you by your first name, brother, duck—and when I say 'duck,' I don't mean 'chicken'! Duck your tail between your legs and make for the tall and uncut!"

I went on to say that I had become a little irritated at the President only the other day when I learned he had written a letter to Senator Elbert Thomas of Utah, addressing him as "Dear Elbert."

"Now think of that," I protested. "I have a patent on this 'dear' business and my patent has not expired."

I was being jocular, of course, about the famous "Dear Alben" letter, which President Roosevelt had written me during the battle to reform the Supreme Court. That letter remains, I suppose, the most tenaciously remembered document of my long political career. One of my prized souvenirs, in fact, is a letter which Harry Truman wrote me after he had been in the White House for several years but before I had become Vice President. I had written President Truman on some matter or other, and had addressed my communication, "My Dear Mr. President." He promptly shot back a reply to me, which began:

"Dear Alben: I'll take the chance on addressing you that way, hoping it will not get into the Kentucky elections as it did once before and don't you be so damn formal when you address me."

He signed it: "Harry."

The "Dear Alben" episode in my life began with a very serious matter: the controversy over the Supreme Court. As far back as 1934 the attitude of the Court toward the New Deal program began to trouble me. I have an almost religious reverence for the Supreme Court. To me it is a sacred institution, and I feel that the men who are honored to serve as justices should remove themselves completely from all areas of partisanship—the Supreme Court and politics simply do not mix. I have always regarded it as unfortunate that the late Charles Evans Hughes, whom I admired as a great American and an outstanding jurist, permitted himself to be drawn from the Supreme Court bench into the political arena. In 1952 I made a special point of expressing my wholehearted admiration to my old friend and fellow Kentuckian, the late Chief Justice Fred M. Vinson, after he had declined to become a presidential candidate; I could not speak, of course, until after he had announced his decision, because I myself was being mentioned as a candidate.

It bothered me, therefore, back in 1934, when the Supreme Court began knocking down New Deal legislation as fast as it reached the Court for constitutional tests. As Charles Evans Hughes, who later became Chief Justice of the Supreme Court, once said, "The Constitution is what the judges say it is. . . ."

I did not wish to think ill of the Court; yet it was hard not to wonder whether the personal philosophy of some of the members was having an overriding influence on its decisions. It was well known, for instance, that one of the elderly members, the late Mr. Justice McReynolds, had an unreasonable personal dislike for President Roosevelt; at one Gridiron dinner in Washington, the justice breached protocol and good manners by turning his back as the President of the United States was leaving the room.

Feeling as I did that it would be a national calamity if the people's faith in the Supreme Court was ever weakened, it was inevitable that I should support President Roosevelt's effort to liberalize the composition of the Court. In fact, even before Roosevelt proposed his plan, which was characterized—unfairly, in my opinion—as the Supreme Court "packing" bill—I was on record as having expressed my concern about the course the Court seemed to be following in its interpretation of social and economic legislation. It was at the 1936 Democratic convention, at which I was again the keynote speaker, that I voiced my views as follows:

I make no attack on the Supreme Court. As an insititution I respect it, and it would be both unfair and unjust if I were unwilling to accord to judges on the bench the right to their views of law and constitutions which I claim for myself.

But there is nothing new in controversies over the Constitution. They began in the convention which framed it, and ten amendments were adopted to it by the first Congress that assembled under it.

I went on to say that "from the exultant voices of the tree-sitters and the devotees of the hitching post, you would imagine that the Supreme Court had never nullified an act of Congress until Franklin D. Roosevelt became President." Pointing out that this was far from the truth, I declared that the Democratic party had sought to treat the Constitution "as a life-giving charter, rather than an object of curiosity on the shelf of a museum." Then I asked:

Is the court beyond criticism? May it be regarded as too sacred to be disagreed with?

The convention answered with a mighty chorus of "No! No!"

Finally I quoted from the inaugural address of Abraham Lincoln, the great President whose memory the Republican party rightfully reveres, in which he said:

If the policy of the Government on vital questions affecting the whole people is to be irrevocably fixed by the decisions of the Supreme Court the instant they are made in ordinary litigation between parties in personal actions, the people will have ceased to be their own rulers, having to that extent practically resigned their Government into the hands of that eminent tribunal.

I received many letters and telegrams after the 1936 keynote speech, overwhelmingly favorable in sentiment. One Wall Street man wrote me that he and his wife heard my speech over the radio at their home in Princeton, New Jersey. "My wife, bred in blackest Republicanism," he wrote, "was completely won over and, for the first time, realized just what the New Deal meant."

It was my active participation in the later legislative efforts to increase the Court membership to fifteen and to retire justices at the age of seventy which eventually led to the "Dear Alben" letter. Of course, what many people failed to realize at the time, and what they probably do not remember now, was that President Roosevelt actually was proposing nothing unprecedented or radical. The number of members comprising the Supreme Court has been frequently changed by Congress. Originally the Court was made up of six justices. Later its membership was increased to ten. Still later it was reduced to its present membership of nine. Mr. Roosevelt's proposal, therefore, was not a new adventure, although his recommendation that it be increased to fifteen members, had it been enacted, would have made the Court larger than ever before.

At the time of the Supreme Court "battle," the late Senator Joseph T. Robinson of Arkansas was majority leader of the Senate, and I was his assistant. As I have said, I agreed in principle with what the President was trying to accomplish. However, I always have regretted that he dropped the measure on us, his Senate floor leaders, rather precipitously, with hardly any advance consultation to work out a strategic plan for piloting the measure through the Senate. Though he carried the ball loyally, Majority Leader Robinson was somewhat dismayed by the way in which it was tossed to him. In retrospect I doubt that we ever could have passed the Supreme Court reform bill; too many inflammatory and emotional issues were injected into the picture. However, had F.D.R., as the "quarterback," given us the signals in advance of the play, not after he tossed us the ball and expected us to run with it, we might have covered more ground.

On the day before the measure was to be debated in the Senate— the Democrats were split wide open on the issue—Majority Leader Robinson called a meeting in his office to discuss plans for combatting a threatened filibuster. After we had "counted noses" and agreed that prospects for the bill's success were virtually nil, Senator Robinson instructed his principal lieutenants that if, for any reason, he was off the floor at any crucial point, my leadership was to be followed implicitly.

Senator Robinson never reached the floor, however. When the meeting broke up that day, he asked me to remain behind. He told me he was not feeling well. He took my hand, put it on his chest, and said:

"Alben, I have a pain—right here. Do you think I ought to consult a physician?"

"Good Lord!" I exclaimed. "You don't mean to tell me that you haven't consulted one already?"

I urged him to call his doctor and to go home and rest. He did so. Next morning I was awakened by a telephone call and informed that Senator Robinson had died of a heart attack. He had been alone in his apartment, as Mrs. Robinson was visiting in Arkansas, and the maid found him slumped over on the floor of the bathroom. Joe Robinson was another casualty in the never-ending "battle of Washington," which has claimed so many good men.

Naturally the floor fight on the Supreme Court bill was deferred, in so far as the Administration was concerned. However, so bitter was the issue that, without even observing a seemly period of truce while the fallen majority leader was being buried, the opposition leaders continued their efforts against the bill.

Some of the maneuvering that took place even before Joe Robinson's body was cold struck me as outrageously indecent. One anti-Administration senator managed to grab the floor as soon as the Senate convened that day—even before we could observe the customary tradition of recognizing the other senator from the fallen leader's home state to make formal announcement of the death. He made a rather venomous speech in which he "warned" other senators not to kill themselves fighting for the Court bill as Robinson had.

Still another senator—he, at least, had the decency to make his statement to newsmen off the floor of the Senate—made the remark:

"If it had not been for this Court fight, Joe Robinson would be alive today.

"I beseech the President to drop this Court fight, lest he appear to fight against God!"

I was shocked by these tactics. I found them in unbelievably bad taste, and such remarks as the last quoted struck me as sacrilegious. As acting majority leader, I felt it my duty to call President Roosevelt's attention to what was going on. He replied in writing to my oral report, and this was the famous and much-misconstrued "Dear Alben" epistle, dated on July 15, 1937, the day after Senator Robinson's death.

In view of the interest that has persisted concerning this particular Rooseveltian epistle it is with some chagrin that I must confess I cannot find the original anywhere among my papers. The text, of course, was released to the press and is a matter of record, but apparently I did not attach any great importance to the letter at the time and have either mislaid it or let it get away from me entirely. It is possible that I sent it, without bothering to have it copied, to the Public Printer for inclusion in the Congressional Record, but I cannot state this with positiveness.

Actually, the President's salutation was "My Dear Alben." He wrote:

"I am glad you called my attention to certain events of yesterday and today. Lest there be any misunderstanding in regard to judicial reform, please let me clarify the situation.

"Since the untimely death of our Majority Leader, I had hoped, with you, that at least until his funeral services had been held a decent respect for his memory would have deferred discussion of political and legislative matters.

"It is, therefore, with regret that I find that advantage is being taken of what, in all decency, should be a period of mourning. . . ."

He went on to say that, because of this situation, he felt "compelled in the public interest, though against every inclination" to write to me as "the acting majority leader in the Senate." Then he spelled out the details of the Court reform bill which the Administration favored.

After the release of this letter by the White House every conceivable misinterpretation was placed upon it. The anti-Roosevelt Democrats in the Senate seized upon it as "proof" that the President was interfering with their choice of a majority leader to succeed Senator Robinson. The anti-Roosevelt element of the press deduced that the familiarity of the salutation meant that the President regarded "Dear Alben" as "his" man; thereafter I was pictured as a sort of rustic, amiable errand boy for the White House. One news magazine even tagged me with the adjective "bumbling"—"bumbling Barkley"—a tricky combination of words that stuck to me like the tar baby did to Br'er Rabbit.

It is not necessary for me at this stage to dissect and demolish the silliness of some of these interpretations, but I am gratified that the record over the years that followed the famous "Dear Alben" letter made it unmistakably clear that I was my own man.

In any event, a contest shaped up between the late Pat Harrison of Mississippi, an outstanding though conservative senator, and myself for the majority leadership. It was during this contest that I had one of my earliest intimate contacts—and it was a revealing one—with Harry S. Truman. He then was a freshman senator, and, without knowing him too well, I instinctively liked him. As the old political saying goes, he "voted right." I solicited no votes for the majority leadership, but many colleagues came to me voluntarily and said they were for me. Among these was Senator Truman.

As the struggle over domestic legislation between the Administration and the conservative Democratic forces grew more intense, a number of senators who had voluntarily pledged me their support switched to Harrison. The only one who told me he was going to find it necessary to switch, however, was Senator Truman. He came to me and said frankly, "The pressure on me is so great that I am going to ask you to relieve me of my promise." Without asking him whence came the pressure I promptly released him. I always admired him for the courage and character he displayed in coming to me as he did. Too often in politics the stiletto is slipped between your shoulder blades, while its wielder continues to smile sweetly and buss you on the cheek.

The vote was taken—by secret ballot, of course—and it was a real horse race right up to the last vote. There were seventy-five Democratic senators voting and, with only one ballot left in the hat, the score stood 37 to 37. When the teller reached in and pulled out that last folded slip, it looked as big as a bedquilt. Then he announced that the last vote was for Barkley. Senator Harrison jumped up immediately and moved to make my election unanimous. I sent my wife a telegram—and it took all my will power to resist the temptation to sign it, "DEAR ALBEN," saying, "WON BY ONE." I have often wondered how I would have felt about Harry Truman if I had lost the majority leadership by one vote!

The White House had kept hands off in the race between Senator Harrison and me, although, after it was over, President Roosevelt personally expressed to me his pleasure at my selection. The President also sent to a "harmony dinner," which we Democrats held shortly after my election to the majority leadership, a note in which he said some nice things. He complimented my "sense of perspective" and "sense of humor," which he implied—all too truly!—would be useful qualities for a majority leader. "Any man who, when the discussion of some picayune subject waxes serious and acrimonious, can rise in his place and sing 'Wagon Wheels,' is a positive genius," F.D.R. wrote. The whole tone of the President's letter was light and pleasant, and, I suspect, shrewdly calculated to soothe the ruffled feelings left in the wake of the Supreme Court fight.

As majority leader, I did my best to carry out the Administration's progressive program, in which I wholeheartedly believed, and at the same time to work for harmony within the Democratic party. It was not easy, however, to steer a harmony course, for the bitterness within the Democratic ranks was extreme, even though, on the very day I was elected majority leader, I took steps in concert with Vice President John Nance Garner to iron out the controversial Supreme Court bill.

In reaching our decision to by-pass this bill Vice President Garner and I took into consideration the obvious fact that we could not pass it. There was nothing to be gained, in our opinion, in splitting the party further by making futile efforts to carry out the President's wishes. Thus the President suffered a legislative block in his effort to change the make-up of the Supreme Court. Before his second term was over, however, attrition within the ranks of the so-called "nine old men" made it possible for him to accomplish his aims of bringing to the bench younger, more liberal-minded men.

There was a time, late in 1942, when I myself was under consideration by President Roosevelt as a possible Supreme Court appointee. A vacancy had occurred on the bench when Justice Byrnes resigned to become wartime Director of Economic Stabilization (later Director of War Mobilization). Entirely without my consent some of my friends in the Senate got up a petition urging my appointment. While I was honored by the suggestion, I definitely was not seeking the post, and, in all sincerity, I would have had to give a great deal of consideration as to whether I would have left the Senate for the bench.

As it turned out, President Roosevelt appointed the late Wiley Rutledge to fill the vacancy, but, in the course of doing so, he voluntarily wrote me a personal note which is perhaps one of the most cordial and complimentary I have ever received from anyone. It read:

THE WHITE HOUSE
Washington

Jan. 8, 1943

DEAR ALBEN:

I do not know whether you will be disappointed or not in this Supreme Court matter. Personally, I would not be. I had really thought a lot about sending your name up but two things happened. First of all, there was no question that your ability, learning and liberality fitted you in every way for the Court. The other consideration, however, tore me apart because of the fact that you are such a very old and close friend of mine.

It related to the fact that the country really needs you just where you are—a good, hard-hitting, yet just, leader of democracy—democracy both with a large "d" and a small "d." You are a sort of balance wheel that has kept things moving forward all these years—and that's that. I had to come to the conclusion that there are nine Justices but only one Majority Leader in the Senate—and I can't part with him in that capacity.

Affectionately,
FRANKLIN D. ROOSEVELT

Honorable Alben W. Barkley
The United States Senate
Washington, D. C.

On February 9—Justice Rutledge's appointment had been announced in the interim—I replied to the President's letter as follows:

DEAR MR. PRESIDENT:

This will acknowledge receipt of your gracious letter about the Supreme Court appointment.

I sincerely hope that nobody bothered you in my behalf. I refused to consent to any effort on the part of any of my friends to bring my name to your attention in connection with it.

Your letter was generous regarding my work in the Senate, although, in truth, I cannot place so high an appraisal upon it.

This account of my years in public life would not be complete if I did not express my affection for that grand old man of politics, former Vice President Garner. I came to differ from Mr. Garner when he broke with President Roosevelt on the third-term tradition, but I respected him for his honest convictions, and nothing ever upset my warm personal regard for him. When I became majority leader and he presided over the Senate, he told me, "You and I are a team—you're the pitcher and I'm the catcher." That was the way it was.

Vice President Garner was famous for his pithy remarks, which were widely quoted around Washington. On one occasion he had to attend some official banquet. Mrs. Garner, who had stayed home because of a cold, asked him when he returned what the ladies had worn.

"Nothing above the table," he growled. "I didn't look under."

"Cactus Jack" has never paid a visit to Washington since his retirement, and he says he never will. I visited him once in the spring of 1952. I was speaking in San Antonio, which is about eighty miles from Garner's home at Uvalde. I borrowed a car and a chauffeur from an acquaintance in San Antonio—he happened to be an undertaker, but he assured me it was a purely personal courtesy—and drove over to see my old friend.

Garner was in wonderful fettle, and he entertained me with a fine barbecue. He was about eighty-three years old at the time, and he lived very simply: he was dressed, as was his usual custom, in a khaki shirt, open at the neck, and khaki pants, and he lived in a small house behind his original home, which he has presented to the city of Uvalde as a library and museum. We reminisced a bit about the days when I would stop in his office with other senators after working hours, and he would invite the group to "strike a blow for liberty," as he called the well-known bourbon-and-branchwater ritual. When it was time for me to leave, he put his arm around my shoulder and said, "Alben, old friend, if I never see you again in this world, I hope to see you in the next." That was my last visit with this grand and rugged old man of politics, but, as I write this, he is still vigorous and strong.

In the days when he presided over the Senate, Vice President Garner was not only a statesmanlike and effective chairman but he added greatly to the color of the United States Senate. I shall never forget the time when he squelched the almost irrepressible Huey Long. Huey, in debate, was like a horsefly: he would light on one part of you, sting you, and then, when you slapped at him, fly away to land elsewhere and sting again. He took particular delight in attempting to bedevil the Vice President, and it was widely known that Garner had little patience with his methods and tactics.

One day, after he had made himself particularly offensive to the chair, Huey jumped up for about the fiftieth time and, in a bantering voice, said:

"Mr. President, I rise to make a parliamentary inquiry. . . . How should a senator, who is half in favor of this bill and half against it, cast his vote?"

Garner glowered at him from beneath his bushy white eyebrows and said:

"Get a saw and saw yourself in two; that's what you ought to do anyhow!"

For one of the few times in his life Huey had no comeback.

Of all the fabulous characters I have known in public life Huey Long was in a class by himself. He was a human kaleidoscope. Always unpredictable, he could play the demagogue, the buffoon, the great pleader; as the mood struck him, he could be hilarious, unscrupulous, or even courtly. It was easy to disapprove of him politically, but hard to dislike him personally—though I was locked in battle with him almost constantly.

One day in the cloakroom I told him, "Huey, you are the smartest lunatic I ever saw in my whole life!" He threw back his head, laughed, and said, "Maybe that is the smartest description I've ever had applied to me!"

I went on to tell him, "You are clever, you are resourceful, you are a great debater: if you only had a balance wheel inside of you, like the little gadget in a piece of machinery, to keep you from doing so many crazy things, you would be a really great man." I meant that then, and

I still believe it. His son, Russell Long, who now sits, as did his father, in the United States Senate, has that balance wheel which was lacking in Huey, and he is both a fine young man and an outstanding senator. Whatever one thought of Huey, he was never dull. My first close contact with him was at the Democratic convention in 1932, when he was still pro-Roosevelt. At that time Long was still Governor of Louisiana, though he had been elected to the Senate. He came to the convention as a member of a contesting delegation from Louisiana which was supporting Mr. Roosevelt for the nomination. There had been a bitter fight before the Committee on Credentials over the seating of the rival delegations and the committe had decided in favor of the delegation opposing the Long forces. There had been much abuse and recrimination in the fight before the Credentials Committee which had disgusted many members of the committee. He approached me in my capacity as temporary chairman, advising me that he and his group would appeal to the full convention from the decision of the Credentials Committee.

"I want to make a suggestion to you," I said. "I know something about your controversy, and I think you have the facts on your side. I suggest that you get up before the convention and present the facts in a dignified manner as if you were arguing a case before the Supreme Court. If you will avoid vituperation and name-calling, I believe you will win your fight."

"You mean," Huey said, grinning, "you think I should act like a gentleman?"

"Exactly!" I said.

"Well," he said, putting on a long face, as if I were making him take castor oil, "if I *have* to, I can be as much of a gentleman as anybody."

He did just as I had advised him, made a forceful and logical, legal argument, and the convention seated his delegation. I think he always respected me for talking turkey to him, for in the years to come, before his assassination, we always remained on amiable terms, even though we frequently were on different sides of legislative matters.

Huey, of course, was a merciless kidder, and he would use his barbs on anyone, even if he liked them. Once he thought he had me set up for a ribbing, and he moved right in. He had come into the senators' dining room one day when I was having lunch with an attractive and very young lady, who was obviously not Mrs. Barkley. He waltzed right over to my table, ogling, smirking, working his eyebrows archly, and doing everything he possibly could to indicate that he thought he had caught

Alben Barkley's maternal grandmother, wife of Captain James Henry Smith, a Confederate soldier who died of injuries received with Morgan's raiders.

Alben Graham Barkley in 1875, at the age of fifty. It was in Grandfather Barkley's home—a log cabin—that Alben Barkley was born.

Barkley's grandmother, Amanda Louise Barkley, stimulated his early political interests. This picture shows her at the age of sixty, in 1890.

Electra Eliza Smith, the mother of Alben Barkley, at seventeen, just before her marriage to John Wilson Barkley.

Electra Eliza Barkley in 1914. rkley still gets lyrical when he nks about the egg custard pie his ther made.

John Wilson Barkley in 1914. The father of Alben Barkley was a strong, hard-working man, a farmer most of his life.

Electra and John Barkley in 1932, rtly before the death of John Bar- y, at seventy-eight.

Barkley's mother at seventy. She was a woman of independence and stamina, and at eighty-eight was tending her own vegetable garden.

The Veep with Jane Hadley Barkley, whom he married November 18, 1949, a little over four months after they met.

For a wedding present the Veep gave Jane a convertible.

Jules Pierlow

Jane Barkley was a wonderful hostess and helpmate during the Veep's remaining term as Vice President. They now enjoy life together on their farm in Paducah.

January 8, 1943

Roosevelt's letter to Barkley on the "Supreme Court matter" was one of the most cordial and complimentary he has ever received.

Dear Alben:

I do not know whether you will be disa pointed or not in this Supreme Court matter. Personally, I would not be. I had really tho a lot about sending your name up but two thi happened. First of all, there was no questic that your ability, learning and liberality fi you in every way for the Court. The other cc sideration, however, tore me apart because of the fact that you are such a very old and clc friend of mine.

It related to the fact that the country really needs you just where you are -- a good hard-hitting, yet just, leader of democracy - democracy both with a large "d" and a small ' You are a sort of balance wheel that has kept things moving forward all these years -- and that's that. I had to come to the conclusior that there are nine Justices but only one Maj Leader in the Senate -- and I can't part wit him in that capacity.

Affectionately,

[signature]

Honorable Alben W. Barkley,
The United States Senate,
Washington, D. C.

TELEGRAM

The White House
Washington
February 23, 1944

MEMORANDUM FOR STEVE EARLY:

Please take the following message in person to Senator Barkley. At the same time ask him if he would mind if I gave it out at the White House through you, or if he prefers, that he give it out himself:

F. D. R.

February 23, 1944

Honorable Alben W. Barkley,
United States Senate,
Washington, D. C.

Dear Alben:

As I am out of the City I am unable to have a personal talk with you. If I were there, of course, that is the first thing I would do.

I regret to learn from your speech in the Senate on the tax veto that you thought I had in my message attacked the integrity of yourself and other members of the Congress. Such you must know was not my intention. You and I may differ, and have differed on important measures, but that does not mean we question one another's good faith.

In working together to achieve common objectives we have always tried to accommodate our views so as not to offend the other whenever we could conscientiously do so. But neither of us can expect the other to go further.

When on last Monday I read to you portions of my tax message and you indicated your disagreement, I made certain changes as a result of our talk. You did not however try to alter my basic decision when you realized how strongly I felt about it. While I did not realize how very strongly you felt about that basic decision, had I known, I should not have tried to dissuade you from exercising your own judgment in urging the overriding of the veto.

I sincerely hope that you will not persist in your announced intention to resign as Majority Leader of the Senate. If you do, however, I hope your colleagues will not accept your resignation; but if they do, I sincerely hope that they will immediately and unanimously reelect you.

When Roosevelt heard of Barkley's intention to resign as majority leader of the Senate, he quickly dictated another "Dear Alben" letter.

The White House
Washington

- 2 -

With the many serious problems daily confronting us, it is inevitable that at times you should differ with your colleagues and differ with me. I am sure that your differing with your colleagues does not lessen their confidence in you as Leader. Certainly, your differing with me does not affect my confidence in your leadership nor in any degree lessen my respect and affection for you personally.

Very sincerely yours,

FRANKLIN D. ROOSEVELT

HOUSE
WASHINGTON

September 5, 1952

Personal and Confidential

Dear Alben:

I am enclosing a memorandum for your file. It
is a photostatic copy of the instructions which I
gave to Tom Gavin to be used at the Chicago
Convention. I also talked with him at the White
House before he went to Chicago and I talked with
several of my friends in the Missouri Delegation.
We were able to line up all of the Delegation on
your side except the Saint Louis people and we had
two of the Saint Louis Delegation on our side. As
you remember, a part of the Missouri Delegation
stuck until the last.

I hope you are having a wonderful vacation and
that everything will go well with you in the future.

My best to Mrs. Barkley.

Sincerely yours,

Harry Truman

Honorable Alben W. Barkley
Vice President of the United States
Washington, D. C.

At the 1952 Democratic convention President Truman
would not make a public announcement that he was backing Barkley, but he did urge his
own Missouri delegation to support him.

THE WHITE HOUSE
WASHINGTON   July 16, 1952

Dear Tom: I hope you
can see your way clear
to vote for Alben Barkley
when nominations for
President are in — and
try to get the Missouri
delegation to go along.

Harry Truman

Hon. Tom Gavin
Kansas City, Mo.

Dear Alben — I've just read you statement. I'm distressed that you feel it necessary to do this.

It is a noble statement which perhaps no one else ~~but~~ in our country could write. Charity, candor and courage are the firm rocks on which you've stood for a long time. And you have again made the rocks more visible to many lesser men, this one included.

God bless you —

Adlai

P.S. But you have made it very hard for me !!!

Stevenson's note to Barkley upon Barkley's withdrawal as a presidential candidate at the 1952 Democratic convention. The postscript still remains an enigma to him.

me *in flagrante delicto.* I let him go on for a while, then rose, bowed, and said:

"Senator Long, meet Laura Louise, my daughter."

"Oh!" said Huey.

It was not often, however, that Huey Long got the worst of any personal exchange. He was not only like a horsefly; he was like a cat—no matter how high you threw him or what you did to him, he would land on his feet. Whenever it became known that he was going to put on a full-dress performance, the Senate galleries would fill up, particularly with women spectators, who seemed fascinated by the spectacle of the Louisiana "Kingfish" in action.

On one occasion he was engaged in one of his famous filibusters, in which he would rant, storm, mimic, pace the floor (in technical violation of the Senate rule that requires a member to stand by his desk when speaking), and carry on about everything from "potlikker" to turnip greens. Senator McKellar of Tennessee, one of the powerful men of the Senate, who was noted for his peppery tongue and temper, was endeavoring to take him on. Long was at his best, and he kept flicking McKellar with humorous jibes, which made the galleries roar. Every time the galleries laughed, Senator McKellar would get madder, swelling up like a poisoned pup. Finally the presiding officer, banging his gavel, threatened to clear the galleries if the demonstrations did not cease.

Seeing an opportunity—I thought—to cool off tempers with a little humor, I arose and addressed the chair:

"Mr. President, I do not think the chair ought to be too hard on the galleries today. When the people go to a circus, they ought to be allowed to laugh at the monkey."

Of course, my jest was directed at Senator Long. But immediately Huey was up on his feet, bellowing in mock anger:

"Mistuh President! I resent that unwarranted remark on the part of the senator from Kentucky, directed toward my good friend, the senator from Tennessee!"

This time everyone laughed, including McKellar, and the tension eased up a little.

Though I have always tried to campaign in all of my political races as if I were being opposed by a candidate who had the combined qualifications of George Washington, Abraham Lincoln, Thomas Jefferson, and Woodrow Wilson, the truth is that I have had only three really formidable races in my life. The first, of course, was my initial race for

Congress, which I have already described. The second was my race for Governor—the only unsuccessful campaign of my career, which I already have described. That was the race in which I acquired the political nickname, "Iron Man," which I have mentioned. My daughter Wahwee used to drive me around the state. In a day that began at 8 A.M. and often did not end until after midnight I would cover as much as 400 miles and deliver as many as sixteen speeches. Those were the days of dirt roads, so, when I turned in at night, I would be covered with dust, perspiration—and hope.

The third good scrap was in 1938, the only year in which I had serious opposition for renomination as the Democratic candidate for the Senate. In that campaign, because of my position as majority leader of the Senate, I became a sort of symbol of the New Deal's strength. President Roosevelt, who was attempting in other sections of the country (with results that on the whole backfired badly on him) to "purge" Democratic candidates who had opposed his measures, decided to come to Kentucky to conduct the opposite of a "purge" by speaking in my behalf. Practically every New Deal-hating periodical in the country ran erudite and authoritative articles on what a black eye it was going to be for the Administration to have "Dear Alben" defeated, and many of them went out on a limb to indicate that I would go under. I have never understood this sort of wishful thinking, particularly when the wisher puts his predictions in cold print where they remain forever to embarrass him.

I was renominated by a comfortable majority, but you can still get an argument in some Kentucky political circles as to whether the President helped me or hurt me. Prior to the President's visit the Gallup Poll had given me approximately 61 per cent of the vote in the Democratic primary, and I won by something like 59 per cent. So, if that poll was any criterion, the President's visit did not affect the result materially one way or the other. However, I was appreciative of the honor paid me by President Roosevelt in coming to my home state to endorse me.

Though strenuous, that campaign in many ways was one of the most diverting in which I ever participated. I was being opposed by Albert B. Chandler, known as "Happy," who was then governor of the state. Though defeated by me, he later went to the Senate when another vacancy occurred. Still later he resigned to take the post of national baseball commissioner, which he held for several years.

Happy's rise to political prominence in Kentucky was an interesting story. A state senator, he had been elected lieutenant-governor on the

Democratic ticket with Governor Ruby Laffoon, taking office in 1931. Under Kentucky law a governor cannot succeed himself, and a man named Thomas S. Rhea, prominent in state politics, was the state administration's candidate to succeed Governor Laffoon. Chandler was determined to oppose Rhea. I was friendly with all three men, but was closer to Laffoon and Rhea.

The Kentucky law of 1912, making direct primary elections compulsory, had been modified by a subsequent legislature, so that in 1935, when the Rhea-Chandler contest came up, it was up to the State Central Committee of the Democratic party to determine whether its candidate should be chosen by primary or by convention. Chandler knew he had a better chance in a primary and was pressing for that alternative. Governor Laffoon, who, of course, had considerable influence in the matter, and Rhea favored the convention method. Although I was not a candidate for any office that year, I favored the direct primary, giving the people a chance to select their candidate, as a matter of principle. I urged Laffoon and Rhea to endorse the primary, and I came down from Washington to present my views to the State Committee. But the decision went in favor of the convention.

Rumblings began to be heard among the voters, and it was obvious that the move was a mistake on the part of the Laffoon-Rhea camp.

Then Governor Laffoon and candidate Rhea made another mistake. The Governor left Kentucky, taking Rhea with him, to make an appeal in Washington for federal highway funds. Almost as soon as the Governor had crossed the border, Acting Governor Chandler summoned the Legislature into extraordinary session to enact a compulsory primary law, which it had the power to do. Laffoon and Rhea streaked back to Kentucky to attempt to block it, but the Legislature passed it anyway, and the Court of Appeals upheld the law.

If the State Committee had gone along originally with the primary plan, I am convinced Rhea would have been elected and the political history of Kentucky would have been different. But even with the Chandler coup, Rhea still would have won had it not been for another mistake. Governor Laffoon insisted—successfully—that a runoff provision be included as part of the primary election. Rhea finished the primary with more votes than Chandler—a plurality but not a majority. And in the runoff Happy defeated him.

In the bitterness that developed both Governor Laffoon and the defeated candidate, Rhea, refused to support Chandler, the Democratic nominee. It was a bad situation, and one that could have led to a Republican victory in the state election. I was urged by Chandler's supporters to campaign for him. Although I had accepted an invitation from President Quezon of the Philippines to visit Manila with Mrs. Barkley and had all my plans made to do so, I canceled these plans, returned to Kentucky, and stumped the state for Chandler. He was elected and became Governor.

Though I had long known that there is not always such a thing as lasting gratitude in politics, I was somewhat surprised in 1938 when, only three years after I had altered my own personal plans so radically to work for him, Governor Chandler decided to try to unseat me. However, he had a perfect right to do so—that is what elections are all about. Both his friends and mine urged me to have a talk with him and try to persuade him to defer his senatorial ambitions until the next vacancy, but this, for obvious reasons, I absolutely refused to do. So the fight was on.

Governor Chandler started off the campaign by charging that I had become too "soft" and too old—it seems that everybody always worries about my age except me! He also said I had been in Washington so long that I was out of touch with Kentucky. Now I enjoy a challenge like that. As soon as my senatorial duties permitted, I went to Kentucky to size up the situation. I had not had a hard primary fight in twelve years, and I thought it possible that some of my political supporters might have drifted away. However, I was gratified to find that a predominantly young and vigorous group of workers sprang up in my behalf. I had plenty of friends and supporters when I began hitting the campaign trail.

Before it was over, I was still going strong, whereas my younger opponent had been hospitalized. He claimed someone—and the implication was plain that it was a deep, dark plot—had slipped him some "poisoned ice water." The chief of police in Louisville, a former Secret Service agent, promptly branded the poison case "a political bedtime story."

I had great fun with the Case of the Poisoned Ice Water. My managers gravely announced the addition of an "ice water guard," also a "food taster," to my own staff. Every time someone would pour me a glass of water at a speaking engagement, I would hold it up and look quizzically at the crowd. With obvious delight the people would take their cue and yell, "Careful! It may be poisoned!" I would shudder fearfully and put it down.

Happy, who is something of a singer, sang a lot of songs during the campaign, including the then popular "Sonny Boy." If he expected me to fire back with "Old Man Mose," I disappointed him; I did not even raise my baritone in "Wagon Wheels," which, as President Roosevelt once reminded the Senate Democrats, I have been known to "perpetrate" on my friends on non-political occasions. At one point, however, after we had had some discussion of where my opponent's campaign contributions were coming from, I did suggest mildly that he change his theme song from "Sonny Boy" to "There's a Gold Mine in the Sky."

This was the race in which I told for the first time a story which has become associated with me. I would relate to the crowds how I called on a certain rural constituent and was shocked to hear him say he was thinking of voting for my opponent. I reminded him of the many things I had done for him as prosecuting attorney, as county judge, as congressman, and senator. I recalled how I had helped get an access road built to his farm, how I had visited him in a military hospital in France when he was wounded in World War I, how I had assisted him in securing his veteran's benefits, how I had arranged his loan from the Farm Credit Administration, how I had got him a disaster loan when the flood destroyed his home, etc., etc.

"How can you think of voting for my opponent?" I exhorted at the end of this long recital. "Surely you remember all these things I have done for you?"

"Yeah," he said, "I remember. But what in hell have you done for me lately?"

Actually, this story—and I cite this as an illustration of how seasoned political humor can be adapted to current times and local conditions—is reminiscent of an old Henry Clay story. Someone once told the great Clay that a certain constituent was going up and down the countryside, denouncing him in vitriolic terms. Clay pondered a bit, then said, "I can't understand why he's against me. I do not recall ever having done him a favor."

President Roosevelt, early in the campaign, made it known from the White House that he was coming to Kentucky to campaign for me, since I, as majority leader, had been carrying the ball for his administration. Governor Chandler did not relish this at all, and accordingly set out to do all he could to counteract it. So when F.D.R. made his speech near Covington, Happy, as governor of the state, was on the platform, sitting as close to the President as he could get. He smiled, called out, and waved to people in the crowd; in short, he did everything that a resourceful candidate could think of to divert attention from Mr. Roosevelt's speech.

Even when the President had endorsed me, Happy would not give up. The President had diplomatically disclaimed any intention of interfering in Kentucky politics, and had said he did not doubt that Governor Chandler, if elected, would make a "good senator."

"But," the President went on to say, "I think he would be the first to acknowledge that as a very junior member of the Senate it would take him many, many years to match the national knowledge, the experience and the acknowledged leadership in the affairs of our nation of that son of Kentucky of whom the whole nation is proud—Alben Barkley."

Governor Chandler, in his subsequent speeches, merely took this and told his listeners, "The President says I'll make a good senator, and that's enough for me!"

The most amusing incident of the day, however, occurred before the speech. Mr. Chandler had boarded the presidential train as it crossed into Kentucky, and he managed to get himself into every news picture that was taken.

When we finally left the train to get into an open automobile, President Roosevelt took his customary place on the right-hand side of the back seat, while I politely walked around to the other side so I would not have to step over him. But my opponent, much to the horror of the Secret Service men, literally leaped over the President and ensconced himself beside him before I could get into the car. So the cheering public along the way saw Chandler in the middle, with Roosevelt and me flanking him.

After the fight was over, and I had won, F.D.R. reminisced with me at the White House about the events of that day, and even gave a hilarious imitation of how Chandler had outmaneuvered me in the car seat. At this point, of course, we could both afford to laugh about it.

A facet of the campaign which I did not appreciate was the introduction of untrue charges that my election had been influenced through improper activities by WPA workers. I fought this by promising publicly to seek the ouster of any federal official against whom charges of attempting to influence relief workers in my behalf could be substantiated. As a matter of fact, my opponent, who had control of the state administration, probably had more influence in this field than I did.

I do not shrink when I am on the receiving end of rough politics, as I have long known that it is not a kid-glove game. However, I have never been able to stomach the deliberate distortion of facts to sully a man's reputation. While the WPA charges were being aired, but before the date of the primary election, I happened to meet the head of the newspaper chain which had been most active in stirring up this issue. "How can you do it?" I chided him, for we had been personal friends for many years. "I have always respected your newspapers as being honest and liberal, and you know I have always had an honest, liberal, and progressive record."

He made the astonishing reply: "Yes, you have a good record. But, if we can beat you, we'll be slapping Roosevelt in the face—and that's why we're fighting you."

I found this a most unworthy admission. In any event, I went on to win that race against Governor Chandler by approximately 73,000 votes out of 520,000 cast, which was a clean-cut, decisive victory.

As the second Roosevelt administration wore on, there was increasingly little to laugh about. In Europe, Hitler was extending his brutal grip. I made several trips to Europe, talking with heads of government, important personages, and plain citizens, and I came back deeply troubled. I had seen the ugly portents: in Berlin the thundering, chanting, semihysterical crowds; in Germany and elsewhere, even the youngsters, who in America would have been boy scouts and girl scouts, being regimented in hatred.

In Budapest, where I attended an Interparliamentary Union conference, I witnessed an incident I have never forgotten. It was a small thing, almost trivial in contrast with other happenings we saw in Europe that year, but the very nature of it made it, to my mind, all the more shocking. In a municipal park there was a flower bed, a beautiful arrangement covering perhaps half a city block. A group of youngsters, in uniforms not too dissimilar to those of boy scouts, stood there, looking at the flowers, while an adult spoke to them. Innocent enough, one would say—what could be wrong about youngsters admiring beautiful flowers? The flowers, though, were arranged to show the Hungarian borders before and after Versailles, and, through this medium, the youngsters were being innoculated with hate for the powers that reduced their country's borders, and exhorted to seek revenge.

This, however, was nothing compared with the things we saw and heard in Germany, where the shrieking voice of Hitler filled the air waves, and young girls were taken away and bred like cattle to produce future soldiers for the Fatherland.

These things I reported to Franklin Roosevelt. Without moving from the White House the President, of course, already knew far more about the seriousness of the situation than any of us. But always he was intensely interested to see the picture through the eyes of those of us who had seen at firsthand the breeding ground of world destruction.

I conferred often with Roosevelt, on important speeches, statements, and legislation pertaining to the gathering war clouds in Europe. I recall with particular vividness my discussion with him in 1937 after he had delivered his famous "quarantine the aggressor" speech in Chicago, for which he was denounced as a "warmonger" by such isolationist senators as Nye, Wheeler, Hiram Johnson, Borah, and others. When I called on him at the White House, I said:

"Well, you certainly suggested a new approach in your Chicago speech."

"Yes!" he said. "I certainly stirred up the animals, didn't I?"

"You certainly stirred 'em up," I agreed.

But F.D.R., despite the informality of his language, was not being either flippant or cynical. As the inevitability of war came nearer, he was deeply troubled. Just as I had witnessed the almost unbearable burden weighting down the shoulders of Woodrow Wilson in the days before World War I, I could see the great change, the agonizing preoccupation, coming over Franklin Roosevelt, who soon was to be our wartime commander in chief.

CHAPTER 12

My Disagreement with F.D.R.

As Senate majority leader, I participated in many private conferences with President Franklin D. Roosevelt, and most of them were
pleasant and mentally stimulating sessions. Usually we would talk in
his bedroom at the White House, and the President, wrapped in his cherished gray bathrobe, which he clung to year after year despite its increasingly disreputable appearance, would interrupt work on a pile of
papers and puff at a cigarette through his long ivory holder as we ex-
changed views. Often the President's conferences with his Congressional
"Big Four"—the Vice President, Speaker of the House Sam Rayburn,
House Majority Leader John McCormack, and myself—were held in
the same setting.

In late February 1944 there were two such bedroom conferences on
successive Mondays between the President and the "Big Four" for the
purpose of discussing a wartime tax bill. It was my custom to ride to the
White House with Vice President Henry A. Wallace in his official lim-
ousine, for at that time the Senate majority leader had no official car of
his own. As we left the Capitol for the first of these conferences, I knew
I was headed for an important meeting. But I had no inkling that the
morning's discussion was to touch off a chain of events that, in the
opinion of many of my political friends, did more than any other event
of my career to keep me from becoming President.

Of course I recognize that all of this is speculative. One's friends frequently attribute unrealistic causes for his failure to achieve some goal
which they think he merits. I am in no position to state with certainty
that the episode revolving around Mr. Roosevelt and me over this tax
bill affected my future political career. Nevertheless it is legitimate to

reflect on what might have happened if this episode had not transpired.

Up to the time of these conferences, which led to my subsequent res-ignation—and immediate re-election—as majority leader, I had enjoyed an intimate and cordial relationship with President Roosevelt. On one oc-casion he had even speculated with me about the "possibility" of my succeeding him. While I never took this conversation seriously, I did have a feeling at that time that, if Henry Wallace should be discarded for renomination for Vice President in 1944, I would be acceptable to Mr. Roosevelt as a running mate. After our temporary breach, however, there was a certain intangible reserve in the President's attitude toward me which did not completely thaw until after the 1944 convention.

Thus, when the time came that year to pick a vice presidential nom-inee, Mr. Roosevelt emphatically dismissed my name from the list of possibilities by declaring, "Barkley is too old—he's even older than I am!" I learned this from friends who heard him make the statement. I never discussed the matter of the vice presidency with him at any time before or after our temporary break; nor, for that matter, did I ever, in all the years of our association, ask him for any personal political favor or ap-pointment.

If it is true that my disagreement with the President led to his decision against me as his running mate in 1944, the incident is a prime example of how history sometimes may be influenced, to say the least, rather capri-ciously. The Vice President chosen that year was Harry S. Truman, who, less than a year later, was to become the thirty-third President of the United States when Franklin Roosevelt passed on.

On that first of the successive Monday conferences, when I went to the White House with Vice President Wallace, Speaker Rayburn, and Rep-resentative McCormack to discuss the tax bill, I was well aware of the fact that the late Wendell Willkie had been needling the President sharply and persistently about the conduct of the war. Mr. Willkie, who had been the Republican presidential nominee in 1940 and who was displaying symptoms of similar ambitions at this particular time, was im-plying that things were not moving as fast as they should, and that more could and should be done. Though the President never admitted it, it was obvious that this prodding had produced a certain sensitivity in him, for he had come along with a recommendation for a tax bill that would raise the staggering sum of $10,500,000,000 in new revenue; if it was money that was retarding the tempo of the war—a premise, incidentally, which I personally never fully accepted—this certainly would provide the material means.

But the House, where all tax bills originate, balked at this astronomical figure. Instead, a bill was passed, which, in its final form, after it had been increased by the Senate, would enlarge the national revenue by about $2,300,000,000.

It was plain to see, on that day of the first conference, that the President did not like what Congress had done. His "Dutch" was up and his jaw was set at its most stubborn angle as he emphatically told us he planned to veto the bill as "inadequate."

We listened attentively to his objections, then Rayburn, McCormack, and I urged him not to veto the bill. We warned him that, unless he signed the bill, or unless Congress subsequently passed it over his veto, there would be no tax bill—i.e., no new revenue—at all. As it looked to the two House leaders, Rayburn and McCormack, at that time, the House would neither raise the ante nor muster enough votes to pass the original bill over a presidential veto.

As events transpired, I did most of the talking that day—in fact, it almost developed into a dialogue between the President and me, with Speaker Rayburn and Representative McCormack backing me up but leaving it largely to me to spell out the details. Vice President Wallace played a strangely silent role, offering no opinion whatsoever.

One of Roosevelt's objections was that the bill did not increase the Social Security tax. He had planned to take the extra revenue from this tax and use it toward defraying the wartime costs of running the government. I argued that the Social Security tax was never intended to be used for this purpose, and that the fact that Congress authorized the Secretary of the Treasury to borrow from the Social Security fund at 3 per cent interest did not transform it into an ordinary revenue fund.

There was no unpleasantness as the first conference ended, though there was no area of agreement, either. The President, without any binding commitment, said that he would think it over and discuss it further with his advisers, and that we would all discuss it again at the next "Big Four" conference on the following Monday. As we left, I felt I might have made some impression, but I was not optimistic.

At the second meeting, almost as soon as we filed into his bedroom and sat down, it was evident that Mr. Roosevelt was more positive than ever. He had a tentative veto message written out in rough form, and he read it to us. Once again I found myself the spokesman for the opposition, with Rayburn and McCormack supporting me and Henry Wallace again taking no part in the discussion. Point by point I took up his objections and presented my arguments against them.

All of this, I should point out, was done in perfectly good humor, and none of us displayed any heat. However, people who know me well say that I have a mannerism which I subconsciously indulge in when I begin to get annoyed. My right shoulder, they say, starts, almost imperceptibly, to twitch, almost as if I were squaring off for whatever might come. I am not aware of this mannerism, but, if it is true that I do this under stress, I dare say that my right shoulder was beginning to twitch toward the end of that second conference when it became apparent that the President's mind was made up and that nothing was going to budge him.

Finally, I said, "Well, Mr. President, it is perfectly obvious that you are going to veto this bill and it is futile for me to argue with you any longer. I must say, however, that if you do so, and assign the reasons which you have given us here, I will be compelled to say something about it in the Senate."

He replied, "Of course, you have that right."

I was acutely depressed as we left the White House. I rode back to the Capitol with Vice President Wallace, and it was a strange ride, for neither of us—literally—said a word. I was deep in study, and, he, sensing my mood, did not intrude upon my meditation.

In due course President Roosevelt's veto message came to Capitol Hill and was read to both the House and the Senate. Whereas I had been troubled by the President's line of reasoning at our conferences, I was profoundly shocked when I heard the message itself read. In its final language it contained phrases that seemed to me unfair; the President seemed to go far out of his way to slap, not only at the tax bill, but to impeach the motives of Congress. Many of the contemporary commentators expressed their amazement at the harshness of the President's language. For example, such an astute and seasoned observer as Arthur Krock, then chief correspondent for the New York *Times* in Washington, remarked on its "violent terms," and said that the language would offend even those of Roosevelt's Congressional supporters who would vote to sustain his veto. "The charge of low motives included his majority leader, Senator Barkley," Krock wrote, suggesting that "the President may, of course, merely have succumbed to a fit of temper."

To me it was a most unfortunate political document, and a highly offensive one. There was one line in the message that I found particularly objectionable. The President asserted that he had asked Congress "for a loaf of bread" with which to carry on the war, and that he had been handed instead "a small piece of crust." Furthermore, he said, the "crust"

contained "many extraneous and inedible matters." To me $2,300,000,-
000 is no "crust."

But there was another line which seemed to me more political than
factual. It stirred deep resentment in me, and it was resented by many
others on Capitol Hill who had worked on the tax bill in good faith.
In commenting on the revenue measure, the President had seen fit to
say, ". . . It is not a tax bill but a tax relief bill, providing relief not
for the needy, but for the greedy."

When I heard this, I knew I could not keep silent; I felt I ought not
to remain as the Administration's floor leader. I had supported the President from the very beginning of his administration. I did this, not
because I was a "yes man" or a "me-too" man, but because I sincerely believed in his program. But, when I was elected majority leader, I made a
personal decision, and I made a public statement to the effect at the
time, that if any fundamental and irreconcilable disagreement with the
President ever arose, I would feel it my duty to resign.

My first impulse was to get on my feet in the Senate and lash out.
But, before I could do this, Senator Walter F. George of Georgia, then
chairman of the Senate Finance Committee, took the floor. While he
was voicing his disapproval of the President's message, I mulled over in
my mind what I should do. I thought to myself, *You had better sleep on
this.* So, when I left the Hill late that afternoon, I went home to think.
Instead of sleeping on it, I walked the floor almost all night.

My first wife was then an invalid. I went into her room and sat down
to talk with her about it. We both agreed it was a serious thing for me
to break with the President. I had helped nominate and elect him; I
supported him, and, in general, I admired and felt a deep affection for
him.

As we talked, however, it became obvious that my only course was to
make a rebuttal speech and then resign as majority leader. "Go to it,
Alben," my wife said. "I'm with you."

In my pajamas I went into my room, where I had an old typewriter.
I still remembered enough of the "hunt-peck-and-cuss" system from my
court reporter days in Paducah, and I tried to type out my own speech.
It came out cold and stilted, however, and I gave it up. At nine o'clock
the next morning I went to my office, called in one of my secretaries,
Miss Lorraine Winfrey, and started dictating. Ordinarily Miss Lorraine
was the model of efficiency, but this day, as it became apparent what
I was doing, she became increasingly agitated. When I reached the point
where I announced I would resign as majority leader, Miss Lorraine

dropped her pencil and exclaimed "Oh, no!" The speech, as I delivered it, was just as I dictated it, with no revisions.

It was about eleven o'clock when I finished dictating, and it was a fairly long speech. I wanted to be in the Senate promptly when it convened at noon, so I could be on my feet and thus be the first man to gain recognition. Only about six or seven pages had been typed when I had to go over to the floor. "Listen," I told Miss Lorraine, "type like the devil is after you! And just as fast as you get a sheet finished, send it over to me by page boy, because I'll be on my feet talking, and I may run out of speech!"

Word had got around that I was going to have something to say on the subject of the President's veto, and both the Senate floor and the galleries were crowded as I began my speech. As I had feared, the rest of the manuscript was slow in coming over from the Senate Office Building, and I began to run out. I leaned over to Senator Kenneth D. McKellar of Tennessee, who sat at the desk next to me, and whispered, "Mac, I'm running out—will you go out and see if you can stir 'em up for me!"

Now the venerable "K.D." and I were old friends, but it so happened that at that time he was harboring the remains of a grudge against me. Our difficulty went back to November 1942, when I was leading the Administration's fight to pass the anti-poll-tax measure. I did not believe in poll taxes. As I told the Senate at the time, "I am a follower of Thomas Jefferson, who advocated equality for all people . . . [not only] . . . for those who could pay $1.50 for the privilege of voting."

My position drew the opposition of some of my Southern colleagues, who organized a determined filibuster against the bill. As majority leader, it was my duty to keep enough senators on the floor so that the filibusterers could not force an adjournment because of the lack of a quorum.

In the course of this skirmishing it became necessary for me to dispatch the Senate sergeant at arms with so-called "arrest" warrants, authorizing him to seize any senators who were absenting themselves from the quorum call and bring them to the Senate floor. This is a power which, with the consent of the Senate, the majority leader has, but which is used only as a last resort.

Unfortunately the first senator to be "arrested" was McKellar, probably the hottest-tempered man in the Senate. At that time K.D., who later became the dean of the Senate, ranked next to Senator Ellison D. (Cotton Ed) Smith of South Carolina in seniority, and he took an almost fierce pride in his position—a feeling which was thoroughly understandable. When the sergeant at arms came to "arrest" him, Senator

McKellar took it as a personal affront. He made a speech on the floor of the Senate complaining of his arrest. I replied to the effect that there was nothing personal in the procedure because I could not foresee whom it might be necessary for the sergeant at arms to arrest in order to produce a quorum. Though our Senate seats were side by side, he did not speak to me for several weeks, although in the meantime I had seen to it that McKellar's "arrest" was erased from the Senate records.

Eventually, my old friend and I broke the long silence by turning to each other spontaneously, after the Senate had reconvened following the Christmas recess, and shaking hands. But K.D. still remained cool toward me, and, after that, was active in another move to deprive the majority leader of his traditional power to appoint members of the majority steering committee. The plan was kept so quiet that I did not get wind of it until it was almost an accomplished fact. I had to block it by firmly telling the Democratic conference that, if it voted to impose such an unprecedented and intolerable curb on its leader, its next step would have to be the election of my successor because I would resign immediately. The move then was defeated by a substantial majority.

But this day as I stood there on the floor, ticking off the points of my indictment against President Roosevelt's veto message, my old colleague from Tennessee was unmistakably on my side. As I whispered my plea for help in rounding up the missing sheets, he hopped up, and, stamping across the floor, went to the cloakroom door and shouted out orders that instilled some life into the page boys. One by one the remaining pages of my speech came in, and Senator McKellar "ran copy" for me, delivering them to me himself as he received them at the cloakroom door.

I pulled no punches. First off, I made reference to the political aspects of the veto by pointing out that the President himself had noted that "persons prominent in our national life" were criticizing his own tax recommendations as low.

"This reference in justification of his veto," I said, "is obviously to Mr. Wendell L. Willkie, the up-to-date Halley's comet darting across the firmament hither and yon to illuminate the heavens with an array of fantastic figures which neither it nor anybody can comprehend. I cannot but wonder, Mr. President, whether this spectacular celestial nomad has frightened the President into the use of figures quite as fantastic, though not as large."

(The "Mr. President" to whom I expressed my wonder was, of course, the presiding officer of the Senate, Vice President Wallace, who, at this point, was seated on the rostrum, listening very attentively.)

Analyzing the President's veto points one by one, I came to the section in which he charged that Congress was granting "special privilege" to the lumber industry by allowing it to treat income from timber-cutting as a capital gain. He had referred to himself as an experienced timber man.

Now, so far as I or anyone else knew, I told the Senate, Mr. Roosevelt's experience with lumber was limited to the sale of Christmas trees from his Hyde Park estate at the Yule season.

"To compare these little pine bushes," I said, "with a sturdy oak, or a gum, or a poplar, or a spruce, which require a generation of care and nurturing . . . would be like comparing a cricket to a stallion!"

Finally, I came to the President's charge that Congress had passed, not a tax bill, but a relief bill "for the greedy."

"That statement," I told the Senate, "is a calculated and deliberate assault upon the legislative integrity of every member of the Congress of the United States. The members of Congress may do as they please. But as for me, I do not propose to take this unjustifiable assault lying down.

"Mr. President," I continued, "this is the first time during [my] long service, which I had thought was honorable, when I have been accused deliberately of voting for a bill that constituted a relief measure impoverishing the needy and enriching the greedy.

"Mr. President, for twelve years I have carried to the best of my ability the flag of Franklin D. Roosevelt. For the past seven years I have carried the flag of this administration as majority leader of the Senate. . . . I have borne that flag with pride because I felt that President Roosevelt in himself constituted a dynamic leader in the great crisis in the history of our country and the world for whom the people yearned."

I went on to say that, during those seven years as majority leader, I had carried the flag perhaps "over rougher terrain than was ever traversed by any previous majority leader," and often with precious little help from the White House.

"But, Mr. President," I declared, "there is something more precious to me than any honor. . . . That is the approval of my own conscience and my own self-respect. That self-respect and the rectitude of that conscience I propose on this occasion to maintain."

As I spoke these words, many of the senators, both Democrats and Republicans, showed their emotion. I learned later that the late Senator Arthur Vandenberg of Michigan, the great Republican leader who was an outstanding and effective advocate of a bipartisan foreign policy, was damp-eyed as I talked. Senator Hattie Caraway of Arkansas, the only woman member of the Senate at that time, also wept.

Up in the gallery, I also learned later, many of my friends, my office staff, and my daughter, Wahwee, had been watching, and some of them were weeping. Leslie Biffle, the Senate Secretary, saw Wahwee—completely unconscious of what she was doing—raking her arm with her fingernails. He sent her up a note, saying:

"WAHWEE: Stop scratching your arm. He'll be re-elected tomorrow."

As I came thus to the end of my talk, I announced to the Senate that I was calling a meeting of the Democratic majority for ten-thirty o'clock the following morning. At that time, I said, I would resign as majority leader.

Then I concluded:

"I have disagreed many times with my colleagues here on both sides of the political aisle, but I have sought to earn their respect and their esteem. . . .

"Let me say . . . that if the Congress of the United States has any self-respect yet left, it will over-ride the veto of the President and enact this tax bill into law, his objections to the contrary notwithstanding."

The Senate chamber was hushed as I concluded. But, as I sat down, a wild demonstration erupted. Even dignified senators violated the rule against applause. I was surrounded by Democrats and Republicans who shook my hand and congratulated me. Arthur Vandenberg rose to speak, but emotion got the better of him and he sat down, unable to finish his opening sentence.

Best of all, and most heart-warming to me, my "copy boy" and erstwhile antagonist, Senator McKellar, jumped up, pounded me on the back, and shouted, "I forgive him! I forgive him everything he's ever done!"

There was no joy in my heart, however, as I left the Senate Chamber. When the newspaper reporters called at my office, I told them, "I have no further comment—my cup runneth over."

My office staff—Flo Bratten, who had been with me since I was a young congressman, Laura Hynds, Marjorie Maxey, Elora Chance, Lorraine Winfrey, and others—were waiting for me, all damp-eyed. Wahwee was there too, and she was frankly blubbering. She took one look at me, threw her arms around me, and sobbed.

When I finally reached my apartment that evening at the end of this arduous day, I found I had a caller. President Roosevelt's trusted press secretary, the late Stephen T. Early, who was my long-time personal

friend, was waiting for me. When I had concluded my speech that afternoon, I had noticed Vice President Wallace leaving the Senate Chamber
rather hurriedly. Even amid all the excitement I thought to myself, "Henry's slipping out to telephone the President." I was right; the President
was at Hyde Park, and Wallace was phoning the secretariat to pass along
the news. This has since been confirmed by William D. Hassett, former
White House Secretary, who, in his memoirs, wrote that he took Wallace's call and personally relayed the news to President Roosevelt.

So I found Steve Early at my apartment with another "Dear Alben"
letter, dictated by the President at Hyde Park. I have the copy in my
possession, typed out on two sheets of the special telegram blanks used
at the White House. The message, in full, as it was handed to me, was as
follows:

TELEGRAM

THE WHITE HOUSE
Washington

Feb. 23, 1944

MEMORANDUM FOR STEVE EARLY:

Please take the following message in person to Senator Barkley.
At the same time ask him if he would mind if I gave it out at the
White House through you, or if he prefers, that he give it out him-
self:

F.D.R.

Feb. 23, 1944

Honorable Alben W. Barkley
United States Senate,
Washington, D.C.

DEAR ALBEN:

As I am out of the City I am unable to have a personal talk with
you. If I were there, of course, that is the first thing I would do.

I regret to learn from your speech in the Senate on the tax veto
that you thought I had in my message attacked the integrity of
yourself and other members of Congress. Such you must know was
not my intention. You and I may differ, and have differed on

important measures, but that does not mean we question one another's good faith.

In working together to achieve common objectives we have always tried to accommodate our views so as not to offend the other whenever we could conscientiously do so. But neither of us can expect the other to go further.

When on last Monday I read to you portions of my tax message and you indicated your disagreement, I made certain changes as a result of our talk. You did not however try to alter my basic decision when you realized how strongly I felt about it. While I did not realize how very strongly you felt about that basic decision, had I known, I should not have tried to dissuade you from exercising your own judgment in urging the overriding of the veto.

I sincerely hope that you will not persist in your announced intention to resign as Majority Leader of the Senate. If you do, however, I hope your colleagues will not accept your resignation; but if they do, I sincerely hope that they will immediately and unanimously reelect you.

With the many serious problems daily confronting us, it is inevitable that at times you should differ with your colleagues and differ with me. I am sure that your differing with your colleagues does not lessen their confidence in you as Leader. Certainly, your differing with me does not affect my confidence in your leadership nor in any degree lessen my respect and affection for you personally.

Very sincerely yours,

FRANKLIN D. ROOSEVELT

This letter, having been sent or dictated over the wire from Hyde Park, then retyped at the White House, was not signed personally by F.D.R.

I read this letter carefully in Early's presence. I felt that, though it was composed in language more formal than the President customarily used in writing to me, it was obviously meant to be conciliatory. I did think to myself, as I read it, that it was strange that the President "did not realize how very strongly" I felt about his proposed veto at the time of our White House conference, for I certainly had made myself as plain as I possibly could.

However, I did not go into these details with Steve Early. I thanked him for the President's message, but told him my mind was made up. We discussed it for a while, and he attempted to persuade me to reconsider. Then he left.

While I was eating dinner alone—Mrs. Barkley was bedridden—I had another caller. It was James F. Byrnes, the President's War Mobilizer and unofficial "Assistant President." Jimmy was one of my oldest friends. We had served together in the House and Senate, and I had gone to F.D.R. in his behalf when Byrnes desired the appointment he held briefly as a Supreme Court justice. For the next couple of hours Jimmy turned the full force of his not inconsiderable persuasive powers upon me. He even went along tacitly with my position when I told him I was deeply offended by the language of the veto message, particularly the phrase that referred to the tax measure as a relief bill for the greedy, not the needy. But he continued to urge me not to resign, and I remember him using the phrase, "If men such as you and I desert the President, he is sunk." Personally I thought this was overstating the issue, but he was saying it, not I.

There is a footnote to this episode. Some years later, during the Truman administration, I happened to be reminiscing about the veto message with Judge Samuel I. Rosenman. He had been one of the President's assistants and advisers, and he remained in that capacity for some time with President Truman.

"When I leave the White House," Judge Rosenman told me, "I will tell you who wrote that message."

I replied, "I will be glad to know, Judge, because, frankly, I always thought you wrote it!"

I saw Rosenman after he returned to private life, and he brought up the subject.

"That message," he told me, "was written by Jimmy Byrnes and Ben Cohen, with Ben doing most of the writing but Jimmy surpervising and approving the finished product."

Even at that late date I found it rather ironic that Byrnes should have come to my home and pleaded so eloquently for me not to be offended by words which he himself had helped to write.

As a further footnote to this incident, Miss Grace Tully, one of the late President's secretaries, says in her book, *F.D.R.—My Boss,* that the President himself wrote that "greedy, not the needy" phrase. To me this confirms by implication that someone else wrote the rest of the message.

The rest was dramatic, yet anti-climactic at the same time. I called the caucus of the Senate Democrats, and resigned. Then I stepped out of the room. Newspapermen besieged me for information as to what was going on.

"Boys," I told the reporters, "I'm afraid I'm like the Swede who proposed to his girl while driving. She said yes, and then they drove along for five miles in silence. Finally she asked him, 'Why don't you say something?' The Swede replied, 'Ay tank Ay say too much already!' "

The Democrats promptly and unanimously re-elected me as majority leader. Though I had proceeded to my own office, I remember reading how my old friend, Senator Tom Connally of Texas, who was designated to head the committee that brought the news to me, came bursting out of the conference room, elbowing his way through the throng of newsmen, and shouting, "Make way for liberty!" Only a short time before, Tom had been one of the senators who complained that my threat to resign as majority leader if stripped of the power to name the Steering Committee put him and other senators in an embarrassing position.

In any event, I accepted the action of the Democratic caucus and resumed my post as majority leader.

Next, the House proceeded to override the President's veto by a thumping majority—something it might never have done had the incident not been so dramatized by the clash between the President and me over the language of his message. The Senate promptly followed suit. Both houses, incidentally, overrode the veto and passed the tax bill with a minimum of oratorical fanfare.

On the same day of my re-election I sat down and wrote the President a reply to his communication to me. My purpose was to assure him, as sincerely as possible, that the incident would be forgotten so far as I was concerned, and that I would continue to work to carry out his legislative and war programs. I thanked him for his disavowal of any intention to reflect upon the integrity of Congress. "I accept your statement in this regard at full value and I am happy to feel that it was sincere," I wrote.

My letter continued:

> I am sure I need not say to you that I have, during these eventful years, worked with you with an inspiration, a devotion and a personal affection which has not been approached by any other man, unless it be Woodrow Wilson, at whose feet I sat as a young member of Congress and learned from him many of the great lessons of liberalism in government and society which I have struggled to advance.
>
> I realize that sometimes language in a written document carries with it connotations not intended by the writer. Sometimes the expressions on one's countenance or the intonations in one's voice indicate a meaning not always carried in the written word. But I

feel that upon reflection you will agree that some of the language contained in your veto message was abundantly susceptible of the interpretation which I put upon it in my address to the Senate and which many others put upon it throughout the country.

I am happy to feel, as you have indicated, that you had no such purpose in mind.

I realize that in these terrific times you are burdened with a responsibility no American President has ever borne. Throughout this perilous period my heart has gone out to you in sympathetic understanding, not only of your great responsibility, but your high purpose in meeting that responsibility. I want you to know that that faith in you endures in me today and will continue to endure because I have recognized in you a spokesman of the people, whose chief desire was to advance their welfare and their happiness.

We have on some occasions disagreed as to policies and we have sometimes disagreed as to methods. Frequently I have submerged my own views in recognition of your more intimate knowledge and your greater responsibility. Sometimes you have yielded your views to mine. In all these circumstances we have maintained a mutual respect which I have deeply appreciated.

But it seems to me there is something broader and more fundamental than any personal acquiescence as between you and me over matters of public policy and fundamental principle. In this great crisis of our nation's history we must all seek some common ground upon which we can meet and have confidence in one another. That applies to all the branches of our Government. If we cannot trust one another in this tragic period of the history of our nation and of the world, how can the people trust us?

I want you to know that you have my utmost confidence and affection and the personal and official relations which have been to me a source of infinite pride, I hope may be continued.

I went on to point out that I had accepted my re-election as majority leader; then I closed with an expression of my fervent hope that the incident would serve to bring the executive and legislative branches closer together, so that victory in Europe and Asia might be speedily won and the task of rebuilding the world for peace might be undertaken.

Thus ended the open clash between the President and me, but, as I have said, he did not quickly forget it. I later learned that the portion of my speech which really stung F.D.R. was the paragraph in which I chided him for representing himself as a timber man on the basis of his experience in marketing Christmas trees.

CHAPTER 13

I Support F.D.R. Again; Another Era Ends

Discussions about "indispensable men" always remind me of a certain tradesman in a small Kentucky town who bought a quantity of goods from a Paducah wholesaler and did not pay up in time. After six months had gone by, and innumerable dunning letters had been ignored, the wholesaler sat down and wrote a final demand for payment. At the same time he addressed several other inquiries to the town where the tradesman operated. He wrote the railroad station agent, asking if the goods had been delivered. He wrote the local bank president, inquiring about the man's credit. Finally he wrote the mayor of the town, asking the name of a good lawyer in case he had to bring suit.

In a few days he received from the debtor himself the following reply:

"Dear Sir: As station agent of this town, I am glad to advise you that the goods were delivered. As president of the local bank, it gives me pleasure to inform you that my credit is good. As mayor of the town, I am compelled to advise you that I am the only lawyer here. And if it were not for the fact that I am also pastor of the Baptist church, I would tell you to go to hell!"

For my part—despite the foregoing convincing example which I have cited—I do not believe in indispensable men. In my opinion Washington and possibly Lincoln were the only men in our history who came close to fitting that description. Nevertheless I did feel in 1940 that Roosevelt, while not indispensable, was the best man to lead us, and, when he asked me for my opinion, I advised him to break the third-term tradition.

I gave him this advice in all sincerity. As a matter of fact, it marked a step in the evolution of my thinking on the science of government for, during the first Wilson administration, I had sponsored an unsuccessful resolution to amend the Constitution and limit the presidency to a single six-year term, a proposal which was contained in the Democratic platform of 1912. Over the years, however, I had changed my mind about the wisdom of this. In 1940, with Europe engulfed in war and the whole world on the brink of it, I felt that Roosevelt was the best available leader, and that we should not be bound by an ancient tradition. I still feel that a good President, or one whom the people want, should not be limited by law to two terms, and, during the Republican-controlled Eightieth Congress, I cast my vote against the resolution by which the Twenty-Second Amendment, limiting Presidents to two terms, came into being.

It was on this occasion in 1940—less than four years before Mr. Roosevelt and I were to have our dramatic collision over his veto message—that the President, according to his statement to me, was viewing me as his possible successor in the White House.

There was already a great deal of speculation as to whether Roosevelt would run again, but he would say nothing publicly. One day, some time before the 1940 convention, which gave him the third-term nomination, we were talking at the White House, and he remarked to me rather casually:

"You know, some of the folks here at the White House are for you for the Democratic nomination as my successor."

"Is that so?" I said. I would not deny that I may even have lifted my eyebrows in showing some interest.

"Yes," he answered, "that's so." He went on to mention the names of several members of the White House family who, he said, favored me.

"Will they agree to stay on and help me run the government if I am nominated and elected?" I asked.

"I think they probably would," F.D.R. replied.

We talked a bit longer, and finally I said to him, "Mr. President, that is very gracious and I appreciate the compliment. However, there is no use for us to kid each other about this thing—you are going to have to run for a third term."

I went on to review the situation which made such a decision necessary. War had broken out in Europe, and there was grave danger of our being drawn into it. "Under the circumstances, Mr. President," I told him, "I think you are going to be compelled to run."

He seemed to be in a thoughtful, reflective mood as we discussed the question further. He asked me what I thought about the anti-third-term tradition fathered by George Washington; it would be a serious thing, he said, to break that tradition.

"That is true," I replied, "but it is only a tradition. The people have a right to elect a President as many times as they please."

Continuing, I told the President that, in my opinion, Washington was not necessarily anti-third-term; he just did not want to be President any longer and made it plain in his farewell address that he thought conditions were such that he could step down. In F.D.R.'s case, I reiterated, conditions were such that he was going to have to run.

As a matter of fact, I have always felt that F.D.R. never really wanted a third term, and would have much preferred to retire from office at the end of his second term. I state this as my carefully considered conviction, despite the relentless efforts of the late President's detractors to picture him as a man with an insatiable appetite for office and power. I firmly believe that F.D.R. ran for a third term only because of the war threat. If his great social program had not been interrupted by war, just as Woodrow Wilson's forward-looking program was similarly circumscribed by World War I, Franklin Roosevelt, in my opinion, would not only have been content to turn over the helm to another man, but would have insisted upon it.

One of the reasons I am so firmly convinced of this was a private conversation I had with President Roosevelt in 1936, even before the beginning of his second term. What he said on that occasion so impressed me that I have always remembered the gist of his statement.

He told me, in effect, that his "great ambition" was to turn over his desk and chair in the White House to his successor, whoever that might be, with the assurance that he was passing on to the new President a nation that was strong, at peace, and prosperous, a nation that clearly recognized its powers to serve its own citizens and did not shrink from using those powers to the fullest in order to move forward and meet the needs of humanity. He went on to say that, as part of the heritage, he wanted to turn over a nation which had proved by the things he outlined that the democratic form and methods of government could and would work. His closing words—and I think I remember them verbatim—were: "In these coming years, I want to get the nation as far along the road of progress as I can."

To me these did not sound like the words of a man who wanted to enshrine himself permanently in office.

I also had occasion in 1940, after I had advised the President that I thought he was going to have to break the anti-third-term tradition, to talk with him about his decision to make Henry Wallace his running mate. As usual, I was being mentioned as a possible vice presidential nominee, but I was not pushing my candidacy because I felt that the President had other ideas. It happened that I was quite fond of Henry Wallace personally. I thought that in many ways he had been an outstanding Secretary of Agriculture, but I had doubts about some of his policies. I was also beginning to be troubled by some of the symptoms Wallace was displaying of the increasing mysticism which later made it possible for some left-wing groups to take advantage of him.

In any event, I felt compelled to speak candidly when President Roosevelt told me he "was weak in the corn belt" and for that reason had decided to take his Secretary of Agriculture as his running mate. "Mr. President," I said, "you know how fond I am of Henry personally, but I must say that *he* is the reason you are weak in the corn belt." I went on to say, "It seems that some of the corn farmers do not exactly appreciate what Henry has done for them, and a lot of your weakness in that area stems from that fact."

But F.D.R. took Wallace anyway, as I well remember; I was permanent chairman of that convention, and a great portion of the crowd in the Chicago auditorium—including a number of delegates—were booing angrily as F.D.R.'s choice was imposed upon the convention. I remember my own Kentucky delegation standing on its feet—I was presiding at the time—shouting and pleading with me to allow my own name to go in against Wallace's.

On the floor James F. Byrnes, then a senator and acting as Wallace's floor manager, was going among the delegations, leaving a strong impression that, if Wallace were not chosen, Roosevelt himself would not accept the nomination. I do not know what authority Byrnes had for that statement, but it sounded to me at the time as if he were putting it rather strongly. I could not possibly conceive of Roosevelt refusing the nomination for such a reason. In any event, I would not allow my name to go before the convention as a vice presidential nominee, because I was standing solidly with President Roosevelt for the program he was attempting to accomplish, and, when he said Wallace was his choice, he became my choice too. I voted for Wallace, and the Kentucky delegation did likewise.

As chairman, I managed to head off what would have been an ugly spectacle by prevailing on Senator Byrnes to keep Wallace from attempting to address the convention after his nomination. I discovered that a considerable segment of those attending the convention intended to boo him and make it difficult for him to speak. The whole nation would have heard the demonstration over the radio. As a friend of Mr. Wallace, I felt it would do neither him nor the party any good to parade his public embarrassment before the convention. One of the strange sights of the convention later was to see nominee Wallace sitting silently on the platform as President Roosevelt's acceptance speech was being piped from Washington via radio to the crowd in the great hall. The man who had been nominated for Vice President uttered not a word to the convention which nominated him.

Incidentally, if there are any political innocents who still believe that vice presidential candidates are chosen by free-and-open convention, let me here and now dispose of such illusions. The 1940 convention was proof that this just is not so. The presidential nominee always is consulted as to his choice in the matter of a running mate. Sometimes he may be swayed if the delegates are vociferous enough about expressing their wishes, but obviously no convention is going to force its nominee to take a running mate who is *persona non grata* to him.

For that matter, I am also skeptical about presidential candidates being "drafted." In more than forty years of convention experience I have seen candidates—Roosevelt included—chosen with much enthusiasm, but I have never seen what I would call a genuine "draft" in the sense that a man is persuaded against his wishes to run. President Roosevelt attempted in 1940, by not announcing his intentions before the convention convened, to create the impression that he was being "drafted." He did this undoubtedly to strengthen his position in defying the anti-third-term tradition once he had made up his mind he would have to run. However, there never was the slightest doubt in the minds of those of us who had talked with him that he was a candidate.

It was a curious performance in 1940. No one can deny that Roosevelt was the popular choice of the majority of the delegates, but the bitterness on the part of those—including some of his old friends—who opposed him was of deep and obvious intensity. Chairman James A. Farley, Roosevelt's old political lieutenant, and the late Speaker Bankhead, the convention keynoter, both ignored the President completely in their opening addresses—a strange situation in view of the fact that Mr. Roosevelt was the Democratic leader. It fell upon me when I delivered my address as permanent chairman to make the first mention of Roosevelt's name, and the wild acclaim with which the delegates greeted it made it quite apparent that—third term or not—he would be the nominee.

As Roosevelt's third term drew to a close, with the war still in progress, and the 1944 convention approached, it became apparent that tradition was going to be defied again and that F.D.R. was going to run for a fourth term. I bore no grudge against the President after our dispute in February 1944. As proof of that, almost immediately after the row, I wrote an article for *Collier's* magazine, telling why I favored Roosevelt's re-election to a fourth term. In it, after outlining his qualifications and weighing them against the demands of the then continuing world conflict, I wrote:

> I am not afraid of a fourth term for the President. *There can be no such thing as a dictatorship,* which some honest people fear and others pretend to fear, so long as the American people have the right of choice. . . .
> It is not a question of sentiment. It is a question of common sense. It is a question of trained and skillful leadership in a world of treacherous crosscurrents and treacherous waters. Tradition must now and then give way to reason and sound judgment in the prosecution of the war to the most speedy and successful conclusion and in the consummation of a peace that will be just and enduring. I believe Franklin Roosevelt is the best qualified of all the men talked about or thought about for President during the next four years.
> Therefore, I support him.

As the 1944 convention neared, the late Robert Hannegan, chairman of the Democratic National Committee, approached me and asked me if I would prefer to serve as chairman of the platform committee, or place the President's name in nomination. I told him I did not wish to head the platform committee, and that it might be embarrassing to the President if I nominated him. My own supporters, I explained, were insisting on nominating me for Vice President, and this might not be to Mr. Roosevelt's liking. Chairman Hannegan told me it was the President's wish that I nominate him, and that he would not have asked me, of course, if the President had not authorized it.

I told Hannegan to see me again in about a week, at which time he came back and I informed him I would do it if the President still desired it. "You've made me a very happy man," said Hannegan. "All right," I answered. "Everything is lovely."

Meanwhile irresistible pressure had been put on Roosevelt to scuttle Vice President Wallace, whom the delegates simply would not take that year. The President finally wrote a letter to Senator Samuel D. Jackson of Indiana, slated to become the permanent chairman of the convention, saying:

> I personally would vote for [Wallace's] renomination if I were a delegate.
>
> At the same time, I do not wish to appear in any way as dictating to the convention. Obviously the convention must do the deciding.

That, so far as Henry Wallace was concerned, was the *coup de grace*.

The Wallace development opened up the vice presidential race, and considerable sentiment began to develop for me. At one stage the distinguished commentator, H. V. Kaltenborn, went on the air and virtually announced my "nomination." While I did not doubt his good faith in either instance, I had cause to recall, with amusement, my "nomination" by Mr. Kaltenborn when this same commentator, on the night of Election Day in 1948, assured the nation with great solemnity and finality that President Truman and I had been defeated. Mr. Truman created much hilarity by giving a public imitation of Mr. Kaltenborn's broadcast. I became receptive to the idea of letting my name go before the convention, and I decided to ask Harry Truman, then United States Senator from Missouri, if he would place my name in nomination. This, I thought, was a fair request for two reasons: in the first place, I had campaigned for Truman in Missouri when he was standing for re-election and thought he needed help with railroad employees, among whom I had many friends; he had thanked me warmly for my assistance and expressed the hope that he someday might be able to return the favor.

In the second place, Senator Truman had just issued a statement in Kansas City, disclaiming any vice presidential ambitions of his own in the following words:

> It is difficult to make my friends believe me when I say I do not want the vice presidency. Frankly, I think I can be of much more help in winning the war continuing the work I have been doing than I could possibly contribute as Vice President.

However, when I telephoned Mr. Truman in Missouri to ask him if he would nominate me, he replied:

"Why Alben, I'd be tickled to death to do it, but I've already promised Jimmy Byrnes I would nominate him."

"Well," I said, "if you've promised Jimmy, that ends that."

I was never sanguine about my chances of being nominated as Vice

President in 1944. I felt that Mr. Roosevelt, though he wanted me to nominate him, did not favor me as his running mate. I further felt that, while he might bow to the delegates by not taking a candidate who was objectionable to them, he would never take one whom he did not want. I knew, too, that word had gone out from the White House that I was "too old."

The denouement was a fascinating political drama. When I reached Chicago for the convention, I had a talk with the late Mayor Edward Kelly, a Roosevelt lieutenant and a friend of mine. He gave me the word that Roosevelt wanted Byrnes and that it was "in the bag for Jimmy." This squared with what Harry Truman had told me of his intention to nominate Byrnes. I settled down philosophically to put the finishing touches on my nominating speech for the President.

Forty-eight hours later Byrnes was dumped as a candidate, largely because organized labor opposed him on his civil rights and labor record. Byrnes was so furious that he prepared to leave the city and return to Washington. Before he left I called him at his hotel room to ask what had happened to him and his candidacy for Vice President. He asked me to come over to his room and he would tell me all about it. He said that Roosevelt had sent word to him to come on out to Chicago as he was his choice for Vice President.

For nearly two hours we licked each other's sores with heartfelt sympathy.

Then he said to me:

"You are going to nominate Roosevelt, aren't you?"

"Yes," I answered.

"If I were you," he said, "I wouldn't say anything too complimentary about him."

Despite my sympathy for him in his disappointment I demurred to this suggestion, pointing out that I could not very well nominate a man, and especially Mr. Roosevelt, without being complimentary to him, but I told him I would think it over. I called Paul Porter, who had already received an advance copy of my nominating speech, and asked him to hold it up for an hour or two in the event I wanted to make any changes. I decided to make no changes and authorized him to distribute the speech to the press. I did place Mr. Roosevelt in nomination, and he must have appreciated my speech, for I received a wire from him, saying, "I AM VERY GRATEFUL TO YOU FOR THAT SPLENDID NOMINATING SPEECH. IT MADE ME VERY HAPPY."

In his memoirs my good friend, Jim Farley, writes that I was so furious at being "by-passed" by President Roosevelt that I "was about to tear up the nominating speech," and that he and a few others, though they were opposed to a fourth term, persuaded me to go through with it. I certainly had conferences with Jim Farley during the course of the convention, but I do not recall any action or statement on my part that should have led him to feel I was about to tear up my speech. A number of my friends were somewhat puzzled over the fact that I was nominating Mr. Roosevelt in view of our recent disagreement and the fact that I was not acceptable to him as a running mate. However, subsequent to our disagreement, I had written an article in *Collier's* magazine advocating his election to a fourth term and I had promised to nominate him at the convention. I felt it my duty to perform this service and did so.

The drama was played out with the vice presidential nomination going to Senator Truman, who did "not want the vice presidency" and who had told me he could not nominate me because he was pledged to propose Senator Byrnes. An added fillip was that Mr. Truman's candidacy was virtually stage-managed from the convention platform by Chairman Hannegan, who had persuaded me to nominate Mr. Roosevelt. Looking back upon the 1944 convention, I suppose I was somewhat naïve about the whole business. The pleasant aftermath, however, was that I came to enjoy such warm friendship and pleasant associations with Harry Truman.

President Roosevelt's reserve toward me softened a good deal after I had campaigned vigorously for the Roosevelt-Truman ticket in the 1944 election. Once again he displayed something of the old warm relationship when I called at the White House for conferences with him.

I shall never forget the conversation we had after the President returned from his meeting with Stalin and Churchill at Yalta: he wanted to bring me up to date on what happened at Yalta, and he wanted me to brief him on the domestic and legislative picture. When I arrived, he was preparing to shave himself, so I joined him in his bathroom.

"Sit down," he said.

"Where?" I asked.

With a whimsical glint in his eyes he motioned to a certain functional stool.

It was the only place to sit, so I sat there for more than an hour while we discussed the world situation. I think one might say that on this occasion I was truly "closeted" with the President. My only regret is that there was no photographer present to record for posterity this highly informal conference between the President of the United States and the majority leader of the Senate.

It was one of the most interesting talks I ever had with Franklin Roosevelt. Every time the President would start to shave, he would become so absorbed in telling me the details of his conversation with Stalin that the lather would dry on his face, and he would have to start all over again. He must have lathered up at least six times.

One of the things he told me was that, when he and Churchill argued with Stalin against fixing the Russian-Polish boundary on the old Curzon Line established after World War I, Stalin reminded them that Lenin had sought to have a more westerly boundary established, but that the post-World War I line had been fixed by Lord Curzon, an Englishman, Clemenceau, a Frenchman, and Dr. Walker,[1] an American. "Can I go back to my people and tell them I am less Russian than Curzon, Clemenceau, and Walker?" Stalin demanded. Roosevelt told me that was an argument which he and Churchill had difficulty answering.

From the talk I had with the President in his bathroom I do not believe that he underestimated Stalin, or was taken in by him at Yalta. Nor was there any diminution in his mental alertness at that time, as the late President's detractors have alleged. Though he was beginning to fail physically, his mind was keen. F.D.R. may have overestimated Stalin's good faith, but this was perfectly natural in view of the fact that the United States and Russia had just been wartime allies. I believe, on the basis of what he said to me that day, that he had a realistic view of what he was up against in dealing with Stalin.

Much of the partisan criticism about Yalta is unfair and has been exaggerated for obvious purposes. When the truth is known about what was intended by the agreements entered into at Yalta—and I do not mean Stalin's later perversion of these agreements—it will be found that President Roosevelt and his associates were trying their best to bring to the Polish people the type of open, independent, free government for which the Poles have been fighting for centuries.

President Roosevelt certainly had the best interests of the Polish people in mind when he insisted at Yalta that they be permitted to determine their destiny as a nation in a free election. That was democracy at work. The trouble was that Stalin and his cynical, ruthless regime did not

---

[1] I was unacquainted with Dr. Walker, and have been unable to identify him, but it is the name President Roosevelt quoted Stalin as using in connection with Curzon and Clemenceau.

carry out the promise to which the Russian dictator had agreed. The Soviet Union did not permit the promised free election in Poland, thus preventing the Polish people from expressing their wishes. The communistic government was imposed upon Poland, not at Yalta, but by the post-Yalta actions of Stalin and the Kremlin autocrats.

To those of us who saw President Roosevelt regularly it was painful to watch his rapid physical deterioration after his return from Yalta. As biographers of the late President have recorded, one could literally see him slipping away. I sat next to Mrs. Roosevelt at a banquet one night and she told me she was terribly concerned about the President's lack of appetite. Just a few hours before he departed on that last journey to Warm Springs, Georgia, in April 1945, the late Senator Elbert Thomas and I saw him at the White House. As we left, I remarked to Senator Thomas, "I'm afraid he'll never return alive."

Whatever I have set down about Franklin D. Roosevelt has been done in the interest of filling out the record on a chapter of political history in which I was a participant. Nothing I have said is to be construed as tinged with any bitterness, disappointment, or resentment on my part. I cherish in my heart a deep admiration for the character of Franklin Delano Roosevelt and a beautiful memory of my association with him.

As I look back over the history of the Roosevelt administration, I am convinced that whatever opinions different categories of people may hold concerning Franklin D. Roosevelt and his contribution to American government and American life, he made a deep impression and left a more indelible imprint on the era in which he served than any other President since Abraham Lincoln.

When one considers the tragic conditions which this country faced at the time of his arrival on the scene, it is not difficult to speculate on what might have occurred in free America if these conditions had not been remedied. Not only did he save American business, which was helpless, but he may have saved American democracy.

That he had great virtues none will deny. That he had great faults his friends must admit. But this is true of all great men. The very attributes of nature which clothe great men with virtues frequently clothe them with glaring weaknesses. This was true of Mr. Roosevelt as it has been true of many of our greatest statesmen. But through the unseen and mysterious processes of nature, which we call the alchemy of human life, the good qualities frequently overwhelm the weaker ones and give a decided predominance to the virtues over the faults. In my opinion this is true of Mr. Roosevelt. In my opinion, also, the great changes which he wrought in the relationship between government and the people will not be easily erased or undone. The American people have accepted them, and they are a part of the warp and woof of our society.

CHAPTER 14

My Relations with President Truman

ONE of the engaging qualities about Harry Truman is his humanness. He had—and has—a great respect for the office of the President; yet, he never allowed himself to become so personally exalted, as some men have done in lesser positions, that a person could not talk to him as a fellow human being. He was a great hand at kidding his intimates on occasions, but he also could take it when the joke was on him.

I have related how, at the fateful 1944 convention, Mr. Truman became the vice presidential nominee, protesting all the while that he did not want the job. Later, when we became President and Vice President together, I used to chaff him good-naturedly about this incident. He was also fond of saying that he never had really been a candidate for any public office but that the offices always "caught up" with him.

So one night, after he had repeated this statement at a banquet which we were attending together, I arose and told our audience that President Truman's statement reminded me of the Republican I had heard about who thought he would get himself a state job when Kentucky elected its first Republican governor in 1895.

This hungry Republican, I related, got on his mule and rode all the way from Somerset to the state capital, Frankfort, a distance of about a hundred miles. He hung around for about six months. Finally all his money was gone and he still had no job, so he saddled up Old Nell and started for home.

On the outskirts of Frankfort he met a friend who asked him why he was in such a hurry to go home.

"Hurry!" exclaimed the disappointed job-seeker. "All my life I've heard that the office should seek the man. Well, I've been here six months and haven't seen an office seeking a man yet. If you happen to run across one after I've gone, will you please tell it that I'm a-ridin' out Somerset Pike, and ridin' damned slow!"

I closed this story—and the President laughed uproariously at it—by turning to Mr. Truman and saying, "You may not have sought any of the many offices you have held, but, whenever they were out looking for you, you were riding mighty slow!"

Shortly after his inauguration as Vice President, Mr. Truman also enjoyed another bit of spoofing which I carried off at his expense. It was at the National Press Club "Congressional Night" party, to which I referred in an earlier chapter. At another Press Club function soon after his inauguration as Vice President, Mr. Truman had attracted a certain amount of attention by posing for pictures at a piano with the beautiful and alluring movie star, Miss Lauren Bacall, perched on top of it. In my talk on the subject of "Advice to Newly Elected Senators," I undertook to give some advice on the non-mixability of politics and piano playing.

"If you are a musician, and have a predilection for playing the piano, and have any vice presidential aspirations," I said, "do not attempt to hold down the lid of the piano with a beautiful girl, caparisoned in an abbreviated skirt automatically revealing an amplitude of shape," I said. "The poet says, 'There is a divinity that shapes our ends, rough-hew them how we will.' I say, there is a humanity that ends our shape, or may end it.

"So, under such circumstances, be careful. You might strike a false note, or take note of a striking posture. Or even strike out altogether!"

There was no lightness, however, in the soul of Harry Truman for a considerable period after fate catapulted him into the White House. I recall that tragic day in April 1945, when the news was flashed from Warm Springs of the sudden death of President Franklin D. Roosevelt. Vice President Truman telephoned me, among other officials, to ask that I attend the hastily arranged and somber ceremony at which he took the oath as President. I missed his call, however, as Senator Tom Connally and I were already on our way to the White House to express our condolences to Mrs. Roosevelt.

As majority leader, I had come to enjoy the same sort of close "catcher-and-pitcher" working relationship with Vice President Truman that I had with former Vice President Garner. This liaison had been less close when Henry Wallace presided over the Senate, not because of any personal reasons, but because Mr. Wallace had so many outside interests other than being Vice President. This was partly President Roosevelt's fault. I occasionally advised Henry in a friendly way to devote more attention to his duties as presiding officer; he always took my suggestions in good spirit and thanked me for them, but it never seemed to make any impression.

Vice President Truman, however, was a "professional" in the best sense of the word; he was well liked in the Senate and was thoroughly interested in his job, so, when he succeeded Vice President Wallace, the old teamwork was restored.

When Truman succeeded to the presidency, he did so in a mood of extreme humility, and some of his repeated statements about his "unfitness" and "inadequacy" for the job found their way into print. While I admired and respected this human quality in the man, I felt he was doing himself an injustice and that it was not good for the President of the United States to be quoted in such terms of self-deprecation.

Finally I went to him—and there were others among his associates who did likewise—and spoke to him along these lines:

"Mr. President, I realize how you feel about this job you have inherited, and I respect you for your humility. But you have got the job, and you have the responsibility. You are President of the United States and I hope you will no longer deprecate your own personal situation or minimize your ability to carry on the task to which you have been called.

"God raises up leaders. We do not know the process, but, in the wisdom of Almighty God, you have been made President. You will have all the help that any of us can give you. Have confidence in yourself. If you do not, the people will lose confidence in you. However humble and contrite you feel, you have got to go forward and lead this nation out of war. Have trust in the God Who brought this about and He will enable you to do what you have to do."

President Truman thanked me soberly for my counsel. Gradually he grew more sure of himself and, commencing to act with vigor and assurance, he became a forceful and confident Chief Executive.

Harry Truman and I worked closely together during the remainder of the late President Roosevelt's unexpired term of office, and it came about, as I shall describe, that in the fall of 1948 we were called upon to do a certain amount of traveling in the interests of the Democratic party. On November 5, 1948, Mr. Truman and I returned to Washington, having been elected three days earlier as President and Vice President of the United States. There were a lot of joyful Democrats and maybe even some surprised Republicans on hand to greet us. The President, who had been having some fun along the way with that famous "DEWEY DE-FEATS TRUMAN" edition of the Chicago *Tribune,* addressed the huge crowd from the White House steps, then called on me for a few words. "Mr. President," I said, "in the language of Minnie Pearl of the Grand Ole Opry, I'm just so proud to be here."

I might have added with perfect accuracy that it had not been in the cards that I should be standing on the White House steps as Vice President-elect when the Democratic convention convened in Philadelphia the previous July. For, despite the fact that we had been the best of friends in the Senate, saw eye to eye on leading issues, and had always worked together as a team, I had not been President Truman's choice as a running mate.

It was no secret that President Truman's preference for the vice presidential nomination was Associate Justice William O. Douglas of the Supreme Court. I knew that the President's legal counsel, Clark Clifford, a good friend of mine, was burning up the wires to the West Coast, where Justice Douglas was vacationing, attempting to persuade him to accept the nomination. But the justice was unwilling. Whether he feared that the ticket could not win, or disliked the idea of involving the Supreme Court in another political contest, I do not know.

All this, in turn, made me reluctant even to consider the vice presidential nomination, for, as I commented to political reporters in Philadelphia before the balloting began, "I never cared for cold biscuits."

My own position at the 1948 convention was rather interesting. I was Democratic leader of the Senate and was being spoken of as "Mr. Democrat." I had been in national politics since 1912, and had been a delegate to every Democratic convention since 1920. Twice before I had been a convention keynoter; I had nominated Franklin D. Roosevelt for his fourth term in 1944, had seconded Governor Smith's nomination sixteen years earlier, and, among other honors, had served as permanent chairman in 1940. At every convention since 1928 I had been mentioned for Vice President, and there were some delegates who viewed me as presidential timber.

In any event, I had been "often a bride'smaid but never a bride," as the old saying goes, and it seemed that if I was ever to achieve the vice presidential nomination, this was the year. But I did not go to the convention as a candidate and I did not become one while there. As I told the delegates later in my acceptance speech, "If anyone had told me when I left my home for Philadelphia a few days ago that I would leave here tomorrow as the nominee of the Democratic party on the national ticket,

I would have pronounced such person as a prophet without honor either in his own or any other country."

My nomination was as unexpected to me as it was to others, because I had assumed that, if Mr. Truman were renominated and had his choice, his running mate would be someone other than myself. However, after the convention, the consensus seemed best summed up in a remark attributed to Jim Farley: "The convention made up the President's mind for him."

In 1948 there had been more than the usual preconvention sentiment for me as the vice presidential nominee, and there were some delegates who even urged that I seek the presidential nomination against Mr. Truman. I was having none of the latter. Not only was Harry Truman my friend, but he was the party leader, and I regarded him as an able Chief Executive.

Some political pundits have written that Truman did not favor me because he was dissatisfied with my record as majority leader. I think that in this instance the seers were daydreaming. I had always enjoyed completely harmonious relations with Harry Truman, and he had been highly complimentary to me on many occasions. Among letters which I have preserved is one which reads as follows:

THE WHITE HOUSE
Washington

July 27, 1945

DEAR ALBEN:

Today marks the eighth anniversary of your service as Majority Leader of the Senate. I understand that this is twice as long as any of your predecessors have served. These years have been eventful ones. They have been years of great moment to the United States and to the world.

In all of the recent events which have meant so much in shaping the future of our civilization you have played an important and effective role. Not only have you helped to fulfill the ideals and principles of our party, but you have been willing and anxious to lay aside all semblance of partisanship or desire for party advantage whenever the welfare of our nation required it.

I congratulate you on your past service as Majority Leader, and, also, on your thirty-three years of service in the Congress. The nation is grateful to you for your patriotic share in the accomplishments of these years, and I know that the years to come will be equally fruitful.

With all best wishes for your continued health and success from your old friend.

Very sincerely yours,

HARRY TRUMAN

Honorable Alben W. Barkley
The United States Senate
Washington 25, D.C.

That President Truman continued to hold this regard for me was indicated by his remarks as we stood together on the White House steps on that November day when we returned to Washington after our victory in 1948. On that occasion he did me the honor of referring to me as "a great leader in the Senate" and "one of the great legislators of all time." Later he warmed my heart further by describing me on several occasions as "the best Vice President a President ever had."

In any event, I never asked President Truman, and he never told me, the reason why I was not his choice. Nor did I ever ask him to support me. The way my nomination came about was this:

Some weeks before the convention Senator Howard McGrath, then chairman of the Democratic National Committee, asked me to serve again as temporary chairman and keynoter. I demurred strongly, telling him I had delivered the keynote speech twice—and practically a third time in 1940, when the anti-third-term keynoter ignored President Roosevelt, leaving it to me, as permanent chairman, to sound "Hail to the Chief." I felt some other man should have the honor, and suggested the names of several, including Scott W. Lucas, then Senator from Illinois, who later became my successor as majority leader. A week later McGrath returned, telling me the Committee—and President Truman—still wanted me to make the speech. I could not refuse such a request.

When I arrived in Philadelphia the Saturday before the convention opened, I found the most discouraged and downcast group I had ever seen. You could cut the gloom with a corn knife. The very air smelled of defeat. "Listen!" I told the Committee officials. "Don't walk on your chins too soon."

I made my speech, and persons who heard it have described it as a rip-snorter. I reviewed what, to me, was the very real and positive record of the Democratic party in sixteen years under Roosevelt and Truman; then, by way of contrast, I paid my respects to the Republican-controlled Eightieth Congress.

I made fighting words out of the phrase, "New Deal," on which the Republicans sought to heap opprobrium. I said:

> They call it the New Deal. At every convention since 1932 and on every political rostrum, Republican politicians have hurled their anathemas at this New Deal as if it were some blight or plague that had poisoned the lives and consumed the liberties of the people and kept them chained and helpless.
>
> What is this cankering, corroding, fungous growth which every Republican orator, save one, denounced with unaccustomed rancor, then in their adopted platform hugged to their political bosom as if it were the child of their own loins?
>
> It was recovery. The new Roosevelt administration breathed into the nostrils of every worthy American enterprise a breath of new life, new hope and new determination. It put old agencies at the people's disposal and, where necessary, inaugurated new ones to make democracy live and work for the American people.

I went on to detail the great accomplishments of the four successive administrations, started under Roosevelt and continued under Truman. Then I derided the boast of the Republican nominee, Governor Thomas E. Dewey, who had announced with what I termed "characteristic finality" that "his administration" would "clean out the cobwebs."

"I am not an expert on cobwebs," I told the cheering Democrats, "but, if my memory does not betray me, when the Democratic party took over the Government of the United States sixteen years ago, even the spiders were so weak from starvation they could not weave a cobweb in any department of the Government!"

When my speech was over—and these are facts which have been reported and interpreted by others—the hitherto apathetic delegates were on their hind legs and cheering. A dead convention had come to life. The St. Louis *Post-Dispatch* reported that my address had "swept the Democratic convention off its feet" and that "it was no secret that many of the delegates would have preferred . . . [Barkley] . . . as head of the ticket in place of President Truman."

I was, in fact, approached by a number of delegates, including several state governors, who urged me to permit my nomination as President. "You're the man," they said. To all such urgings I replied with an emphatic *no*, saying:

"If anybody puts my name in nomination before this convention for President, I shall arise and renounce it. I did not come here as a candidate; I am not a candidate, and I will not take advantage of whatever enthusiasm I may have generated here to get the nomination—certainly not against Mr. Truman."

Next day President Truman himself was on the telephone congratulating me on my address.

"Why didn't you tell me you wanted to be Vice President?" he said. "I didn't know you wanted the nomination."

"Mr. President," I answered, "you do not know it yet."

"Well," said the President, "if I had known you wanted it, I certainly would have been agreeable."

"Mr. President," I replied, "I appreciate that, but I know that you have considered other men for the nomination, so I just did not calculate upon it at all.

"But now," I continued, "from what I hear, it looks as if the convention wants to nominate me as your running mate. I am not going to lift a finger to get the nomination, but, if the convention does nominate me, I think I should accept."

"I think you should accept," Mr. Truman cordially replied, "and I hope you will."

By this time a Truman-Barkley ticket was a foregone conclusion. Of course, there were many pessimists who thought it was an empty honor, because they did not believe that we, or any Democrats, could be elected that year. I never held that belief; I was always confident we could win, and this confidence grew as the campaign progressed.

In retrospect the many clouded crystal ball comments on the impending "defeat" of the Democratic ticket in 1948 are rather amusing. For instance, the St. Louis *Post-Dispatch*, in commenting that I might have been the Presidential nominee that year, observed, " . . . Many hold that he would have been the best possible choice to weld the scattered fragments of the party together and rebuild it for 1952." Regardless of the speculative predictions, the result indicated that Mr. Truman and I were fairly good welders.

On the final night of the convention President Truman came over to Philadelphia in his private train. We sat outside by the railroad track behind the convention hall, waiting to be notified of our nominations. Someone brought out a couple of wooden chairs for us—they were not too comfortable—and we sat there until the early hours of the morning. While we waited, we had a very agreeable visit, which reminded me of the old song, "Here Am I, Waiting at the Church." We talked about many things: politics, trivia, how to bring up daughters—everything that might come into the minds of two men who not only were shortly to become the standard bearers of their party, but who were congenial friends with many common interests.

I was with Mr. Truman on the platform, of course, when he made his acceptance speech. I greatly admired his bold stroke in announcing there and then that he was summoning the Republican-controlled Eightieth Congress into special session eleven days hence, and that he would call upon it to pass some of the laws which the Republican convention platform had just declared were urgently and immediately needed. It was a typical Truman challenge, demonstrating the courage and the initiative of the man. That Eightieth Congress really had made a deplorable record. In so far as the welfare of the general public was concerned, the slogan of the Eightieth Congress might well have been, "We feel for you, but we just can't reach you!"

I enjoyed every minute of the campaign. I knew it was going to be a lively one. When I saw President Truman off on the start of his campaign, I shook hands with him and said, "Good luck—and mow 'em down!" He responded, "I'm going to fight hard, and I'm going to give 'em hell!" His daughter, Margaret, who is a lovely young lady and, as a certain music critic knows, the apple of her father's eye, was standing by. She shook her head disapprovingly and said, "Daddy, you shouldn't say 'hell.' "

While the President was off whistle-stopping, I was making the first full-dress "prop stop" campaign in national political history. I covered the country in a specially chartered airplane, the Bluegrass. I visited thirty-six of the forty-eight states in six weeks, traveling some 150,000 miles back and forth, and delivering more than 250 speeches. I addressed so many small gatherings that one national news magazine dubbed me "the poor man's candidate." By my display of energy I settled, at least for the time being, the propriety of the tiresome refrain that "Barkley is too old." Unfortunately I was destined to hear it once more in 1952.

In addition to the natural issue—the record of the Democrats versus the Republicans, the latter exemplified by the Eightieth Congress—we had some of our best help that year from the Republican candidates, Messrs. Dewey and Warren. Governor Dewey, who had fought a hard battle as the losing candidate in 1944, made the mistake of conducting this campaign as if he were already "Mr. President," and I suppose Governor—now Chief Justice—Warren had no choice but to go along. I used to poke a little fun at them by telling my audiences that "I wrote my speeches in the air and delivered them on the ground" while the Republican nominees, who traveled by train, "were always up in the air so far as their speeches were concerned."

In fact, Governor Dewey's performance reminded me of old "Fiddlin' Bob" Taylor's campaign for Governor of Tennessee in 1896, when the free-silver issue was hot. Taylor was one of the finest of the old-fashioned Chautauqua type of orator; many a time, as a boy, I saved up my nickels to buy a ticket to hear him lecture on "The Fiddle and the Bow," "Love, Laughter and Song," and "The Paradise of Fools." But Taylor was making this race by playing his fiddle, using his magnificent voice, and saying as little as possible about anything specific.

One day a heckler demanded to know where the candidate stood on the money question. "My friend," intoned "Fiddlin' Bob" in his most sonorous and mellifluous voice, "I am glad you asked me that. I am a candidate for Governor of this great Volunteer State . . . yes, sir . . . and I am glad . . . mighty glad . . . to explain my position on any issue. Yes, my friend, I am glad you asked me my position on this gr-reat economic and social question that is troubling the American pee-pul!"

He paused dramatically, and said, "Here is where I stand. I am for a little more gold, a little more silver, a little more greenback—and a sprinkling of counterfeit!"

Dewey's 1948 campaign, in my opinion, was just about as specific as "Fiddlin' Bob's" stand on the money issue, and it was no surprise to me that he was defeated.

CHAPTER 15

At Last, the "Veep"!

So, FINALLY, on January 20, 1949, I came to be the "Veep." On a crisp, sparkling day I took my oath of office on the steps of the Capitol, placing my hand on a beautiful Bible which had been presented to me by the Broadway Methodist Church in my home town of Paducah. The oath was administered by a fellow Kentuckian, Justice Stanley F. Reed of the Supreme Court. President Truman, too, was sworn in by a Kentuckian, the late Chief Justice Vinson.

The President and I had thought we had had a rather tumultuous reception when we returned to Washington after our election, but, thanks to the Republicans, we had ourselves quite an inaugural parade. The Republicans, it seemed, had overreached themselves with their own overoptimism on this inaugural business. Some months before the election the Republican chairman of the Senate-House Inaugural Committee, Senator C. Wayland (Curly) Brooks, had announced that this was going to be "the biggest damn inaugural in modern times." He saw to it that the Republican Congress provided $80,000 for grandstands and so forth along the parade route, as compared with $39,000 in 1941. Mr. Brooks, of course, did not foresee that the Democrats might win, and that he himself would be retired by the voters of his home state of Illinois in that same election. Anyhow, it was a very lovely parade, and we Democrats tried to show the proper appreciation by always referring to the ample and lavish grandstands along the parade route as the "Curly Brooks Memorial Stadium."

About the only flaw in the inaugural festivities, so far as I was concerned, was that, through some mix-up, the sturdy men of the Mose Green Club, a proud old political club of Louisville, who had come all the way from Kentucky with their green hats and canes, were not allowed to march in the parade.

An amusing bit of family byplay on Inauguration Day was the difficulty encountered by my daughter, Mrs. Max Truitt, in persuading one of her sons, Stephen, to attend the ceremony. Steve—he is the grandson who, as I related in an earlier chapter, invented the nickname of "Veep"—is quite an individualist, and did not think he should miss school. He also had protested in similar fashion against being "dragged" to the home-coming parade with which President Truman and I had been greeted after our November victory. "Aw, Mom," Steve had argued, "I've got a spelling test. Besides I consider this whole thing embarrassing!"

At the big inaugural ball that night the President paid me the compliment of saying to the assembled Democrats:

"I can't tell you how much I agree with you on your choice of the first citizen of Kentucky. You can't give him too much honor in my book. I don't think this country ever had a President and Vice President who were more congenial or whose adherence to the principles of the Democratic party was so much in parallel."

In my response I jested that, in Senate days together, Mr. Truman used to call me "Boss," and that "when Mrs. Truman is not around, I am going to hold him to it."

There has been quite a change in the public attitude toward the office of Vice President. In the Constitutional Convention of 1787, Benjamin Franklin ridiculed it by proposing that the occupant be addressed as "Your Superfluous Highness." John Adams, later to become President, belittled the position as a sort of fifth wheel to the executive branch, and James Monroe, himself a future President, also opposed creation of the office.

For many years the vice presidency was considered such a dead end that the nomination sometimes was employed as a kiss of death to sidetrack the careers of rising figures whose popularity or independence was becoming a threat to the powers in control of their political parties. For example, Theodore Roosevelt, who became President via the vice presidential route, was maneuvered into the position by New York State Republican leaders. Teddy had been a strong-minded New York governor, and the bosses—Thomas Platt and others—simply wanted to get him out of the way. Unfortunately for their plans they did not count on the assassination of President McKinley.

In earlier days John C. Calhoun, the only man in history ever to do so, actually resigned as Vice President under Andrew Jackson, whom he disliked. According to tradition, the great Henry Clay, who had a consuming ambition to become President, twice spurned offers of the vice presidential nomination; ironically, had he accepted either time, he would have become President, for both of the men who headed the ticket on these occasions—William Henry Harrison and Zachary Taylor—were elected and died in office. Former Governor Frank O. Lowden of Illinois, who also had been disappointed in his presidential ambitions, actually turned down the vice presidential nomination after he had been formally nominated on the second ballot at the 1924 Republican convention.

It was Woodrow Wilson's Vice President, Thomas R. Marshall of Indiana, who, at his inauguration, produced chuckles by remarking that he thought he was entitled to make a few remarks since he was "about to enter upon a four-year period of silence." Vice President Marshall later enriched the national lore with his deathless quip, "What this country needs is a good five-cent cigar," which he whispered to a clerk during the course of some long-winded, unscintillating Senate debate.

In my own Senate days I recall being summoned to the rostrum by President Coolidge's salty Vice President, "Hell-and-Maria" Dawes, who, like Marshall, suffered frequently from the occupational boredom of presiding over some droning, interminable debate. "Barkley," he growled, "this is a helluva job! I can do only two things: One is to sit up here and listen to you birds talk, without the privilege of being able to answer you back. The other is to look at the newspapers every morning to see how the President's health is!"

When I became "Veep," I did my best to shun the example of the unhappy "Throttlebottom" of the musical comedy, *Of Thee I Sing,* who mourned that the Vice President "sits around in the parks and feeds the pigeons, and takes walks and goes to the movies." One day "Vice President" Throttlebottom thought he would join the library, but found he "had to have two references" so he couldn't get in.

With President Truman's active concurrence—he was one of my "references"—I became a working Vice President. From his own experience Truman knew how little opportunity had been given in the past for Vice Presidents—"separated from the presidency by only a heartbeat"—to acquaint themselves with the job they might have to take over, and he wisely set out to rectify this situation. He had me attend his Cabinet meetings, and, with his approval, Congress passed an act making the Vice President a member of the National Security Council.

I suppose I traveled, mostly by air, more than any Vice President had up to that time, making speeches in all parts of the country. Many of these speeches were of semi-official nature, for I often represented the President, who, naturally, was limited in his ability to accept engagements. I enjoyed these appearances. I like to travel, and I enjoy meeting people and talking with them. I have always believed it to be the duty of those who are elected to high office to report to the people at every opportunity. The people cannot all come to Washington to witness their government in action and I firmly believe in carrying information to the people by all available legitimate means.

Of course, for a certain period, I seemed to be much in demand as a crowner of "queens" at various celebrations—Apple Blossom Festivals, Cherry Blossom Festivals, and just about every sort of festival that one can think of. It seemed an inevitable—and not entirely unwelcome—part of the ritual that the visiting Vice President should kiss the queen, after crowning her. I knew this would expose me to a certain amount of ribbing, but I manfully faced up to my duties.

This osculatory business became such a problem that on one occasion —I believe it was the crowning of one of the Cherry Blossom queens in Washington—I sought to get by with merely giving the queen a dignified peck on the forehead. The crowd—and the press photographers—roared objections. I then kissed her on the cheek. More objections. Finally I saluted her on the lips. The spectators—and photographers—now were satisfied, but, by this time, as I later remarked in an interview, I had got into the spirit of my work and was beginning to enjoy it! Let no man ever allege that Alben Barkley shirked his duty!

On another occasion the Vice President's office was visited by a beautiful movie actress, Miss Marie McDonald, who was known in the cinema world, for reasons not too difficult to discern, as "The Body." This time, thank heaven, I withstood the importunings of the photographers to kiss Miss McDonald. I say "thank heaven" in no derogation of Miss McDonald or her charms; the simple fact was that, a day or so later, the beautiful lady came down with the measles.

On my trips around the country I always sought to travel with the least fanfare and the greatest possible freedom of movement. This freedom was circumscribed somewhat after the unfortunate attempt upon President Truman's life by misguided Puerto Rican nationalists in 1950. The Secret Service learned that the fantastic scheme also included a plan to assassinate the Vice President, and the President insisted on assigning a guard to me.

I was making a speech in Illinois when I received the news about the attempt on the President's life; it stunned me, and shocked the crowd when I announced what had happened. Five Secret Service men were detailed to guard me, but I finally persuaded the chief of the service, U. E. Baughman, to reduce the number to two. I could not argue him into calling it off altogether, which is what I wanted, for I always had the feeling that if anyone wanted to take a pot shot at me, not even the most efficient vigilance, which is what the Secret Service, a very efficient organization, provides, could prevent it.

I became very fond of the two agents who became my shadows, but this did not prevent me from trying at every possible opportunity to slip off from them. It became a sort of game, and the agents became resigned to it after a while. Once I refused to buy a pair of shoes in my favorite Chicago shoe store because they would not let me go alone. On another occasion, however, I eluded them by jumping into a Washington bus and taking a ride by myself.

The Vice President's principal duty is to preside over the Senate. I enjoyed this, though I came to sympathize with Vice President Dawes's feeling of frustration, as I often itched to get back into the fray of debate. The presiding officer witnesses many fascinating passages—and many amusing ones, too. I remember once when, in the heat of debate, my old colleague, Senator McKellar, who was opposing the Administration viewpoint on some issue, hotly addressed the chair and objected to the conduct of the majority leader, Senator Lucas. The gentleman from Tennessee complained that the majority leader actually had dared to "yawn" while, he, McKellar, was speaking. I considered the objection, then solemnly ruled, "The yawn of the Senator from Illinois will be stricken from the record."

As presiding officer, I performed many functions, once even substituting for the Senate chaplain. The Senate had adjourned briefly and reconvened, which, under the Senate rules, created a new calendar day. The chaplain was not at hand to open the session with a prayer. I volunteered to fill the breach, and some of the senators who had heard my speeches at the conventions were surprised when I delivered one of the shortest prayers on record.

"Lord," I prayed, "in these days of uncertainty, we ask for and thank Thee for the boon of Thy guidance and direction. Endow us with wisdom and light to see the path of our duty and courage to keep our feet within it. Amen."

I was proud to occupy the historic room in the Capitol assigned to the Vice President. I liked to keep a wood fire burning in the fireplace and to smell the good smell of wood smoke which reminded me of the innumerable open hearths at which I had warmed myself in my youth. I enjoyed being surrounded by the priceless relics which enhanced the office: Theodore Roosevelt's chandelier; the Rembrandt Peale portrait of Washington; the famous Dolly Madison mirror; a desk once used by McKinley and Wilson, and so on.

I knew all the lore about these relics: the mirror, for instance, was the one which the beauteous Dolly had purchased in France for $50, provoking an outraged Senate to spend about $2800 investigating her "extravagance."

One day, alas, I unwittingly defiled—or maybe enhanced?—the McKinley-Wilson desk. I sat there to sign a $3,000,000,000 appropriation bill; someone slipped me a ball-point pen with which I was unfamiliar, and I pressed so hard that my name is scratched into the surface.

I kept guest books for the signatures of all who called at the vice presidential suite during my four years in office. The books contain the names of more than 22,000 adults and youngsters from forty-eight states and fifty-two foreign countries. We had our share of the famous: there were such visitors as Winston Churchill, Gloria Swanson, Pandit Nehru, Dinah Shore, Madame Chiang Kai shek, Jane Russell, and "Cousin Minnie Pearl" from the Grand Ole Opry.

Once my good friend, Bob Hope, came by to join me on a trip to crown a queen at the Apple Blossom Festival in Virginia. We stepped outside of the Capitol for a picture and, when the wind ruffled his locks, Bob commented, "Windy out here." I answered, "You ought to see it inside."

Another time the girls in my office were much excited when the British Embassy called and said a certain visitor wondered if he might come by my office and have someone take him to the Senate gallery and also give him a ride on "that little subway train" that runs between the Capitol and the Senate Office Building. When the visitor appeared, the entire feminine contingent of my staff insisted on escorting him. He was the Duke of Windsor.

When Prime Minister Churchill came to address a joint session of the two Houses, I reminded him of the luncheon I had given him during the war, when I was majority leader and he was visiting President Roosevelt, and I told Mr. Churchill a story I had not told him then. It seems that Churchill was a most energetic guest at the White House, bustling around everywhere in his dressing gown, and bursting in on the President at all hours. So when I called the President and asked if I might borrow Mr. Churchill for a little luncheon at the Capitol, he let out a whoop that practically shattered my eardrums, and said:

"For heaven's sakes, do! Give him a glass of scotch and a good lunch, and, while you're entertaining him, I will get rid of some desk work."

Churchill hugely enjoyed this story on himself. I also reminded the Prime Minister of the crowd that besieged us later on the Capitol Plaza, and how one lady had grabbed him, shrieking excitedly, "Mr. Churchill, my little baby looks exactly like you!" To which Churchill had replied magniloquently:

"Madam, all little babies look exactly like me."

Once a delegation of Methodist clergymen from the Midwest called on me, and the girls in my office were surprised when rather uproarious laughter came resounding from my office. The girls asked me what I had done to get the ministers to laughing. I explained that the subject of "equivocation" had come up in our conversation, and I had simply told the clergymen one of my favorite stories about the preacher who was delivering a sermon to a congregation composed of influential parishioners whom he did not wish to offend. He preached on "Sin"—always a reasonably safe subject—and concluded his remarks with the cautious exhortation:

"And so, I say unto you: Repent of your sins—more or less; ask forgiveness—in a measure; or you will be damned—to some extent!"

One of the "Veep's" official duties was to attend a lot of functions of all sorts. One day I had to go to a special showing of a European art exhibit, and I decided to take my five secretaries along. I was standing there with the girls, admiring some "old master," when Lady Astor, who was visiting in this country, broke in and buttonholed me. "When are you going to give England another loan?" she demanded peremptorily. "What," I replied, "did you do with that last billion we just gave you?"

As I have indicated, relations between the White House and the Vice President's office were exceptionally cordial. President Truman was extremely gracious in arranging to have ceremonies conducted at the White House on the occasion when a gold medal, which Congress had authorized in recognition of my long public service, was presented to me. Another pleasant occasion for me was when he paid a surprise visit to the Senate to present me with the gavel made from a timber taken from the White House during its restoration. The presentation occurred on the thirty-eighth anniversary of my service in Congress. I was greatly affected by the gesture, and, in responding to Mr. Truman, I said:

> This gavel is one of the evidences of the human quality which you, Mr. President, possess, and which makes so many people love you and appreciate you and respect you because you are human. As Artemus Ward, the great American humorist, once said, "One man has as much human nature in him as another, if not more." Sometimes you may appear to have more, Mr. President. That is a quality which all of us admire.

On still another occasion the President, ever solicitous of the prestige of the office of Vice President, decided that the "Veep" ought to have his own flag and seal. He set the Heraldic Branch of the Department of the Army to work designing them for me. When they were finally ready, I received a hand-written note from the President stating, "I think they are beauties. You can make 'em step aside now!"

In due course a two-star general called at my office to present me with the new adornments. The general felt impelled to explain at some length the characteristics of the flag, and, in the midst of his discourse, for some unfathomable reason, he blurted out, "I do not know whether the eagle on this flag is a male eagle or a female eagle." At this point I closed the proceedings by remarking with finality, "What difference would that make except to another eagle?"

I want to say for the record that I admire Harry Truman and think in many respects he made an outstanding President. I recognize that he made some mistakes, but so does every man and woman who was ever born. It is regrettable that the petty things about the Truman administration are the things, that, for the moment, may be best remembered. I think that Mr. Truman was far too kind and loyal to certain old friends who took advantage of him and whose actions sometimes were no credit to his administration.

I am confident, however, that history's judgment on Harry Truman will be favorable, and that he will be given his due recognition as a courageous and progressive President. As we both approached the end of our terms as President and Vice President, I sent him, at his request, an autographed picture, and I fully meant what I inscribed upon it: "To my friend and fellow laborer in the vineyard of the Lord."

He may have displayed on occasions an all too human tendency to speak or write hastily. I can sympathize with this quality, for I often flare up myself over petty irritations. However, I have worked out a sort of personal safety valve which I would occasionally urge President Truman to emulate: I would write "mad" letters, but put them away for a "cooling off" period in a special drawer; after a few days I found I no longer wanted to send them.

President Truman, however, did not "pop off" on the big issues. His big decisions were invariably taken only after serious consideration, in which he invited the opinions of his Cabinet and advisers. Among the big issues which, in my opinion, Truman met wisely and courageously were the decision to employ the atomic bomb in Japan and thus end the war; the decision to act in Korea, which, although it has since been subjected to base and ignoble criticism by political partisans, was applauded at the time as a brave and necessary act; the Berlin airlift, which probably saved Europe for us; the Truman Doctrine in Greece and Turkey and the Marshall Plan, which also held off the advances of world communism, and the decision to recall General Douglas MacArthur.

The MacArthur situation was an embarrassing problem for the President and all his advisers. The general is recognized as a great soldier and patriot. Personally, I had long admired him and felt a sort of family connection, as my youngest daughter is married to his nephew and namesake. General MacArthur, at that time Chief of Staff of the Army, had attended their wedding in my home at Washington.

However, the decision to relieve him from his command in the Far East during the Korean conflict was taken after much deliberation. The matter of General MacArthur's practical defiance of instructions issued to him by the President, who is Commander in Chief of the military forces, had been the subject of many prior discussions at Cabinet meetings and other high-level conferences. In order not to draw General MacArthur away from the scene in Japan and Korea by having him come to Washington, President Truman had even flown to Wake Island to confer with him on the conduct of the campaign.

As the controversy finally approached an unavoidable climax, President Truman called me by telephone at the Naval Hospital in Bethesda, where I had undergone an eye operation. He wanted me to meet with him, the late Chief Justice Fred Vinson, Speaker Sam Rayburn, and several others to discuss the MacArthur situation. I told him it would be two or three days before I could leave the hospital. The President then proposed that he would come out to the hospital to see me. I was willing, but pointed out that, if he did that, it would become a matter of public knowledge and would touch off speculation as to what our conference was about. He agreed it would be better if he did not come.

Two or three days later when I left the hospital, one of my first matters of business was to attend a meeting at the White House to discuss the MacArthur matter. The President meanwhile had already had his meeting with his advisers. At the conference which I attended, Secretary of State Acheson, General Omar Bradley, then head of the Joint Chiefs of Staff, and several others were present, including, to the best of my recollection, General George C. Marshall, former Chief of Staff. The President solicited opinions from all of us. When it came to me, after ascertaining from the military men present that there was no possibility of compromise, I declared that if it were a choice between relieving General MacArthur entirely or allowing him to continue in command in the face of his virtual defiance of the Commander in Chief, I saw no other course but to relieve him.

The sensation which this created is well known, and the details need not be repeated. However, in the wake of the general's famous "old soldiers never die" speech to Congress, there was a full-dress Cabinet meeting at the White House. President Truman went around the table, asking each of us our reaction. When he came to Dean Acheson, the urbane Secretary of State, whose comments were always a delight, leaned back in his chair and stroked his elegant mustache. Then he opined that the MacArthur situation reminded him of the story about a man who had an exceptionally beautiful daughter.

"All her life," he related, "the father took pains to protect the girl from any harm. He saw to it that she led a sheltered life and went with the right people. Finally, when she was eighteen, the girl came to him weepingly and said:

" 'Father, I have to confess something to you. I'm afraid I'm pregnant.' "

"Whereupon," the Secretary of State concluded, "the old man threw up his hands and shouted:

" 'Thank heaven, that's over! I've been fearing something like this all my life!' "

CHAPTER 16

Cupid and I

IN THE FALL of 1949 the Chicago *Tribune*, a newspaper not ordinarily amiably disposed toward Democrats, published a cartoon by Joseph Parrish about me which I found most pleasing. It pictured me with a rather benign expression, leaning from the Senate rostrum and inquiring of someone who was attempting frantically to capture my attention, "For what purpose does the gentleman wish to be recognized?" The "gentleman," of course, was none other than our ubiquitous little friend with the wings and the lethal bow and arrow, the "Hon. Dan'l Cupid." The title of the cartoon was "WILL THE CHAIR STATE THE QUESTION?"

In November there was another cartoon, drawn by the famous Daniel Fitzpatrick and published in the St. Louis *Post-Dispatch*. It has always been one of my favorites. It showed a spunky songbird, perched in a bare tree over the wintry St. Louis sky line, singing, "Veep! Veep!" The title was "Kentucky Melody."

These drawings were only an infinitesimal part of the thousands upon thousands of words and pictures, to which tons of newsprint were sacrificed (not to mention the incalculable clutter on the air waves) for the purpose of memorializing one of the happiest events of my life. I refer, of course, to my marriage to Jane Rucker Hadley, which took place during my term of office as Vice President.

When we met in Washington on July 8, 1949, I had been a widower almost three years, and Jane had been a widow for five years. Her late husband, Carleton S. Hadley, had been general counsel to the Wabash Railroad in St. Louis, and Jane was supporting her two teen-age daughters by working as private secretary to her husband's successor.

Jane had not had a real vacation in five years, and, having four days off, she decided to accept a long-standing invitation from her friends, Mr. and Mrs. Clark Clifford, formerly of St. Louis, to visit Washington. Clark Clifford was counsel to President Truman, and he and his lovely wife, Marny, were among the most popular members of Washington's younger married set.

Originally Jane was supposed to come to Washington during the first week in June, but her employer suddenly became ill and she was forced to postpone her trip until July. Here again enters the "fate" theme, which so fascinates me: It so happened that I was doing a great deal of traveling at that time, and the only week that I was actually in the capital uninterruptedly was the period when Jane came for her postponed vacation. If her employer had not become ill and Jane had come as originally planned, I would have been away from Washington and might never have met her. I have always said that I was never so thankful in my entire life for another man's bad fortune. (Happily it was only a slight indisposition.)

The Cliffords gave a first-night party for Jane aboard the *Margy*— named for Margaret Truman—a small boat occasionally used by the President and the White House staff. The guest list included several senators, an ambassador or so, some cabinet and sub-cabinet members, and influential journalists, but Jane says that from the moment I greeted her at the top of the gangplank, I took over. She says I held her hand much too long, backing up traffic behind me. I do not deny anything she may say about our first meeting; the gentleman from Kentucky freely admits that, in the popular vernacular, he "fell"—promptly, immediately, and instantaneously.

As a matter of fact, I had missed catching in our introduction whether this charming visitor from St. Louis was "Miss" or "Mrs." Hadley, and I did hope—again selfishly—that she was unattached. When we were talking later that evening, she saw me looking at the wedding ring on her left hand, and she cleared up my confusion by telling me that she was *Mrs.* Hadley and that she had been a widow for five years. I told her immediately that I simply could not understand the men of St. Louis, and then she called me "fresh!"

I also told her I had been in St. Louis a short time earlier to address the Democratic Jefferson-Jackson Day dinner.

"Oh," she said, "I know you were there—I read all about it in the papers."

"Why weren't you there?" I asked.

"I couldn't afford it," she said. "It cost $100 a plate."

"Well," I said, "they didn't show me anything like you in St. Louis, or I would have arranged for you to be there!"

At this point, Jane now tells me, she thought to herself: *Oh, boy! We're off to a good start!*

The boat was a little late in taking off that night. The reason was that the party was waiting for another guest, Sam Rayburn, then Speaker of the House, who was detained on Capitol Hill. We finally had to sail without him. While Sam is one of my oldest friends, I did not miss him at all and, in fact, was glad he did not show up, for Sam is a bachelor and on that evening I did not want any competition whatsoever.

I managed to keep Jane beside me on a little leather-cushioned seat in the stern of the boat. She says that I was very attentive, but that, whenever anyone else attempted to join our conversation, I was distinctly cool to the intrusion. Well, that was all right with me: so far as I was concerned, we were on the high seas and I was prepared to repel piracy!

Finally dinner was served, buffet-style, and I went to bring Jane and me two plates of food. When I returned, she was gone. She later told me that she became conscience-stricken over neglecting the other guests— among them, Secretary Acheson, Under Secretary of Commerce Cornelius Vanderbilt Whitney, Baron Silvercruys, the Belgian Ambassador; Senators Fulbright and Tydings, and Arthur Krock—and decided to move on.

The party sailed to Marshall Hall, an amusement park on the Potomac below Mount Vernon, and we all had a delightful, old-fashioned time riding the merry-go-round and the little cars that bump into each other. I say we had a "delightful" time, but I felt I had been slightly "stood up" because Jane had left me at dinner. I confined most of my efforts at the amusement park to the shooting gallery, but so far as I was concerned Cupid had already scored a bull's-eye on me.

I must have voiced my disappointment, for Senator Fulbright, who had known Jane in Missouri, went up to her on the return trip and, exercising the prerogatives of an old friend, lectured her: "Jane, what in the world have you done to the 'Veep'?"

"What do you mean? "she said.

"Well," he answered, "you've been awfully rude, leaving him as you did."

"For heaven's sakes!" she said. "Tell him to come on over."

So I rejoined her, and the rest of the evening brightened up again. All the way home we sat on the deck and sang old songs, while Jerry

Wadsworth, son of the late former congressman and senator from New York, played his guitar.

At this period, I might interpose, the society columnists had been marrying me off with monotonous regularity to almost every eligible widow in the country. If I had entered into matrimony with every charming lady with whom my name was linked in print, I would have made Brigham Young look like a woman-hater.

Actually, however, after the death of my first wife, I never dreamed that I would ever remarry. My children were all married and had their own families. I was occupied with my duties as a senator and later as Vice President, and was absorbed in my work. My daughter, Mrs. Max O'Rell Truitt, was my official hostess, and I confined my social engagements strictly to official functions. When Jane came to town, however, all that was changed.

On the morning after the Potomac cruise Jane was still asleep when I awakened her by telephoning her at the Cliffords' residence. I wanted to ask her to have dinner with me the following night, which was a Sunday. The Cliffords had already accepted an engagement, but Marny, who has all the perceptions of the beautiful woman that she is, promptly managed to ring me in on that engagement.

That Saturday night, however, I saw Jane again at a garden party given by Gwendolyn Cafritz, the Washington society hostess, and her husband, Morris. I monopolized her company all evening, and I did so again on Sunday night. In retrospect it is rather amusing to recall that, at the Cafritz party, the photographers dogged me and took pictures of me with almost every lady to whom I talked, except Jane.

Before Sunday night was over, I had asked Jane if I might give a luncheon for her at the Capitol on the following Wednesday, which was the first day I had open.

"Oh dear!" she said. "I'm supposed to go home and get back to work Tuesday."

"Well," I suggested, "call your boss and see if you can get a reprieve."

Jane did get her vacation extended—she admits she had made up her mind to stay over for it even if it cost her the job—and I had the luncheon for her. While I was at it, I followed it up late Wednesday afternoon with a little party in her honor at my apartment, to which I invited a number of friends. And that managed to stretch out into an evening of dinner and dancing at the Shoreham Hotel terrace. That day the society columnists were really buzzing!

While we were dancing that evening, I saw Leslie Biffle, Secretary to the Senate, and his wife, Glade, seated at a nearby table. I danced Jane over near them, leaned over, and whispered to Les, "How am I doing, boy?"

"You're doing fine—mighty fine!" he answered.

On the afternoon when Jane left Washington, I persuaded her to come to my office so I could drive her to the train. While we were talking in my office, Secretary Biffle walked in on a matter of business and started to say, "By the way, have I told you about——" Then he saw Jane, stopped in the middle of his sentence, and walked out again. When he got home that night, he told his wife, "Glade, our Vice President is going to get married." He probably was the first to predict it, for even Jane and I did not suspect it at the time.

Before she left, I asked Jane if she would mind my calling on her in St. Louis if "I just happen to be passing through some time."

"Why, certainly," she said. "In fact, I'd be hurt if you didn't call."

"Well," I said, "I would like to call on you, but I am thinking of your feelings, as there might be a lot of publicity about it."

"Oh no, there won't be any publicity," she said. "We just don't have things like that in St. Louis. You only get your name in the papers when you're born, when you're married and when you die."

I thought to myself, *Poor girl, she doesn't know what she's letting herself in for!*

But if she was willing, so was I. Almost immediately I found it convenient to accept a speaking engagement in Minneapolis. I decided it would be highly logical to return by way of St. Louis. After all, it is really only a few hundred miles or so out of the way—hardly any distance at all.

Jane met me at the St. Louis airport and took me to a luncheon party to introduce me to some of her friends. It was a lovely and enjoyable occasion, and there were no reporters or photographers around. As she was driving me to the airport I remarked how wonderful it had been that there had been no publicity. "Didn't I tell you we don't have publicity in St. Louis?" said Jane. Next morning the newspapers in both St. Louis and Washington, and I have no doubt elsewhere, had headlines proclaiming: "VEEP VISITS ST. LOUIS WIDOW!"

From then on the fat was in the fire. I courted Jane assiduously, and everywhere we turned there was a barrage of reporters, photographers, radio microphones, and sometimes even newsreel and TV cameramen. Now I am no shrinking violet, and all my life I have been genuinely appreciative of the attentions bestowed upon me by the public information media. But this was one time when, like Garbo, I wanted to be alone.

In between my increasingly frequent week-end flights to St. Louis I would write lengthy letters to Jane in longhand while presiding over the Senate. In those days I think I would have tolerated anything, even the most outrageous sort of filibuster, to keep the senators talking so I could get my love letters written. I would give the sealed envelopes to William Vaughn, my administrative assistant, to dispatch by air mail from the Senate post-office substation. He would take them to the post-office window personally, clutching them to his bosom, address side down, so the small parade of news hawks who inevitably shadowed him could not see to whom they were going. One day the little lady at the post-office window inadvertently let the cat out of the bag by weighing the letter, address side up, in the presence of a sharp-eyed columnist.

On my trips to St. Louis I met some of Jane's family, including her mother, Mrs. Estle Rucker, who is an accomplished pianist and music coach. Jane's father has been in the hospital for some years, having suffered a stroke. I felt an attachment to the family, incidentally, for I had been a young congressman when Jane's grandfather, Judge W. W. Rucker, a Missouri Democrat, had served in the House, and I had voted for many of his bills.

In fact, I sometimes teased Jane about her political affiliations. Although she came from a good Democratic family—and is back in one now—it leaked out that she had been a Willkie supporter during the 1940 presidential election. Her milkman at that time was a Roosevelt man, and one day she left him a note in an empty bottle, canceling future orders with the explanation: "NO WILLKIE, NO MILKIE!"

I met Jane's oldest daughter, Anne, who was then seventeen, but I had some difficulty in catching up with Janie, the fourteen-year-old. Every time I came to St. Louis, Janie was busy with the girl scouts or her high-school sorority, and she considered these engagements of much more urgent priority than staying home just to meet some Vice President who happened to be very attentive to her mother.

On one occasion, while attending a festival of some sort and crowning the queen, I excited the reporters by quipping, "Some of these days, I am going to crown a queen of my own." This caused such furor that, shortly after, when I took Mrs. Hadley and Anne, along with my daughter, Mrs. Truitt, to Paducah with me to the dedication of Barkley Field, an airport which was being named in my honor, I made a point of crowning my little granddaughter, Dorothy Anne Barkley, as "Queen of Queens."

On the return trip from the Paducah airport dedication, incidentally, I had the only near-mishap of any consequence that I have ever experienced during all my air travels. Coming in over Washington for a landing, the plane in which I was flying was almost hit by a blimp. This inflated gasbag, which was trailing some advertising slogan, came within fifty feet of hitting us. This was soon after a fatal crash over Washington between a fighter plane and an air liner, and people were jittery on the subject of air safety. Jane was quite worried when she heard about it, but the incident did not bother me, as I did not even know about it until after we had landed. I had been happily relaxing in the plane, thinking about what a lovely day it had been. I would have been very annoyed to have had anything spoil it.

I might interpose that I believe thoroughly in air travel. I never take out insurance when I fly, and, outside of this blimp incident, which was of a rather freakish nature, the only mix-up I have ever had in all my air travels was one time when I boarded a plane to go to Rochester, Minnesota, and wound up in Rochester, New York. And that was my fault.

Three months and twenty-two days after our meeting on the *Margy*, Jane and I announced our engagement. Eighteen days later—November 18, 1949—we were married in St. Louis.

Jane and I have always had a little joke between us as to who proposed to whom. First, we blamed it on each other. Judiciously—after all, I once was a judge in McCracken County, Kentucky, and at one time was considered for appointment to the Supreme Court of the United States— I finally ruled that we had proposed to each other. Equally judiciously Jane humors me in this ruling.

I think I am stating it mildly to say that the public evinced some interest in our courtship and marriage. The night on which we announced our engagement, the press, radio, TV—and neighbors—took over Jane's little apartment. There were even people peeking in through the window blinds.

Of all the reams of copy written about our courtship and impending marriage, I rather liked an editorial run by the Milwaukee *Journal*. It quoted a remark attributed to one of my predecessors, Woodrow Wilson's Vice President, the dryly humorous Thomas R. Marshall. "The Vice President," Marshall had once observed, "is like a man in a cataleptic state; he cannot speak; he cannot move; he suffers no pain; and yet he is perfectly conscious of everything that is going on about him." I am quite certain Mr. Marshall had something entirely different in mind when he uttered this gem of wisdom and wit, but, to me, it seemed peculiarly appropriate at the period just before my marriage.

Our wedding was a beautiful, dignified service in the small Singleton Memorial Chapel of St. John's Methodist Church, conducted by Bishop Ivan Lee Holt, Methodist Bishop of Missouri, with the Reverend Dr. Albea Godbold, pastor of the church, assisting. It was conducted in the presence of our families, a few friends and representatives of the press. My son, David, was my best man.

Outside, however, a crowd estimated to number as high as 10,000 people thronged the streets. Jane was almost startled when she saw them, and I myself had never seen anything quite like it. Our honeymoon car, which was my wedding present to Jane, was almost turned over; my administrative assistant, William Vaughn, was knocked down and trampled, and the chief of police, who was inadvertently blocking the view of a female spectator, got stabbed with a hatpin.

Eventually, however, we were able to drive away from the church, and we got off on our honeymoon and the start of a wonderful life together.

Jane and I have been very happy. We share many interests. She was a wonderful hostess and helpmate during the remainder of my term as Vice President, and, since I have left Washington, we have had much fun together, traveling, meeting new people, and making plans for the future. I feel I have been doubly blessed in life, having had the good fortune of being married to two lovely and wonderful women. No man could say more.

CHAPTER 17

The 1952 Convention: My Relations with Adlai

I COME now in my narrative to the climactic drama of my forty-seven years in politics—the Democratic convention of 1952. In that year, having held for the past four years the second highest office in the land, I decided, after much soul-searching, to make myself available for the Democratic nomination for the presidency.

Never in my long political career had I been under any illusions about the nature of politics. I had ample reason to know that it is always a good idea in politics when someone tells you something to get it in writing; then to read not only between the lines but on the other side of the paper, and, finally, to give the paper an acid test to determine if there are any "whereases," "and/ors," or "maybe, ifs" written on it in invisible ink. This sort of precaution, of course, is also frequently necessary and wise in other walks of life and other occupations.

This is neither disillusionment nor cynicism; it is merely practicality born of long experience. I love politics; I think public service is an honorable, stimulating, and rewarding career, and, if I had my life to live over again, I would follow exactly the same course.[1] I am merely stating the facts when I say that, on taking the plunge into the 1952 preconvention scramble, I soon found myself neck-deep in political skirmishings, some of which, to say the least, were rather curious.

While I did not achieve the presidential nomination, I came close! Whatever disappointment I experienced was not caused by my failure to win the grand prize, but on account of some of the circumstances sur-

[1] In fact, as this is written, I have yielded to repeated urgings by many friends and well-wishers in Kentucky, and have entered the race for election to the United States Senate in November 1954.

rounding the manner in which I was dealt out early in the convention. There was much personal satisfaction in the support I received and the reaction of the delegates and the public to the situation which developed. Whether I, or any Democrat, could have won the presidential election in 1952 is, of course, subject to speculation, as General Eisenhower undeniably was a candidate of great personal popularity.

Long before the convention I was approached by many individuals and delegates and urged to seek the presidential nomination. It was no longer a "favorite son" boomlet, confined to my home state or to any particular area of the country. I was better known nationally than at any period of my political career, and there were many influential Democrats who regarded me as a candidate who could unite all elements of the party. The feeling was widely held, and widely expressed, that I had become, indeed, "Mr. Democrat," though this is a title which I never assumed or aspired to.

The first issue to be decided, however, was whether President Truman would run again. In my eyes he was the party leader. I felt that he deserved the nomination if he wanted it; never in my political career had I sought to advance myself at the expense of others, and I did not intend to start playing an underhanded game at this stage.

For quite some time the President kept his counsel. I had several talks with him and urged him to run. I told him that regardless of who the nominee was, the Truman administration and its record would be the issue, and he was the best man to uphold it.

I also told him that, if he made the race and wanted me as his running mate, I would accept the vice presidential nomination again. At the same time I told him frankly I would not run for Vice President with any other candidate, and that, if he did not seek re-election, I myself would give serious consideration to seeking the presidential nomination.

The President remained noncommittal, but there soon followed a period during which he put out feelers to interest the late Chief Justice Fred M. Vinson in becoming the Democratic standard bearer. Fred Vinson, a fellow Kentuckian and a great American, had managed one of my early races and was one of my closest friends. In fact, when Fred decided he wanted to retire from Congress and seek a position on the bench, I went to President Roosevelt in his behalf and urged his appointment to a vacancy then existing on the Circuit Court of Appeals in the District of Columbia. (It seems that I was always going to F.D.R. in behalf of someone other than myself. There was no appointment within his power to confer that I ever sought or wanted.) Although President

The Veep received early recognition for his oratorical ability. At nineteen he was awarded a medal, which he still has, for a speech he delivered while attending Marvin College.

Three Paducah lawyers in 1902.
Barkley is the one to the lower right.

In 1903 Barkley was embarking on
his political career and also marriage
to Dorothy Brower.

Congressman Barkley in 1914, after
his first year as a member of the
House of Representatives.

(Above) *Shown with America's Sweetheart, Mary Pickford, at a Liberty Loan campaign, in 1918, is Congressman Barkley. To the right of Barkley are Marie Dressler, Charlie Chaplin, Douglas Fairbanks, and Champ Clark, who was then Speaker of the House.*

(Below) *Barkley in 1934, during a broadcast.*

The Veep is an inveterate traveler. Here he and Mrs. Barkley are returning from a trip in 1938.

Ella Barnett

In 1934 the Barkleys visited the land of the Nile, traveling to the pyramids camelback.

Jane Hadley (lower right) brought out the Veep's most jovial spirits at a party given by Mrs. Morris Cafritz, July 9, 1949, the day after they first met. Also present at the table was Bob Taft.

Jane and Alben Barkley honeymooned n Sea Island, November 1949.

The Veep introduces Tom Connolly and Representative Daniel Reed to the Pope, September 1948.

William Duke the Third, a Hereford bull, was presented to Barkley as a fee for an address given at a high school commencement in Glasgow, Kentucky, May 25, 1951. He still has the bull on his Paducah farm.

The Veep, on his seventy-fourth birthday, November 24, 1951, sits on a ration case and balances a mess kit on his knee as he shares field rations with troops on the Korean battle front. In the center background is General James A. Van Fleet, Barkley's host for the day.

The tenth anniversary of the attack on Pearl Harbor: Vice President Barkley honors the veterans buried in National Memorial Cemetery of the Pacific, in Hawaii.

(Above) *Angles, the Barkleys' home in Paducah, is a fine old pre-Civil War mansion, furnished mostly with antiques. Barkley had admired and dreamed of owning Angles as a young man, and in 1937 his dream was realized.*

(Below) *Private citizen Alben Barkley looks over his Paducah farm, April 1954.*

Roosevelt protested that he hated to see such a valuable man as Fred Vinson, who was an outstanding authority on tax legislation, leave Congress, he made the appointment. That was the beginning of the judicial career which, after he had filled several high administrative posts in the interim, eventually led Fred Vinson to the highest judgeship in the land.

Despite our close friendship, I forbore from advising Chief Justice Vinson on the presidential race, because of my own interest in the nomination. However, on account of my firm belief that the Supreme Court should be completely divorced from politics, I later congratulated him when he announced he would not consider becoming a candidate.

Then began the boom for Adlai Stevenson. In an earlier chapter I told how the Barkley and Stevenson families were related through a common ancestor known as "Little Gabriel" Stevenson, an early settler in North Carolina. I also told how my paternal grandmother fanned my youthful interest in politics by telling me how she used to play barefoot in the creek with the Adlai E. Stevenson—the present Adlai's grandfather—who served as Vice President under Grover Cleveland. As a matter of fact, when I made my first campaign speech for Adlai at Louisville after he had won the nomination, I introduced him by saying that, when I found out "I could not get the nomination myself, I was determined to keep it in the family."

Cousin Adlai responded by pointing out, not only that he and I were related, but that the wedding of his great-great-grandparents was the first marriage recorded in Kentucky, before the Blue Grass country was even a state.

"I trust it is still legal," said Adlai, "but, if anything was wrong with it, it affects Alben as much as it does me."

I used to see Adlai occasionally in Washington when he was an assistant to the late Secretary of the Navy Frank Knox and later an official of the State Department. I have already mentioned how, the first time I spotted him at a Washington gathering, I recognized him as a Stevenson by his distinctive way of walking, a sort of loping canter which was peculiar to all the Stevensons I had known in my early days in Kentucky. Over the years Adlai and I had become quite friendly. While campaigning for the Democratic ticket in Illinois in 1948 I had spoken in behalf of his election as governor, and I since had spoken many times at various meetings in Illinois at his invitation.

It was after Chief Justice Vinson had removed himself from the political arena that President Truman asked Stevenson, who had then announced he would be a candidate to succeed himself as governor of Illinois, to come to Washington to see him. In the published reports of the forthcoming meeting there was not much mystery as to what the conversation was going to be about.

On the day after his visit at the White House, Governor Stevenson telephoned me and asked if he might come and see me. "Come on, Adlai," I said.

So he came to my office and confided that the President—without quite eliminating himself from the picture—had suggested that Stevenson consider becoming a candidate. "You and I are pretty closely related," Adlai told me, "and I came here to talk to you because there is so much confusion of tongues here in Washington—I wanted to talk with someone I could trust."

I told Stevenson I was somewhat embarrassed, because, if Truman should withdraw, I was considering seeking the nomination myself.

"Well," said the governor, "if you were ten years younger, you would be the nominee by acclamation, no question about that."

I, of course, had heard this "too old" refrain before, so I patiently responded with an abbreviated version of my "recitation" which I always give when this subject is brought up, closing with the roster of world-famous figures, from Gladstone to Churchill, who did their best work after seventy.

We talked a while longer, and I finally told Stevenson that the decision would have to be his.

"But there is one thing certain," I added. "You cannot run for President and for governor of Illinois at the same time."

I went on to say that I was sure he would be renominated for governor without opposition, but that, if he tried to hold on to the gubernatorial nomination while seeking the presidential nomination at the same time, he would be hurt in both races.

Our discussion ended with Stevenson saying, "I think I probably ought to announce right now that I will not accept the presidential nomination under any condition."

"No," I advised him, "do not do that. You cannot tell what will happen between now and July. Mr. Truman has not made his position clear yet, and there is no need for you to take any stand at this time."

So Adlai left, thanking me for my counsel.

The next step in the political drama was the Jefferson-Jackson Day dinner in Washington on March 28. This was the big Democratic turnout, with President Truman as principal speaker. The opening ceremony called for President Truman to proceed with Mrs. Barkley to one of the head tables, while I, in turn, escorted Mrs. Truman to the other.

As we entered the banquet hall and I put my foot on the steps leading to the speaker's table, President Truman, who was walking ahead with Mrs. Barkley, asked her to excuse him for a moment while he stepped back and spoke to me. Speaking softly, so no one else could hear, he said to me:

"I am going to announce tonight that I am not going to be a candidate."

I was so surprised that I almost lost my footing on the steps. "No!" I exclaimed. "No, you are not going to do that!"

"Yes, I am," the President whispered back.

And he did exactly that in his speech to the stunned Democrats, many of whom shouted, "No! No!" His unexpected announcement was carried to the nation over the television and radio networks, and, in so far as the Democratic presidential nomination was concerned, it opened up a Pandora's box.

In my own talk to the Democratic assemblage that night I stressed the gains that the nation had made under the Democratic party and under President Truman. I declared that the foundations of government had been strengthened "to a point never approached by this or any other people in the history of man." I also struck back at what I considered grossly unfair criticism of the Truman administration which had been made by General MacArthur in a recent speech. The newspapers reported that I received an exceptionally enthusiastic ovation and that I was interrupted by applause twenty times during the course of my speech.

Before the evening was over the political reporters, of course, were diligently scurrying through the crowd of assembled Democratic leaders, seeking opinions as to whom the party would turn to since the President had removed himself. Many party stalwarts were quoted as declaring themselves, then and there, for me.

Soon there were a number of Democratic names in the race. Up to this time the principal contender, who had not waited for President Truman's withdrawal, was Senator Estes Kefauver of Tennessee. He had become a nationally known figure as a result of his chairmanship of the Senate Crime Investigating Committee—a chairmanship, by the way, to which I, as presiding officer of the Senate, had appointed him, since he had been the sponsor of the bill setting up the inquiry. Senator Kefauver was making a favorable showing in popularity polls and, in fact, a few days before the President's withdrawal, he had scored a surprising victory over Mr. Truman in the New Hampshire primary.

However, with no reflection upon Kefauver's personal ability, I felt he could not win the nomination. I had the same feeling about the other leading contenders—Senator Richard B. Russell of Georgia; Senator Robert Kerr of Oklahoma, and Averell Harriman—all of whom were good friends of mine. Senator Russell, by the way, shared a common link with Adlai Stevenson and myself: that first Stevenson, "Little Gabriel," who settled in North Carolina, was also his ancestor.

Governor Stevenson was among those present when the President made his dramatic withdrawal. On the following day Stevenson was interviewed on a television network, and he avoided making a clear-cut statement of his intentions. On the same visit to Washington, the day after the President's withdrawal, when an interviewer asked him if he would support Barkley, Adlai was quoted as promptly replying, "I would support Barkley for anything."

Some weeks later, however, Governor Stevenson did come out with a statement that he would not seek the nomination; that he "could not accept" it, and that he desired only to be re-elected governor of Illinois. It sounded on the surface as if he were eliminating himself, and most commentators interpreted it in this fashion. However, it was not a clear-cut declaration like General Sherman's "I will not accept if nominated, and will not serve if elected," which is my idea of an unequivocal withdrawal.

Frankly I thought that Stevenson's announcement at this time was a political mistake, but, taking him at his word that he was not a candidate, I sent him a telegram congratulating him on his candor.

My next contact with Adlai was at a testimonial dinner in New York City designed to boost the candidacy of Averell Harriman, who was popular with the administration but not very well known to the people. I was seated at the speaker's table near Governor Stevenson, and I went over and told him:

"Your announcement the other day was a very courageous and frank thing."

He replied, "I don't know whether I did the right thing or not."

"Well!" I said, somewhat surprised. "Whatever it was that you did, you did it! It's too late to worry about it now."

There is no question that, after Justice Vinson eliminated himself, Governor Stevenson was the candidate whom President Truman wanted to lead the ticket. But finally the time came when Truman—never a man of inexhaustible patience—became irked at Stevenson's attitude, which reflected an apparent unwillingness to emerge as a "Truman candidate."

Meanwhile, with Congress in adjournment, I had left Washington and gone to my home in Paducah. Sentiment began to accumulate in my favor, and the Kentucky State Democratic Convention practically threw my fedora into the ring for me by formally endorsing me and pledging to my candidacy the votes of Kentucky's twenty-six delegates. The Kentucky Democrats even sought to coax me further by publicly presenting me with a fine new hat in case I aimed to do any throwing on my own.

Finally, two months to the day after the President's withdrawal, I issued the following statement:

> While I am not a candidate in the sense that I am actively seeking the nomination, I have never dodged a responsibility, shirked a duty, or ignored an opportunity to serve the American people.
>
> Therefore, if the forthcoming Chicago convention should choose me to lead the fight in the approaching campaign, I would accept.

I then began busying myself with my own situation. If all the complimentary things that were said about me and written about me had been convention votes, there is no doubt that I would have been the nominee on the first ballot. One little tribute that particularly tickled me came from an old colleague of early New Deal days, Raymond Moley, who had not found too many pleasant things to say about Democrats in recent years. Should I be nominated and elected, Moley wrote, he would like to propose a simple inaugural address in rhyme, "taken from the golden age of jongleurs and attributed to the great Raimbaut," to wit:

> In heat or cold, to come and go,
> To trot and gallop, run and leap,
> To toil and suffer, scorn to sleep,
> This is the life I'm now to know.

About two weeks before the convention the drama began to heighten. I received a telephone call from Colonel Jacob M. Arvey, the national committeeman from Illinois and Chicago Democratic leader. Arvey was the man who was largely responsible for bringing Stevenson into the Governor's chair, and he was a leading promoter of the Stevenson presidential boom.

"Mr. Vice President," Arvey told me, "Stevenson is 'not going' . . . He's not going to be nominated; he's out. We want to be for you."

"How do you know he is out," I asked. "Has he told you?"

"He has told me," Arvey replied. "Furthermore, I think Stevenson ought to place your name in nomination, if it is agreeable with you and your delegation."

"It is agreeable with me, and I am sure it will be agreeable with my delegation," I said. "But have you spoken to Governor Stevenson about nominating me?"

"No," said Arvey, "I haven't spoken to him about it yet, but I'm sure he'll be glad to do it."

I still had my doubts, but, on the strength of Arvey's call, I talked with Governor Lawrence W. Wetherby, chairman of the Kentucky delegation, who was scheduled to nominate me. We agreed that Governor Wetherby would be delighted to yield if Stevenson desired to place my name in nomination. As events transpired, however, that was the last I heard of the matter.

Practically on the echo of the Arvey conversation I received another long-distance call. This one was from Leslie Biffle, then Secretary of the Senate and a leading Truman political aide. "The President," he said, "wants you in Washington for a conference on Sunday. This is a 'must.'"

So I returned from Paducah to Washington on that Sunday—eight days before the convention—and went with Biffle to the White House for an 11 A.M. conference. There with the President were Frank McKinney, then chairman of the National Committee, Clayton Fritchey, a high-ranking Democratic Committee publicist, then a member of the White House secretariat, and about eight other members of Mr. Truman's official staff. Among them was Dr. Wallace Graham, the President's physician. I never did quite understand what the good doctor was there for, unless it was to look me over covertly and render a professional opinion as to whether I would survive a campaign. Anyhow, he never took his stethoscope out.

Chairman McKinney opened the parley by telling me right off that President Truman had decided to back me for the nomination. This statement was made in the presence of Mr. Truman, with his implicit approval. The President himself, during the course of the conference, remarked that it had been traditional in this country that any outgoing President, if he so desired, could virtually nominate his successor. I took this remark as a clue to his then current impatience with Governor Stevenson's apparent reluctance to accept the mantle as an Administration candidate.

President Truman would not make a public announcement that he was backing me, Chairman McKinney went on, but he would urge his own Missouri delegation, of which he was a member, to support me. Furthermore, he would personally ask his own alternate delegate, Thomas Gavin of Kansas City, to vote for me. Mr. Truman has since given me a photostatic copy of his handwritten note to Tom Gavin, written five days before the opening of the convention. It read as follows:

THE WHITE HOUSE
Washington

July 16, 1952

Dear Tom: I hope you can see your way clear to vote for Alben Barkley when nominations for President are in—and try to get the Missouri Delegation to go along.

HARRY TRUMAN

Hon. Tom Gavin
Kansas City, Mo.

I listened to all of this talk with interest, but I had a question to ask of the President and his political advisers. "What about Governor Stevenson?" I inquired. "In my judgment, he has not eliminated himself. I do not mean any reflection upon his sincerity, but he has never said positively that he would not accept the nomination, and I think he still has his foot in the door."

No, the conferees told me, Stevenson was definitely out: he would not accept the nomination. I said, "I do not know what authority you have for that, but all right, let's get on."

We discussed the various contenders, and McKinney went on to tell me how the situation looked to his group. On the first ballot Kefauver would lead with about 350 votes, Russell would be second, and I would be third. On the second ballot I would gain about 150 votes moving ahead of both Kefauver and Russell, and on the third ballot I would be nominated. On paper it looked good. It sounded pretty easy.

With this almost intoxicating background—the word from Arvey that Adlai was out, and the White House conference at which I was told I was the administration's hand-anointed candidate—I went to Chicago. I should have been highly elated and optimistic. But there were stubborn doubts persisting in my mind that it would not be as easy as Chairman McKinney presented it to me on paper. Some things, I kept telling myself, might go wrong in Chicago.

As it turned out, several things did go wrong.

CHAPTER 18

What Happened at Chicago

I ARRIVED in Chicago for the 1952 Democratic convention with the assurances of party leaders from President Truman down that Adlai Stevenson would not take the presidential nomination and that I would be the convention's choice. Governor Stevenson himself had repeatedly insisted he did not want the nomination, and Jacob Arvey, the Illinois committeeman who was behind Stevenson's political career, had told me he thought it could be arranged for Adlai himself to nominate me. Yet, when the convention was finished, I had been passed by and Mr. Stevenson was the nominee.

I left Chicago a somewhat wiser man—even at seventy-four, which was my age then, a person can learn—but I still had my basic philosophy on life and my sense of humor. As I drove back to Paducah with my wife, Jane, I reflected that the role of Cousin Adlai at the convention reminded me of a story that former Congressman Frank Clark of Florida once told about an old fellow from Mississippi who was on his deathbed.

Clark, a realist, was chiding his colleagues in the House for their reluctance to pass a perfectly justified bill raising the salaries of congressmen. I was a member at the time and was present during the debate. The bill had been argued all day, and there was a strong suspicion that many of those speaking against it were hoping it would pass over their dead bodies. In fact, at one point, a certain representative who had spoken against the salary raise pushed into the cloakroom and exhorted, "Get out there and do something, boys—I'm afraid our side is going to win!"

Finally Congressman Clark got on his feet and said that the attitude of those who opposed the bill reminded him of this old fellow in Mississippi who thought he was dying. As the sun sank slowly in the west, casting its benign rays over the horizon, he motioned to his wife to come over to his bedside.

"Mary!" he whispered. "You remember that old trunk in the basement?"

"Yes, John," she answered tearfully, "I believe there is an old trunk down there."

"Well, Mary," he whispered, "there's a quart of bourbon—fine, old bourbon—in it. Go down and get it."

"Yes, John," she said. "What then?"

Well, John gave her specific instructions. He told her to fill a glass with finely crushed ice, to bruise some mint and stir it up in the glass, with just a pinch of sugar. Then he told her to pour the bourbon liberally over the concoction, and to decorate it with sprigs of mint and set it aside until a frost formed on the outside.

"And then, Mary," gasped the old man, his voice now all but extinct, "bring it up here—bring it in here to me. And when you bring it in here, Mary, no matter what I do or say—make me take it!"

After Congressman Clark told that story, the House passed the salary increase bill overwhelmingly. One might say that the congressmen wanted to be "made to take it." It might also be said that Governor Stevenson's attitude was reminiscent of old John's admonition, "No matter what I do or say, make me take it!"

Adlai Stevenson and I are the best of friends, and I greatly admire his brilliance and his many other outstanding qualities. I campaigned for him in 1952, and I would gladly help him again if the party should again nominate him for high office. After his unsuccessful campaign for the presidency he too kept his philosophical sense of humor, and he and I have had several pleasant post-mortems on the events that transpired before and after the convention.

"Adlai," I once told him jestingly, "if I had it to do all over again, I'd go after the nomination in the same manner in which I buy antiques: I'd act disinterested, as if I didn't really want the thing—just as you did!"

When I arrived in Chicago, ready to do battle for the Democratic nomination, the camps of the leading contenders—and of some of the hopeful would-be dark horses—were already well entrenched. The early arrivals among the delegates and alternates were being wooed with everything from cardboard coonskin caps to charm bracelets and iced soft drinks.

My own candidacy had achieved sufficient momentum to alarm some of the rival captains, so they were already tuning up for another chorus of that tiresome old refrain of "Barkley's too old." Some of my friends decided that we should slip a little sour note into that tune, and they thought they knew how to do it. It was a sweltering July day, and a motorcade was on hand to meet me. But, instead of my getting into the lead automobile and riding comfortably to my Chicago hotel, I set out on foot and hiked the half mile over the hot city pavements. Jane walked along with me, and so did Colonel Arvey, the Chicago Democratic leader, who had advised me earlier that he was switching to me because Stevenson was "out."

Some of the younger members of my impromptu parade were fatigued by the heat and by the pace I set, but I arrived at the hotel in fine fettle. It was obvious that this little demonstration convinced my doubters that there was a lot of mileage left in me yet. For myself, I knew that there was.

Almost immediately I was caught up in a rash of interviews, press conferences, and radio and television appearances. The tempo of modern conventions leaves the candidate himself little time to engage in any real grass-roots "politicking" with state leaders and individual delegates. This was a particular handicap to me, for, with the exception of a few individuals who were working for me on their own, I had no formal organization at all. As I look back on it, it is rather amusing to recall that when I arrived in Chicago I did not even have that supposedly indispensable, all-important element of a modern campaign, a professional publicity man. Nor did I have anyone to handle my public relations until Charles Sawyer, then Secretary of Commerce in President Truman's cabinet, sent over to assist me an able gentleman, Ludwig Caminita, Jr., a Washington public relations counselor who was not a federal employee.

There was an encouraging display of Barkley buttons, decorated with a dramatic bolt of streaked lightning, when I arrived on the Friday before the convention. Soon, however, trends began to develop, which, when I could fend off the circus atmosphere long enough to contemplate them, disturbed me.

For one thing, late Sunday afternoon—the convention opened on the following morning—I received a personal visit from Arthur X. Elrod, a commissioner of Cook County, Illinois, and a politically knowledgeable gentleman. He said he came as an emissary from Jack Arvey to tell me that Governor Stevenson that day had advised the Illinois delegation in a "closed" but highly publicized conference that he did not want the nomination. Stevenson went on to say, Elrod related, that if he were free to cast his own ballot for a presidential nominee, he would vote for Averell Harriman.

This did not sound to me as if things—particularly from the Administration viewpoint—were shaping up behind my candidacy.

On the Sunday night before the convention opened, the blow fell. I had gone to Chicago, confident of the support of organized labor. During my entire career as a liberal congressman and senator I had espoused the cause of organized labor, in which I thoroughly believed. Before leaving Washington I had talked about my prospective candidacy with William Green, since deceased, then president of the American Federation of Labor. Mr. Green told me, "We hope you do allow your name to go before the convention, and we will be glad to do anything we can for you."

Likewise, at a convention of the CIO's United Steel Workers in Atlantic City the previous spring, which I addressed by invitation, I had a similar talk with the late Philip Murray, president of both the United Steel Workers and the CIO. "If you get into this presidential race," he assured me, "you can count on us 100 per cent."

In view of what happened later in Chicago it is ironic to recall the ovation that was given me by another CIO union, the Amalgamated Clothing Workers of America, which also held a convention in Atlantic City in the spring of 1952. I was cheered for fifteen minutes before I could even start my talk. The union delegates marched up and down the aisles, just as if they were at a political convention, shouting, "We want Barkley!"

All these developments, naturally, had made me confident of labor's support. Late on the evening before the opening of the convention news that I could hardly believe came to me in my hotel room. A little group of labor men, purporting to speak for the AFL and the CIO, but acting, so far as anyone has been able to learn, with no mandate from their respective organizations, gave out an announcement that "organized labor" could not support me because of my age.

This, so far as my candidacy was concerned, was a kiss of death.

There was, and still is, some confusion as to just how this situation came about. The spokesmen who were principally quoted were Jack Kroll, director of the CIO's Political Action Committee, and George M. Harrison, an AFL vice president and president of the Brotherhood of Railway Clerks. Walter Reuther, president of the United Automobile Workers and now Philip Murray's successor as CIO chief, and Joseph Keenan, former director of Labor's League for Political Education, also were prominently mentioned among those who had conferred on Sunday afternoon and decided I was "too old." [1]

In any event, after the joint CIO-AFL parley, Mr. Kroll was quoted in the newspapers as saying, "We have the utmost respect, admiration and affection for Vice President Barkley. It is a matter of extreme regret and concern that we are not able to support his candidacy." (Later, in the *CIO News*, this statement was printed almost verbatim, with the addition of the qualifying clause, "because of his age.") Harrison was quoted as saying more bluntly, "We can't sell Barkley to labor, not because of his record but his age."

Mr. Kroll and Mr. Harrison have since disclosed that on that same Sunday afternoon they passed the word to President Truman, through a White House aide, that labor would not support me. This has been confirmed by the *CIO News*. Whether the President received this word I have no knowledge. All I can say is I received no word from the White House concerning this message to the President.

It so happened that on Sunday, while the self-appointed labor group was meeting to praise me and bury me at the same time, I was in touch with another old labor friend, Jacob Potofsky, president of the CIO's Amalgamated Clothing Workers. I told him I would like to invite a group of labor leaders to have breakfast with me on Monday morning to discuss my candidacy. He called back later to say that a group of ten would come over. In retrospect it seems to me that he sounded strangely reticent, as if embarrassed, for—though it was not known to me—the decision to go against me had already been taken.

On Monday morning the labor group came over. Among them were Kroll, Keenan, Reuther, and six or seven others. Harrison, though invited, did not come. It was the most unappetizing repast I have ever attended. Even Mr. Kroll was quoted later as saying, "I couldn't swallow my breakfast for thinking of what I had to tell an old friend."

When they all sat down around the table, I quietly laid the morning papers, carrying the news of what the labor group had done, on the

[1] The official *CIO News* has since stated that the question of my candidacy was "discussed at length" by CIO officials in Chicago on the Sunday of that conference. In addition to Kroll and Reuther it named the following as having participated in the discussions: Allan Haywood (since deceased), then executive vice president of the CIO; James B. Carey, CIO secretary-treasurer; O. A. Knight, president of the Oil Workers International Union; Joseph Beirne, president of the Communications Workers, "and others." The article, however, did not specifically identify which of these men attended the joint conference with Harrison, Keenan, and presumably others of the AFL.

table along with the scrambled eggs, and said, "Gentlemen, I never thought I would live to see the day when I would read such a headline."

Was I, I asked, really "too old"? I reminded them I was four years younger than Churchill; that Gladstone was Prime Minister of England at eighty-four; that Goethe completed *Faust* at eighty-two, and that Oliver Wendell Holmes did not retire from the Supreme Court until he was ninety-one. I also cited my lifelong record as a fighter for the interests of labor, which I believed were also the interests of the nation.

They listened politely, not demurring to anything I said. Finally, Walter Reuther spoke up and, to his credit, he was candid, though, from my viewpoint, not logical. What Reuther said, I suspect, began to get closer to the meat of the matter, for the *CIO News*, in its published post-mortem on the affair, while still bearing down on my "age," admitted to dark suspicions that I was liked by such *"professional politicians"* as Jim Farley and that *"the Dixiecrat wing might jump onto the Barkley coat-tails."* I have supplied the italics to indicate my astonishment at such reasons for dealing such a blow to a man whose record was so well known.

Reuther told me that no one criticized my liberal record, but that the group "did not like" a statement that Jim Farley had given out, linking my name with that of Senator Russell of Georgia, whom labor regarded as too conservative, as a possible presidential-vice presidential ticket.

I replied to Reuther that I had not seen Farley's purported statement and that I had not authorized any statement by anybody. Furthermore, I pointed out that, while I had great respect for Senator Russell, I was sure that neither this convention nor any other in its right mind would nominate two candidates from the same section of the country.[1]

[1] Weeks after the Democratic convention, after he had succeeded Philip Murray as CIO president, Walter Reuther gave out his own version of what had happened in Chicago. It was rather interesting. The Associated Press on September 6, 1952, quoted him as saying in Cleveland, that the reports that he and other labor leaders had "killed" my candidacy were "vicious stories." The AP story continued, as follows:

"Certain political fixers approached labor leaders at the convention proposing that they persuade labor delegates to come out for a Barkley-Russell ticket.

"We had nothing against Barkley but we wouldn't take Senator Russell (Ga.) under any circumstances. We consider Barkley our very dear friend and under no conditions did we want to hurt his feelings."

Then—saying "fixers" arranged the breakfast meeting—Reuther declared labor men spent two hours telling Barkley that many delegates friendly to labor could not be swung over because they were morally bound to support other candidates.

I was in no mood for humor on this occasion, otherwise I might have remarked to my labor friends that I felt like the man in Abraham Lincoln's story who was being ridden out of town on a rail. Someone asked him how he felt about it and he observed, "If it weren't for the honor of the thing, I would just as soon have walked."

The action of the Kroll-Harrison-Reuther-Keenan group precipitated a serious protest in the ranks of labor. George Meany, then secretary and now William Green's successor as president of the AFL, and CIO Secretary James B. Carey came to see me. If Mr. Carey had been apprised of what was brewing, as the *CIO News* later implied, he certainly did not indicate it to me that day, for both he and Mr. Meany forcefully expressed their dissent. "They had no authority to make that statement— neither from Green, Murray, nor from the executive committees of the AFL or the CIO," Meany and Carey told me.

The maverick nature of the "too old" statement was further indicated in many ways. At a meeting of members of the American Federation of Labor, who were attending the convention as delegates, Vice President Charles J. MacGowan bitterly assailed the action of those who had proclaimed my ineligibility. He said he spoke for the majority of the Federation's executive council, "most of whom are in town and have never taken any position on the Barkley matter," and that it had been "tragic" for such a blow to be dealt to "a great champion of labor."

John L. Lewis publicly denounced the action, and personally urged

"We said, 'We love you, you have been a real champion of organized labor.'

"Barkley said, 'I understand your position. I made the mistake of getting into the race too late.'

"Jack Kroll said, 'It wouldn't be fair to you as an individual. It's a killing job. The President at 68 thinks he's too old.'

"We left under friendly terms, but the political fixers don't want it that way. They began to circulate these vicious stories and the newspapers deliberately misrepresented our position."

I have never seen any denial by Mr. Reuther of the above statement, so I assume it was an accurate representation of his opinion, to which, of course, he is entitled. For my part, if this interview was correctly reported, I have not the faintest notion as to what he was talking about in his references to "political fixers." If such "fixers" approached him in regard to a Barkley-Russell ticket, it was completely without my knowledge, as I told him at the breakfast. As for the breakfast itself being arranged by "fixers," it was I, personally, who extended the invitation through Jacob Potofsky, a very fine gentleman and an official of the CIO, as I have related.

me to "stay in there and fight—we'll beat them!" In his public statement he declared:

> Vice President Barkley has always been a friend of organized labor. He has led a distinguished career, deserving of the eternal gratitude of every man in America who works for a living as well as all other citizens.
>
> The rank and file of organized labor throughout the United States are grateful to Vice President Barkley for his lifetime record and for his espousal of the interest of the common man.

To this Lewis added that it was obvious that "the self-anointed political leaders of labor who took it upon themselves to attempt to disqualify him . . . were engaged in a small-time political intrigue with other candidates." He also followed it up by making public a telegram which he sent to a United Mine Workers official who was a member of the Kentucky delegation. In a portion of his wire, the doughty John L. declared:

> EVERY KENTUCKIAN KNOWS THAT FOR AN HONORED LIFETIME ALBEN W. BARKLEY HAS TAKEN THE SALT WITH THE BREAD . . . HE . . . IS THE MAN THAT SHOULD BE SELECTED TO LEAD THE FIGHT OF THE COMMON PEOPLE. . . . BARKLEY IS A LION-HEARTED CHAMPION AND A PROVEN DEFENDER OF THE PEOPLE'S RIGHTS. . . .

Then the telegrams began to pour in on me from labor union locals and from individual union leaders from all over the country. I shall not attempt to reproduce them in full here, but excerpts from these messages, all signed by union officials, were as follows:

> "The sentiments of labor are with you; the men that were against you were a segregated few who took upon themselves their action. . . . We of labor feel grieved. . . . A great injustice has been done to you by some labor leaders. . . . We would have supported you for anything you desired to run for. . . . Neither Kroll nor Harrison speak for organized labor. . . . The people of organized labor, Republicans and Democrats alike, will support you at the polls; go after it. . . . We of labor desire to voice our objections most emphatically to the action of the so-called labor leaders who are attempting to speak without our authority. . . . It is inconceivable that a person of your stature should be cast aside by the very persons whom you befriended. . . . We are amazed and disappointed by the statement that labor cannot support you for the nomination. We believe you are much stronger mentally and physically than most men many years your junior. . . . Please do not be misled

by new labor leaders who say they are speaking for all labor. We of the rank and file of labor are back of you 100 per cent. You have been our champion in labor for years and God help us when our labor leaders let you down. . . . Action of so-called labor leaders in undermining your candidacy does not reflect thinking of overwhelming majority of working men and women. It is a betrayal. . . . You got a dirty deal from so-called top-flight labor leaders. Do not give up. . . . The very labor leaders who claimed that seventy-four is too old are within that age group themselves and are still holding down jobs in their own unions. . . . You have more vigor and stamina than most of those who made the insulting proposal that you withdraw. Had you been in your thirties, I am convinced the attitude of those gentlemen would have been the same because some of them were pledged to other candidates months before. . . . The blunt, crude way in which the so-called representatives of organized labor made their proposals to you has cost the Democratic party probably a million votes."

And so it went. As these messages came in, it became increasingly obvious that the rank-and-file members of organized labor, as well as many of its leaders, were with me as they had been throughout the years of my public life. But the damage had been done, and, with the convention under way, there was no time to repair it.

I remained close to my headquarters on Monday, the opening day of the convention, keeping in touch with developments. For the time being my only statement on the labor situation was the following noncommittal bulletin, which I gave out when pressed for comment:

I had breakfast with a group of labor leaders. I enjoyed sitting down and discussing their problems with them, as I have done over the years.

On the opening morning of the convention Governor Stevenson, in officially welcoming the convention to Illinois, made an excellent speech that stirred up much enthusiasm. One senator from a state which had a "favorite son" candidate in the race telephoned to ask me what I thought of Stevenson's speech, and I told him it was very good. "Well," he said, "it sounded to me like a nominating speech—like a bid for the nomination."

Late that afternoon I had some callers. I was visited by Senate Secretary Biffle and by Kentucky's Senator Earle Clements, Governor Lawrence Wetherby and Lieutenant Governor Emerson Beauchamp. All had been active in urging my candidacy, and Biffle, as I have related, had arranged the conference at the White House a week earlier, when I had been told I would be the Administration's candidate. They came to tell me that the labor statement was having an adverse effect on delegates from the big industrial states who had been counted on to support me.

"Do I understand that you have come here to urge me to withdraw?" I asked.

That, they answered, was the way it was.

So that evening I prepared a statement which was read to the assembled newsmen by my designated representative. In it I gave what amounted to a thumbnail synopsis of my lifelong political credo. I said:

I would be derelict in my responsibility to the American people and to myself if I failed to state the reasons which caused me to withdraw my name from the consideration of the convention. I shall state them now.

It has always been my belief, and my record supports this, that the Democratic party should serve without favor the best interests of all segments of our life, the rich, the poor, the Negro, the Jew, the Catholic, the Protestant, the laborer in the field, the laborer in the factory, the businessman, the farmer and the oppressed, wherever they may be.

I have never believed and do not now believe that any one of these groups should be permitted to dominate or control either of the great political parties of our nation.

However, since arriving in Chicago I have learned that certain self-anointed political labor leaders have taken upon themselves to announce their opposition to me as a Democratic nominee for President. They have admitted to me that weeks ago they committed themselves to a program and to candidates other than myself which would give them greater control of the machinery and policies of the Democratic party.

I went on to say:

At the same time, the leaders of certain large delegations, who have been encouraging my candidacy, now find it expedient to withdraw their proffered support of me.

If, by taking myself out of this race, I have contributed to the progress of the Democratic party and the future welfare of the United States, and, thereby, have rendered a service to my country, then I am most happy.

As a private citizen, I shall always seek to promote the welfare of my country, as I have tried to do in public life for the past forty years.

And so I withdrew.

At seven o'clock the next morning a special messenger brought me a note from Governor Stevenson. It was on official stationery in his own handwriting, and it read as follows:

DEAR ALBEN—I've just read your statement. I'm distressed that you found it necessary to do this.

It is a noble statement which perhaps no one else in our country could write. Charity, candor and courage are the firm rock on which you've stood for a long time. And you have again made the rock more visible to many lesser men, this one included.

God bless you—
ADLAI.

P.S. But you have made it very hard for me!!!

Now this was a gratifying but rather cryptic note—particularly the postscript. Though I have never asked him, I have often wondered exactly what Adlai had in mind. If he meant that my withdrawal made it more difficult for him to refuse the nomination—implying that he favored my candidacy—why had Arvey's emissary told me on Sunday that Stevenson was insisting he was not a candidate but favored Harriman?

In any event his note required no answer, so I did not send one.

I was now through at the convention so far as being a candidate for anything was concerned. I had withdrawn from the presidential race, and I meant it. I would not accept the vice presidential nomination under any circumstances and I meant that, too. There seemed nothing left for me to do in Chicago except to stick around as a bystander, and read the interesting post-mortems that were being served up in the papers.

My first impulse was to leave Chicago and return to Paducah. Before I made a decision, however, I was invited by the National Committee to appear in the convention hall and address the delegates. It was suggested that I speak at noon on Wednesday.

I decided to accept the invitation, but I demurred at the time assigned me to speak. The great convention hall is less than half filled at noon, and the radio and television audiences at that hour would be limited. If I were to sing a swan song on the national political stage, I wanted it to be under appropriate circumstances. So time was assigned me on Wednesday evening.

All day long I had a stream of callers and telephone messages and telegrams from all parts of the country, urging me to change my mind. I had no opportunity to write out my remarks to the convention, and hardly any time even to consider what I might say. At one point during the day, however, Jane, who was a wonderful soldier during our hour of disappointment, prevailed on me to go with her to a quiet place for a late lunch, so I might think about the evening's speech. While we sat there alone, I reflected on what I might say.

What happened that evening in the convention hall moved and touched me very deeply. It would be immodest for me to attempt to assay the degree of the demonstration when I entered the hall, but veteran reporters have described it in words and in print as one of the greatest political ovations of history. "BARKLEY FOR PRESIDENT" banners —a little ironic at this point—broke out all over the hall. I was cheered for more than thirty minutes before I could begin speaking.

As I have said, I had written no part of my speech, not even any notes, and the words as they emerged were impromptu, spoken from the heart.

I began my talk by making it plain that I was not a candidate for any office. The great crowd set up cries of "No, no!" But I diverted this demonstration by relating a story. I told them I felt much like the country gentleman who used to go to town every Saturday in his farm wagon drawn by two mules. On each occasion, he would come home late at night in an intoxicated condition, but the mules knew just what to do. They stopped in front of the house, and the farmer's two sons would come out, unhitch the team, and put the old gentleman to bed.

One Saturday night, I went on, the boys thought it was time to teach their father a lesson. They put the mules in the barn, but left him in the wagon. As the sun came up over the horizon, he aroused himself, stood erect, and rubbed his eyes. Then he saw his plight. As he looked out over the muleless tongue and hindgate of the wagon, he observed to himself, "I have either lost a damn good pair of mules or I have found a damn good wagon!"

"They [the American people] know, and you know and I know," I told the convention, "that truth will make the people free; that they can only be enslaved by falsehood, and it is our duty as Democrats and as Americans, charged with the responsibility of bringing government to the people . . . to bring that truth to them . . . in all of its nakedness and all its sheer austerity so that they may know from us, and not from our enemies alone, the record of the Democratic party under the Roosevelt and Truman administrations for the last twenty years.

"My friends," I went on, "democracy is not a mere political formula. Democracy and the yearning for democracy among the people not only of America but of the world is not bound by state borders or by national borders or international boundaries. Democracy and freedom, as we understand them and want to enjoy them, are not circumscribed by religious denominations. They are not circumscribed by economic conditions. They are not circumscribed by race, creed or color, either here or elsewhere, in the entire world. . . .

"We have been taught to believe in and revere freedom of worship, freedom of speech, freedom of the press and freedom of assembly. These are the fundamental four freedoms of our democracy and our civilization. But, my friends . . . [these freedoms] . . . are but idle words unless we have freedom of thought so that men have the right to think and to think out loud. . . ."

Turning attention to the campaign ahead, I reminded the convention that the Republican presidential nominee, in his acceptance speech, delivered from the same platform from which I spoke, had said he was going to lead a "great crusade." We Democrats, I asserted, were not beginning, but were continuing, "a crusade that we began twenty years ago and more." The Democratic crusade was, I continued:

. . . a crusade first to lift the American people out of the depths of a despair which had befallen them after twelve years of Republican inefficiency and mismanagement in the affairs of our nation; a crusade that set the farmer out of the ditch of despondency, and placed his feet upon the firm foundation of economic equality, with all other groups of our peoples; a crusade to establish a sound and stable banking system; a crusade to give to the American people honest, free and efficient industry; a crusade to give to labor a new charter of liberty so that it might have the right, with equal power and representation to sit around the council tables with its employers and discuss the differences in wages and working conditions fairly and honestly in the American spirit.

A crusade to see that every American has a decent home in which to live, with not only all of the necessities of life, but some of the luxuries of life as well.

A crusade to see to it that every child born of woman under the American flag should . . . live in normal, wholesome atmospheres, with a chance for education to prepare himself for the burdens and responsibilities of life.

A crusade for all of our people; a crusade to preserve the soil of our land, a crusade to protect our river valleys from . . . waste and damage; a crusade to give to every American farm home the boon of electricity and to lift the burden of housework in part from the backs of the wives of farmers, and give them the power with which to produce the necessary things upon which we subsist.

Not only a crusade to make our lives happier, fuller and freer, but likewise a crusade to increase peace and hope and cooperation among the nations of the world so that our inventive genius might not be turned towards the destruction of man, but towards the constructive things that might mean a happier and fuller life to all mankind in the years that lie before us.

I went on to say that this was the sort of crusade which the Democratic party had waged for twenty years, and that I was proud to have taken a part in it. Then I declared:

"I do not know what the fate of the world holds for us. I have no crystal ball. I am no prophet. I cannot see into the future any more than any other man, but I know one thing: in spite of the deficiencies, in spite of the acknowledged mistakes and defects, the administrations of Franklin D. Roosevelt and Harry S. Truman have given the American people a greater share in the enjoyment of the fruit of their labor than any other administration in the history of the United States."

When the tumult with which the delegates greeted this declaration died down, I turned my thoughts to the international scene. I thought of Korea and of some of the snide and slanderous things that political opportunists were saying about our efforts to halt the advance of communism by fighting there. I reviewed what had happened in the tragic interim between two World Wars, and of how it might have been otherwise had Woodrow Wilson's great dream come true. After World War II, I said, we sought to organize the world for peace through the United Nations.

"As every man and woman in this audience and in America knows," I declared, "if the United Nations goes the way of the League of Nations, the last hope of mankind to organize the world for peace will perish in our day. . . .

"That is why we are in Korea. We are in Korea because we pledged our word in San Francisco that, as a member of the United Nations, we would come to the defense of any member nations under aggressor attack anywhere in the world."

Then I told the delegates of the trip which I had taken with my wife, Jane, into Korea on the previous Thanksgiving, and of how I had celebrated my seventy-fourth birthday on the snowy mountains of Korea, eating from a mess kit with the men in uniform. I had conceived the idea of the trip as a means of letting the fighting men know they were not forgotten by the American people, or by the Administration. Although President Truman would have loved to make this trip himself, but could not do so, he approved my mission.

Perhaps the account of my trip to Korea, as I told it to the delegates, is worth repeating here, in part. Here it is, as the convention stenographer recorded it:

Last November my wife and I journeyed into Korea. I had my Thanksgiving dinner with our men in uniform in Korea. Two days later I celebrated my birthday on the snowclad mountains of Korea with the men in uniform. It was the best birthday I have ever had, but it is not the last one I will ever have by a number of years! [Laughter and applause and cheers]

Before we got to the mountain beyond the Thirty-Eighth Parallel, I said to General Ridgway, "I will eat my birthday meal with the boys at the front."

And when we arrived they had arranged a tent for me in which to eat my meal. I said, "I do not want to eat in this tent. I want to take my place in line with the rest of our soldiers, and with my mess kit take my share of food with them."

I got my share of food and on that snowclad mountain we sat around in groups, eating that food. Over to my right was a Negro soldier from Birmingham, Alabama; to my left was a white soldier from Cincinnati, Ohio; in front of me was another Negro soldier from one of the Carolinas, and behind me were white soldiers from all over the country.

As I sat there and ate our food, I said to this Negro soldier from Birmingham, Alabama, "How do you like it over here?"

"Well," he said, "if I had my 'druthers' I would rather be back in Birmingham. But if they give me the green light, I am ready to march to that Yalu River, no matter what the sacrifice may be."

As I listened to that colored soldier in the uniform of the American Army, telling me that he was ready, upon the flash of the green light, to march to the Yalu River, I said, "I wish to Almighty God I could transmit some of his stout heart to some of the cowards in our country who for some reason . . . [Applause and cheers] . . . who for small and petty political reasons would make it harder for him to march to the Yalu or for him to march to any other river which means the defense of our institutions of civilization and the democracy of which we are proud!

I brought my speech to an end soon after the above passage. My closing words were, "Thank you—and good-by." Again I was cheered for forty-five minutes or more. It was all I could do to maintain my composure, and, when my wife came to the platform to join me as the bands played "My Old Kentucky Home," I would not have trusted myself to have attempted to say another word.

That night, I planned to leave for home on the next day. My part was played, and I did not want anyone to think I was hanging around there like a dog at a kitchen door, hoping someone would throw him a bone. But my friends insisted that I stay and see it out. I was sentimental about it, as I had attended every Democratic convention as a delegate-at-large from Kentucky since 1920, so I decided to see this one through to the end.

Since I had withdrawn, I was greatly surprised when Senator Thomas Hennings of Missouri, without my knowledge, placed my name in nomination. The nomination was seconded by House Majority Leader John McCormack and Lieutenant Governor Pat Taylor of North Carolina. While I sincerely appreciated these tributes from my friends and the warmth with which the convention greeted my name, I would have preferred not to have been nominated.

The outcome of the convention, however, was a foregone conclusion. Adlai Stevenson was nominated—and the delegates thus chose an outstanding man whose race, though not successful, reflected high credit upon himself and his party.

I played no part at all—and I was not consulted—in the selection of the nominee for Vice President. I had made it plain to both President Truman, Governor Stevenson, and to all others that I was not interested in running again for Vice President. On the night before the convention ended I was called to the stage to take a bow with President Truman and Governor Stevenson, who had just been nominated. After his acceptance speech, Stevenson retired to a room behind the platform with President Truman, Chairman McKinney, Jack Arvey, and some others to confer on the selection of a running mate. I encountered Arvey in the passageway, and he suggested, "Why don't you go in there with them in regard to this vice presidency?" I did not know whether he meant for me to go in and seek it for myself, or to undertake to advise them about someone else.

In any event, I said, "I am not interested in being nominated myself, and I have not been invited in for consultation." Mrs. Barkley and I then went on to our hotel.

Next day my wife and I set out to drive in leisurely fashion to Paducah. All along the route we were recognized and greeted affectionately. I had no bitterness in my heart, and I have none now. At the time, however, I did feel aggrieved and offended that I should have been dealt such a blow.

As I look back on these events I have become reconciled to the conviction that the men who issued the statement against me were acting in good faith in what they thought was the performance of their duty. I had up to that time regarded them as my warm personal and political friends. I so regard them now and shall be always willing and anxious to co-operate with them in the preservation of the rights which labor has secured and for which I have fought throughout the years.

All that is now water over the dam, and it gives me no concern. My only regret at this point is that I withdrew as I did. If I had it to do all over again, I would not have withdrawn. Whether I would have been nominated is not important. All my political life, however, I have never been a quitter. I did not quit in 1952 because I was afraid to risk defeat; I did so, in the heat of the moment, when my principal advisers urged me to do so. I wish now I had remained in the race, even if it had meant going down in defeat.

Though I was not a candidate, the 1952 election found me back on the campaign trail, working hard for the Stevenson-Sparkman ticket.

There was one phase of the 1952 campaign concerning which I must briefly express my disapproval. That was the defection from the Democratic ranks of certain party stalwarts, principally from some of the Southern states, because of their disappointment in the selection of Governor Stevenson as the nominee. I could not look with approval upon the so-called "Dixiecrat" movement in 1948 when Mr. Truman and I were candidates, nor could I look upon it with approval in 1952 when some delegates who participated in the convention that nominated our candidates departed from the ranks and councils of the political party which had done so much for their section of our country. I accord to any man the freedom to entertain and express his own opinions. I myself disagreed with Franklin Roosevelt on a matter of principle in 1944. But my disagreement was on the basis of my personal convictions. I did not on that account seek to destroy the political party in which I believed and of which I had been a lifelong member. I could not reconcile my views with the attitude taken by men who had been given high honors by their party and their states.

I shall call no names, but will rest on a brief excerpt from a speech I made while stumping the South in Governor Stevenson's behalf. On this occasion I declared:

I am more proud to be a Democrat today than I have ever been in my life.

How any man who has been honored all of his life by the Democratic party in holding high and responsible office . . . can now go wandering off after Eisenhower and Nixon is beyond my comprehension and beyond yours.

In the year 1952, however, the Democrats for the first time in twenty years were destined to lose. The combination of General Eisenhower's great and well-deserved popularity and the "time for a change" psychology was too much to overcome. It is no reflection on Mr. Eisenhower's prestige to say that his was an overwhelming personal victory rather than a sweeping Republican triumph. The narrowness of the Republican margins in the House and Senate confirms this. In other years of great party land-slides—Woodrow Wilson for the Democrats in 1912, for example, Herbert Hoover in 1928, and Franklin Roosevelt in 1932—the winners carried with them large majorities in both houses of Congress.

So, on January 20, 1953, I became a private citizen again for the first time since I was sworn in as prosecuting attorney of McCracken County, Kentucky, in January 1906.

That afternoon—the inaugural ceremony was over—we had a farewell luncheon at Dean Acheson's house. It was a cheerful gathering; we were not a gloomy crowd. I do not recall that anyone told any stories, but I think we all felt like the bereaved French husband in the story I related in an earlier chapter; at his wife's funeral he remarked to her broken-hearted and sobbing admirer, "Do not take it so hard, my friend. I shall marry again."

If my colleagues in the outgoing Truman cabinet had insisted that I tell them a story somewhat relevant to the occasion, I think I might have let my mind go back to the time when I was a young lawyer and defended a man for murder. Possibly he should have been hanged, but I got him off with a life sentence. One week after he had gone to the penitentiary, his father came to me and said, "I want you to get my boy out of the penitentiary."

"Get him out!" I exclaimed. "He's got a life sentence and has only been in there a week! What's the trouble?"

"Well," the father said, "I had a letter from him this morning and he's a little dissatisfied."

The moral I would have put to this story is that dissatisfaction can work in either direction, and what has been done can be—and frequently is—undone.

Anyhow, a throng of well-wishers gathered outside of Dean Acheson's house that afternoon. After a while the people set up a call for Harry Truman, Dean Acheson, and me, and we went outside and thanked them for their good wishes.

As I stood there, I recalled to myself the last time I had been a part of such a crowd: it was on Inauguration Day in 1921, when I stood on the sidewalk in front of Woodrow Wilson's house on S Street to join the people in telling him good-by.

On that faraway day in 1921 I had seen the end of an era. On this day in 1952, I was again witnessing the passing of a great Democratic administration. But I felt it would not be long before we would "marry again."

CHAPTER 19

The Attic in My Edifice: Some Random Notes

IN EVERY HOUSE there is some nook—a closet, an attic, or a basement—where the odds and ends of the household are stored: the furnishings that are not in use at the moment but are "too good to throw away"; the old pictures and family albums, the souvenirs that cannot be discarded because of sentiment, and maybe a box or two of old love letters and correspondence from cherished friends, past and present. In my own home at Paducah there is a basement room and a loft in the old red barn, both filled with just such memorabilia.

A man's memoirs are a sort of edifice. As I come to this point in my story, I find I have a number of furnishings and souvenirs and pictures left over, for a man accumulates a great many experiences in a busy life stretching over three quarters of a century. I would like, therefore, to treat the remaining portion of this volume as the closet, attic, or basement, wherein I shall store a few choice memories, and a few observations on some things in which I deeply believe.

Perhaps, since this is a volume of memoirs written largely from memory, it might be appropriate to start this particular chapter with a story I once told to a gathering of newspapermen—a story having to do with memory.

It seems that a baby, a fine, healthy, husky baby, was born in Kentucky. Its parents were inordinately proud of their new child, and they invited the neighbors from all around to come and see the baby. Among the visitors was a ninety-two-year-old matriarch, who approached the crib, examined the baby carefully and at great length, and finally, from the wisdom of her years, pronounced judgment.

"It's a fine baby, a splendid specimen," she said as the parents and neighbors listened breathlessly.

Then, leaning closer to accommodate her tired old eyes, she added: "And—if my memory serves me correctly—it's a boy."

It has been a wonderful experience, serving for forty years on Capitol Hill as congressman, senator, and Vice President. Congress has changed a great deal over the years. There was a time, prior to 1906, when senators and representatives did not even have offices; if a constituent went to Washington to see them, he had to catch them in the cloakrooms or the corridors, or track them down at their homes or boardinghouses. Even when I went to Congress in 1913, representatives were allotted only a single room in the House Office Building. If anyone wanted to have a private conversation with me at my office, I had to send my one secretary out in the hall, or step out there myself.

My longest period of service was in the Senate. That body has been called "the most exclusive gentlemen's club" so often that the term has become almost a cliché, but it is still an apt description. When a man goes to the Senate, he has the feeling that he *is* associating with gentlemen, and, with rare exceptions, he is. Now and then some bad apple gets into the barrel. Usually, however, the unpleasant characters do not last long on the public scene, and the country survives just the same.

The Senate floor, of course, is supposed to be a sacrosanct place. When the Senate is in session, no one who has no business there is allowed upon the floor. Funny slips sometimes happen, however. Once, when I was Vice President, I was busying myself with some papers during a roll call when I felt my hand warmly grasped and pumped up and down. At first, without looking up, I thought it was some senator, so I responded to the greeting. Then I discovered it was an inebriate, who somehow had managed to stumble past all the guards in order to wend his way up to the rostrum and greet the "Veep." Faces were very red around the portals of the Senate Chamber for some time thereafter.

Some old friends still insist that the most diverting speech I ever made in my entire career was the impromptu opus entitled "Advice to Newly Elected Senators," which I delivered at the National Press Club's reception for freshmen members of the House and Senate in 1945. On the chance that they may be right I shall quote a few excerpts from the address:

I have been asked to give you Baby Senators some good, sound, wholesome advice, and I hope you will take it with the degree of seriousness and solemnity with which I give it.

Do not entertain on anything approaching a lavish scale. I am sure most, if not all, of you have rented, furnished, decorated, embellished, contracted for, purchased, mortgaged or otherwise mismanaged some stately mansion, or other form of baronial estate here in Washington, with a view of unseemly, if not vulgar, entertainment. Let me dissuade you from this. You cannot afford to entertain one senator unless you entertain all senators, because, being prima donnas, they are very jealous of one another. Furthermore, do not get it into your heads that you can advance your senatorial, vice presidential or presidential ambitions, or your judicial aspirations, by entertaining all the members of the House of Representatives. They have no influence in conventions. Neither have senators, regardless of the length of their tenures. I know!

Moreover and furthermore, do not make the mistake of beginning the ordeal of feeding the members of the Press. It is in this field where habit-forming is most frequent and most persistent. If you feed one member of the Press, you will have to feed them all, and they are more "prima donnical" even than senators. If you ever feed all of them once, you are sunk, for it is a continuous performance. And they are all healthy and usually hungry. . . .

Another thing. Never give a newspaperman a drink. . . . Not only will your beneficiary, or victim, as the case may be, return himself for another, or others, but, as a rolling stone gathers moss, especially when subjected to the dampness of *spiritus frumenti*, he will return with a pal or pals, depending somewhat, but not always, on the brand of the case under consideration.

This is important. Avoid all publicity. What you do or what you think, or what you think you think, if you think, or if you think you think, is your business. . . . There is one exception to this particular instruction: If you can find a newspaperman who is foolish or idle enough to listen to you, talk hell out of him, with the understanding that he is not to report back to your constituents what you think, and especially what you say.

Never act as a judge at a beauty contest or a baby contest. It is impossible to be impartial. If it is a beauty contest, you may have designs on the beauty. If it is a baby contest, the chances are that the unsuccessful babies will become voters before you quit running for office, and you will have built up a bloc of opposition which may prove disastrous.

Accept no gratuities of any kind—unless you need them. Accept no stock market tips, unless you know you are going to win, and, if you make investments under these circumstances, make up your mind that you will be happy as a loser.

Do not ride in any Government-owned or operated car . . . unless you are willing to seal your lips against the practice on the part of others, which you do not intend to do.

Forget that you have the franking privilege. Forget that you have a mileage allowance for every trip you make to and from Washington, especially if you come from the Far West.

Follow this advice and you will be different—yes, sir, you will be damned queer!

When giving constituents your Washington address, do not fail to spell out in full "Senate Office Building." If you give him the abbreviation—S.O.B.—he will not know whether you are calling him one, or expect him to call you one.

If, on official trips, you put bay rum on your expense account, then, put it on your hair. Otherwise, it is petty graft. . . .

Do not permit yourself to go on junkets. It is a waste of time and it costs money that comes from the taxpayers. Avoid all such excursions, unless your remaining in Washington in the usual performance of your duties would involve greater waste of time and the people's money.

When in the Capitol or the Senate Office Building, walk up and down the stairs or ride in the public elevators. Pay no attention to elevators marked "Senators Only," and never ring the buzzer three times, which is the senatorial password for "haste." If you get into this habit, you will find yourself doing it in hotels and office buildings wherever you are. When doing it around the Capitol, some constituent is liable to see you at it and accuse you of enjoying special privileges not accorded to others—and, whether a Republican or Democrat, you will be guilty.

Never agree or disagree with a constituent who writes you his views on pending legislation. Always tell him there is something in what he says, which you will be glad to consider, if and when and under whatever circumstances the pending measure may never come up.

This is confidential among us senators. If you think one of your colleagues is stupid in debate, which you will think if you are here long, refer to him as "the able, learned and distinguished senator." If you *know* he is stupid, which you probably will, refer to him as "the *very* able, learned and distinguished senator." This form of address conceals a multitude of shortcomings.

Do not worry too much, if at all, about preparing your speeches. The one you prepare is never the one you make; and the one you make, everybody knows you did not prepare, and it bears no resemblance to the one you prepared, the one you made, or the one you wish you had made. It is the one your friendly and partial newspaper friend sends hot over the wires to his newspaper or his news association as the one you prepared and delivered amidst the enthusiasm of your colleagues, though he knows all the time he is lying in your behalf.

I shudder to think how many speeches I must have made in my time: the figure must be astronomical. I have spoken at every type of gathering from a political meeting in front of a blacksmith's shop to national political conventions, interparliamentary union assemblies and White House functions.

In the course of my speechmaking career I have often received fees for speaking, which is not uncommon, but I suppose I am one of the few speechmakers who was ever presented with a bull calf as a "fee" for making a speech. I addressed the commencement class of the Glasgow (Ky.) High School one year when I was Vice President, and, to my surprise and pleasure, was presented with a Hereford bull calf of prize stock, named William Duke the Third. I still have William Duke the Third on my Paducah farm; in fact, he inspired me once, when posing with him for photographers, to draw a parallel between livestock and oratory—"a point here and a point there, and, in between, a helluva lot of bull!"

My favorite definition of an orator, however, is contained in another story I frequently relate. Two friends met on the street. One was dressed in handsome, rich garments; the other was tattered. "You must have a good job," said the tattered one.

"No," said the fashion plate, "I don't have a job; I have a position. I am an orator."

"What is an orator?"

"Well," the fortunate one continued, "if you meet a man and ask him how much is two and two and he says it is four, he is not an orator. But if you ask *me* how much is two and two, I will respond to you in the following language, viz., namely, to wit:

" 'When, in the course of human events, it becomes necessary to take the second numerical and superimpose it upon the figure two, then I say unto you, and I say it without fear of successful contradiction, that the consequential results amount to four.'

"*That*, my friend, is an orator, which I am."

The art of old-fashioned oratory, which flourished half a century ago, has passed out of existence almost completely. There are only a few practitioners left, and almost none on Capitol Hill, which is all to the good. Hardly ever does one hear and see—for it was both an aural and a visual performance, the flamboyant, flowery, arm-waving, foot-stamping, shouting, roaring type of oratory that once flourished. When I was a boy, I can recall that if a man came to the courthouse to deliver a Fourth of July or any other kind of oration, the crowd went away feeling cheated if he did not put on a ripsnorting, acrobatic spectacle. The same was largely true of the pulpit, also.

From the standpoint of unadulterated eloquence William Jennings Bryan was the greatest orator I have ever heard. However, he swayed his audiences with his deep, resonant tones, and with his beautiful language, rather than with pyrotechnics and gestures. Actually, he made few and comparatively restrained gestures. His most frequent mannerism was a pounding of one fist into the palm of his other hand, a platform gesture which I have adopted. Bryan, it must be remembered, spoke in a day when there were no microphones, and a man had to have a voice capable of being heard in the raw, a voice with carrying power.

My own predecessor in the House, Ollie James, of Kentucky, was a desk-pounding orator of the school which could twist the tail feathers from an eagle. The late Senator Borah of Idaho was one of the all-time great orators of the Senate in my day; not only did he have a beautiful flow of simple English, but his gestures were as expressive as his language.

The late Senator Charles W. Tobey of New Hampshire, whose death occurred as I was preparing these memoirs, also was an interesting speaker, but he was more evangelical than oratorical. Of all the men serving in the Senate in recent times, my good friend, the late Clyde R. Hoey, of North Carolina, looked more as if he should be an old-fashioned orator than any man in that body. He wore his silver hair rather long, almost to his collar, and he invariably appeared in a high, stiff collar and a long-tailed gray coat. However, he was a quiet, effective, logical speaker, rather than a foot-stamper and a shouter.

Another political technique, once widely practiced but one which happily has become gentler (at least, on the surface) over the years, is the art of invective. Politics is still a rough business; political throats are severed as efficiently as ever, but, with the exception of the verbal antics of a few political brawlers, it is done in a more subtle way.

In the old days it was not unheard of for fist fights, and occasionally a shooting or knifing to break out on the floor. In addition to such acts, which did not occur too frequently, the language used in debate was often really terrible. Finally, both Houses were compelled to adopt rules against invective which impugned the character of a member.

In the Senate, for instance, if a member utters any statement reflecting upon the honesty, integrity, or moral character of a fellow member, any senator may call him down, and the offender will have to take his seat and remain silent, until someone moves that he be allowed to proceed "in order" and the Senate votes such permission. This rule is sometimes carried to extremes; it can be applied in such ridiculous fashion that, regardless of whether there has been any real attack on the integrity of another senator, any senator who wants to object may call down a colleague. I presided over the Senate for four years, and I have often remarked that, under this rule, a senator could be held out of order and made to sit down if he merely recited The Lord's Prayer. However, on the whole, the rule does have a desirable effect in preventing undignified and unbridled outbursts.

One of the most gifted verbal barbists who ever served in Congress was Congressman Thomas B. Reed of Maine, who was Speaker under three Presidents, Benjamin Harrison, Cleveland, and McKinley. He became known as "Czar" Reed, because he was a very positive parliamentarian and ran the House with an iron hand. Once, after ramming through a rule to limit time allotted to oratorical outbursts, Reed delivered the classic remark: "Thank God, this House is no longer the greatest deliberative body in the world!"

I never knew Reed personally, because he was before my time, but I have listened with fascination to stories which men who served with him have told about him. My favorite of all Reedisms is the remark he made in 1896, when he aspired to the Republican presidential nomination. Someone asked him if he thought he was going to be nominated, and he replied, "They might go further and do worse, and they probably will!" (I was sorely tempted to borrow this line from "Czar" Reed at several of the conventions in which I was involved!)

That convention, incidentally, nominated McKinley, whom Reed detested. After he had lost the bitter fight, Reed philosophized, "They were for me till the buying started."

Reed is credited with being the originator of the withering description of McKinley, which others, including Teddy Roosevelt, appropriated:

"He has no more backbone than a chocolate eclair." In floor debate he was a master of invective. "The gentleman never opens his mouth without subtracting from the sum total of human knowledge," he once said of an opponent.

On another occasion, Reed, who was an enormous man physically as well as a dynamic and devastating speaker, was engaged in acrimonious debate with a small, wiry congressman from Georgia. As the tension mounted, the Georgian, who was fiery as well as wiry, exploded and shouted at the massive Reed, "I will say to the gentleman from Maine that I will chew him up and swallow him in this controversy!" Old Reed drawled out, "If the gentleman from Georgia chews me up and swallows me, he'll have more brains in his belly than he has in his head!"

Once Reed deflated a pompous speaker who was sonorously quoting the remark attributed to Henry Clay, "I'd rather be right than be President." Said Reed, "The gentleman needn't worry. He'll never be either."

In speaking of Clay, who was always one of my heroes of American political history, that distinguished Kentuckian was no mean hand at the art of invective himself. Some of his most famous tilts were with the vitriolic John Randolph of Virginia, whose tongue could drip pure poison. Randolph once said of Clay, "Like a rotten mackerel in the moonlight, he shines and stinks!" Clay got back at Randolph more subtly when they met on a narrow plank walk that was laid across the mud near the Capitol. There was only room for one man on the plank walk, and Randolph, planting himself furiously in the center of it, said to Clay, "I never get out of the way of a damned scoundrel!" Clay said, "I always do," and stepped aside.

Finally there came the time when Randolph viciously attacked Clay's character on the House floor, implying, among other things, that he was a cardsharp. Clay challenged him to a pistol duel, which ended bloodlessly, and their enmity gradually abated. When Clay was about to deliver his final speech in the Senate, Randolph, who was ill, asked to be brought into the chamber on a stretcher in order that he might hear him.

One of the greatest men whom I have ever known in Washington is Cordell Hull of Tennessee. I served with him in both the House and the Senate, and knew him intimately when he served as Franklin Roosevelt's Secretary of State. He was outstanding in all his positions. The income-tax law which he sponsored as a congressman was a model of clarity and fairness. While he was Secretary, his influence, his logical mind, his adherence to what he called fundamental principles in dealing with national and international matters shone out like a beacon light. I think it can be said that, outside of President Roosevelt himself, no man made a greater contribution to the United Nations and the concept of international justice than did Cordell Hull.

Although Hull, as I related in an earlier chapter, was the virtual organizer of a committee of senators to work for Franklin Roosevelt's first nomination, apparently there was some question at one time as to whether Roosevelt would appoint him to the Cabinet. I learned of this early in 1940, when Daniel Roper, who had retired as Roosevelt's Secretary of Commerce, arranged a meeting between the late Colonel Edward M. House and me. It developed that Colonel House, who had been Woodrow Wilson's chief lieutenant for many years, was interested in ascertaining whether Roosevelt planned to run for a third term, and he wanted to suggest that, if Roosevelt did not run, I seek the nomination. I told him that, though I knew nothing of the President's intentions, I felt that Roosevelt would be compelled to run and that he should do so.

In the course of our conversation Colonel House told me that it was he who suggested to Roosevelt that Cordell Hull be appointed Secretary of State, and that Roosevelt originally was not anxious to do so. I know nothing further about this incident, as I never discussed it with Roosevelt, but I would surmise that the reluctance which Colonel House reported was based, not on any hesitation about Mr. Hull's qualifications, but on a possible unwillingness on Roosevelt's part to deprive the Senate of a valuable member.

I was not present, of course, on Pearl Harbor day when Cordell Hull treated the two perfidious Japanese ambassadors to a taste of his famous Tennessee mountaineer temper, but I did witness one occasion when, under great provocation, he held his temper admirably. Late in July 1939, with the European situation becoming increasingly threatening, Congress was on the verge of adjourning without taking action on President Roosevelt's urgent plea to repeal the Embargo Act. One evening the President called a meeting at the White House, and we discussed the situation from 9 P.M. until midnight. Among those present, in addition to the President, were Secretaries Hull, Stimson, and Knox; myself as majority leader, Minority Leader Charles McNary; such key senators as Warren R. Austin, of Vermont, Pittman and Borah, and, from the House, Speaker Rayburn, Majority Leader McCormack, and others.

Secretary Hull gave a lucid résumé of the danger and the explosive character of the world situation; then F.D.R. called for expressions from the conferees. When it came his turn, Senator Borah spoke up very positively. "There is not going to be any war in Europe," he asserted. "All this hysteria is manufactured and artificial. I have listened to what the Secretary of State has had to say about the information he has, but I have sources of information in Europe that I regard as more reliable than those of the State Department, and I can say to you that there is not going to be any war."

As Senator Borah uttered these words which challenged the accuracy of everything Secretary Hull had told us, I stole a look at the expression on the face of that old Tennessee mountaineer-statesman. I could see he was restraining himself with the greatest difficulty. But he exercised the greatest poise as he went on to differ from Borah in diplomatic terms.

I recall that, of the Republicans present, Senator Austin was most co-operative, insisting that "the time has come to repeal this impossible act." Minority Leader McNary was cautious about expressing himself, though he later told me privately that he thought President Roosevelt was right.

Finally, about midnight, F.D.R. turned to me and said, "Alben, do you have the votes in the Senate to repeal the Embargo Act?"

"No, Mr. President," I replied, "we do not have the votes."

So on August 5, Congress adjourned without repealing the act. On September 1, Hitler invaded Poland and the war which Senator Borah promised us would never occur burst upon the world.

I thought of Senator Borah on Sunday, December 7, 1941, late in the afternoon, when I got the news of the Japanese attack on Pearl Harbor. The first Mrs. Barkley and I were driving up from Paducah, and had been unable while on the road to get any satisfactory radio reception. As we neared Washington, I turned on the car radio again and heard the flood of words about the terrible calamity. We hurried home, where I learned that President Roosevelt had called a meeting of Congressional leaders for that night to discuss the step he must take the following day. I hastened to the White House.

Next day, as I listened to the President call for a declaration of war against Japan in response to the treacherous attack upon our forces, I remembered the emphatic promise of the senior senator from Idaho that there would be no war.

One of the finest tributes to Cordell Hull I ever heard voiced came from the late Senator Arthur Vandenberg, Republican, of Michigan, who, after his evolutionary conversion from isolationism to internationalism, became one of the pillars of strength in molding the bipartisan policy that existed under Roosevelt and Truman. In a private talk with me Vandenberg told me, "I would be perfectly willing for Cordell Hull to chart the course of our affairs internationally from now on, and I would be willing to follow him anywhere."

Vandenberg was a great Republican leader, and so were former Senator Austin, who resigned to become United States Ambassador to the United Nations, and the late Senator Wallace White of Maine. Wallace White succeeded the late Charles McNary as Republican minority leader in the Senate, and he was as sweet a human being as I ever knew. A lot of Republicans, bent on harassing the Roosevelt administration at any cost, made life utterly miserable for Wallace White by constantly prodding him to do things which he felt he could not and should not do. Some of his colleagues could not have been rougher on him had they actually stuck him with a pitchfork. He used to come to me frequently and tell me of the treatment he was getting from his own party. Eventually he retired voluntarily from the Senate.

The Republican who succeeded him as leader was the late Kenneth Wherry of Nebraska, a man who was sincere and honest in his opinions, but an entirely different type. He was almost a freshman senator when he became party whip, and he was typical of a new, bare-knuckled school that was coming into the Senate at that time.

I worked opposite Senator Wherry when he was minority leader and also when he was majority leader during the Eightieth Congress. Privately he was not hard to get along with, but on the floor he seemed to feel he had to put on a show for his party, and he would rant, rear, snort, and pound the desk with his fist. One day, when I was replying to him, I could not resist the opportunity, and I walked across the aisle and put on an imitation of him, almost splitting the top of his desk by pounding on it. The Senate roared, and even Ken went along with the laughter.

In speaking of Borah, both he and the late Senator J. Hamilton Lewis of Illinois, one of the Senate's most colorful characters, used to tell me, with variations, a story about how they first became acquainted. The story, which is rather hilarious in retrospect, got better over the years.

"Ham" Lewis, as he was called, was the senator who was noted for his sandy-pink whiskers and his loud green suits. In his earlier years "Ham" was practicing law in Seattle, Washington, and he had a client who had struck it rich, to the extent of several millions of dollars, as a gold prospector. The client was desirous of ending marital bonds with a female from Boise, Idaho, with whom he had become entangled in his earlier, less prosperous days, so "Ham" set out from Seattle to take depositions in Boise. What he did not know was that the female in question was a rather forceful woman.

"Ham" was quite a dude in those days, and, as Borah used to tell the story, as he stepped off the train in Boise he was dressed in a silk hat, Prince Albert tail coat, striped pants, spats, kid gloves, and a tightly rolled black umbrella. The lady was waiting for him on the platform with a horsewhip. She proceeded to batter in his silk hat, muss up his hair, mark his face, and dust off the seat of his pants, while he tried futilely to defend himself with the umbrella. It was very humiliating.

Lewis was most anxious that there be no publicity about the incident, so he sought out Borah, who had a reputation as a brilliant lawyer and an influential citizen. Borah went with him to the local newspapers and press associations, and finally persuaded them that it would serve no useful purpose to publish the item. Lewis was always grateful and they became great friends when both later went to the Senate. After Borah told me the story for the first time and I asked "Ham" about it, he admitted, "Well, Bill may have embellished it a little bit, but substantially it's true."

Dignity is a desirable quality, but sometimes it can be overdone. Those of us who served in the Senate during the Hoover administration sometimes reminisce about the curious change that came over Charles Curtis after his election to the vice presidency. He had been a senator from Kansas for a long time, and was quiet, effective, and well liked. He had served as majority leader, and practically everyone called him "Charlie." One day, soon after his election as Vice President, an old Senate colleague addressed him in the old familiar manner. Curtis turned on him and demanded, "Where do you get that 'Charlie' business? I'm Vice President now, and I want you to address me as 'Mister Vice President.' " We had a lot of fun with that one in the cloakroom!

One of the most delightful personalities who served on the opposite side of the aisle from me for many years was the late Senator Arthur Capper, Republican, of Kansas. Arthur was deaf, and frequently he would come on the Senate floor while a vote was being taken and would not know precisely what was being voted on. He would then ask in tones loud enough to be heard all over the Senate Chamber:

"What is it we're voting on?"

Then, on being told, he would inquire:

"Well, which side are we on?"

Not all experiences during my long career on Capitol Hill left pleasant tastes, however. I remember distastefully the incident which occurred when I was a member of the Banking and Currency Committee, investigating the stock-market debacle of the late twenties, and some publicity man managed to plant a midget on the lap of the dignified J. Pierpont Morgan. It was an affront to the Senate to let this hearing be converted momentarily to a side show. Much good, incidentally, came of these proceedings, as the investigations led to establishment of the Securities and Exchange Commission, and to legislation regulating the sale of securities by corporations engaged in interstate commerce.

I also served as chairman of the marathon Pearl Harbor-disaster hearings by a joint Congressional committee in late 1945 and 1946. I recall with no pleasure the efforts made to introduce partisan political motives into these hearings. It was a matter of record at the time, commented on by many objective reporters, that our work was impeded by the two Republican senators who were members of the committee.

The situation finally became so impossible that the distinguished chief counsel to the committee, William D. Mitchell, a Republican, by the way, who had been Solicitor General of the United States in the Coolidge administration and Attorney General under Hoover, finally resigned, with his entire staff, in protest. In resigning Mr. Mitchell pointed out that a full month had been consumed in examining only eight witnesses, and that the long suffering General George C. Marshall, wartime Army Chief of Staff, had been kept on the stand nearly five days. Mr. Mitchell commented:

> Since the start of the hearing it has become increasingly apparent that some members of the Committee have a different view than that entertained by counsel, either as to the scope of the inquiry or as to what is pertinent evidence. This has been reflected in extensive examination by some members of the Committee far beyond what the legal staff anticipated.

Mr. Mitchell also made it clear that there had been no effort on the part of the Administration to whitewash or conceal any facts about the Pearl Harbor disaster. He said:

> I want to make it clear that there has been no restriction placed upon counsel by any member of the Committee or by any agency of the Government as far as presenting pertinent evidence is concerned. We have had access to all pertinent records and have received complete co-operation from all Government departments concerned.

At one point during the hearings before he resigned Counsel Mitchell clashed openly with one of the Republican senators, who had practically snatched a document out of the hands of a general who was testifying, without giving Counsel opportunity to examine it. The senator, realizing what he had done, tried to make amends by handing the document to Counsel, but Mr. Mitchell openly turned his back on him and stared bleakly in another direction. I have never seen anything quite like it at any hearing in which I have participated.

At another point former Senator Scott Lucas, Democrat, of Illinois, felt constrained to protest bitterly at the open coaching of one of the Republican inquisitors by a man who was identified as a onetime employe of the Republican National Committee.

For my part, I became so depressed by the proceedings that, when Mr. Mitchell and his staff resigned, I announced that I was seriously considering resigning with them. But I stuck it out, and we produced a report, signed by the majority of the Committee, which I think performed a service to the nation. In it, among other conclusions and numerous recommendations, we disposed of what I regard as one of the most deplorable partisan charges of all time by declaring:

> The committee has found no evidence to support the charges, made before and during the hearings, that the President, the Secretary of State, the Secretary of War, or the Secretary of Navy tricked, provoked, incited, cajoled or coerced Japan into attacking this nation in order that a declaration of war might be more easily obtained from the Congress. . . .
>
> The President, the Secretary of State, and high Government officials made every possible effort, without sacrificing our national honor and endangering our security, to avert war with Japan.

The two Republican senators, of course, filed their own dissenting report.

Another experience, the horror of which shall be engraved on my memory as long as I live, was my trip to Germany early in 1945 as chairman of a joint Congressional committee to inspect Nazi extermination centers. As the American Army began to drive into Germany, General Eisenhower, then the Allied commander, recommended to General Marshall, Chief of Staff in Washington, that Congress be asked to send a committee to view these camps, because they were so atrocious and horrible that it was hard to believe, without seeing them, that such things existed. General Marshall discussed the matter with me as majority leader of the Senate, and in two days a committee of six senators and six representatives was on its way. We visited Buchenwald, Nordhausen and Dachau, names that will remain forever infamous. What we saw was loathsome beyond description: looking at the starved, dead bodies, piled in courtyards like cordwood, even hung on hooks like cattle in a slaughterhouse, made one want to reach out and seize a club or a gun and start punishing the guilty parties.

There were two members of the minority party in our committee who, on seeing the first camp, were skeptical. They openly expressed their doubts as to whether it was real, or whether a "show" had been arranged to "sell" Congress on the idea of German atrocities. After we had visited the next two camps and seen the brutal evidence at its worst, they were as sick and as indignant as any of us. "We've seen enough; we're convinced," these two senators told me. "You write the report—we'll sign it." This time our committee's report to the Senate was unanimous.

Three background incidents in connection with the atom bomb stand out in my memory:

The first was the day when the late Secretary of War Stimson asked me to assemble a picked group of senators, Democrats and Republicans, in my office—I was majority leader at the time—to discuss an unspecified "top secret" matter with us. There were eight or ten of us: McKellar, Walsh of Massachusetts; Austin, Vandenberg, and others. Secretary Stimson swore us to secrecy, then guardedly gave us a hint as to the terrible weapon that was being developed which later ended the war in Japan. He did not use the word "atom bomb" or "atomic energy" but discussed it in general terms. The purpose of the conference was to give the key leaders of the Senate an idea as to the importance of the project under way, so we would not be in the dark when the requests for the huge secret appropriations were sent to the Senate.

The second incident is a story that former Senator McKellar, then the chairman of the Appropriations Committee, tells about how he received news of the atomic project. In his inimitable fashion the Tennesseean relates that he was tossing in his bed one night, unable to sleep because he had dined on country ham, which always upsets him. He began thinking about some of the matters before his committee, and suddenly started to wonder why the Senate was being asked to appropriate $2,000,000,000 "for something mysterious."

Next day, he relates, he made a trip to the War Department and told Secretary Stimson that he ought to be given at least an inkling of what was going on. The Secretary pondered, allowed that Mr. McKellar's request was only reasonable, and then asked, "Can you keep a secret?" "Mac" assured him that he certainly could; that, if necessary, he would even eat country ham every night before retiring so there would be no danger of his talking in his sleep.

Then Secretary Stimson leaned forward and dramatically whispered, "We are about to split the atom!"

"After we finally dropped the bomb and the news became public," Senator McKellar related, "I told a friend about this encounter with Stimson, and the friend asked me how I took the news. I confessed that I must have taken it rather waspishly, for I turned to Secretary Stimson and said indignantly, 'Here we are in the middle of a big war, and you are fooling around trying to split an atom!'"

The third incident involved the day on which President Truman called the National Security Council, of which, as Vice President, I was a member, to the White House to tell us that we had learned the Russians had exploded an atomic bomb of their own. When I got back to my office, my staff knew I was terribly depressed about something. All I could say was a phrase I sometimes use when I have received bad news— "this is one of those days when I feel as if I should never have left Lowes crossroads."

I wish the geniuses of this country would sometimes turn their attention momentarily from atom bombs and such and get to work on a much-needed invention—a political divining rod by which one can determine whether a man who says he is not seeking an office really means it, or whether he is just being coy. As I have related in these memoirs, I have seen quite a few examples of the latter, whereby men have been nominated for high office—sometimes elected, sometimes not—all the while protesting that they really did not want it.

I think this chapter has gone too far without my saying something about one of my favorite subjects—catfish. As I indicated in my chapter of reminiscences about President Roosevelt, with whom I occasionally went fishing, I am more of a theoretical than a practical fisherman. I thoroughly approve of fishing as an institution, but I rarely go. However, as a boy, I used to fish in the Mississippi River and catch catfish—channel cat, mud cat, and blue cat. I have always maintained that one of the best eating fish in America is catfish, and I resent the snobbish, discriminatory attitude in certain quarters against catfish. Some people would have you believe that catfish is plebeian and common. Well, there are a lot of us common people. Further, I have always said that if you would change the name of catfish to *filet de féline* and put it on the menu of a fancy New York restaurant at four dollars per serving, the whole Mississippi River couldn't supply enough of it for them to sell.

In my various travels overseas I have had a number of experiences which I have not touched upon.

On a trip to Germany in 1921—the year of the terrible inflation when you literally got a satchel full of German marks in exchange for a small number of American dollars—I was sight-seeing in Berlin and was looking for a certain location. I walked up to a big German policeman, who was stationed on the Unter den Linden, twirling his Kaiser Wilhelm mustache, and started to ask him a question in my primitive German. In perfect English, he responded to me, "What the hell do *you* want?" I told him, and he took me where I wanted to go.

"Where in the world," I asked him, "did you learn that good English of yours?"

"Oh," he said, "I used to be a cop in Brooklyn!"

In 1930, on another trip to Berlin, I met old Marshal von Hindenburg, then eighty-two years old and President of Germany. This was prior to Hitler's seizure of power. As an indication of the hard times through which Germany was passing, there were moth holes and rips in Von Hindenburg's old-fashioned Prince Albert coat that had been patched and sewed. Through an interpreter he told me that he had always had an ambition to hunt bear in Colorado, and that, when he finished out his term of office, seven years hence, he thought he would make the trip. I told him that his name once had been anathema to Americans, but that if he came to the United States for any reason he would be received in friendly fashion. The old soldier smiled when my words were translated to him. Von Hindenburg, of course, did not live either to finish out his term or to see the full force of the misery his maniacal successor was to bring upon Germany and the world.

I have had other trips to Berlin, but the most thrilling of all was at Christmas, 1948, when I flew in, via the Berlin airlift, along with Bob Hope, Irving Berlin, and their wives, Jinx Falkenberg and her husband, Tex McCreary, the Rockette girls, and others to bring a touch of Christmas to our airmen and soldiers who were defying the Russians and keeping the blockaded city open.

On a trip to London once I was walking by myself one evening in Hyde Park, marveling at the freedom of speech accorded the soapbox orators there. Imperturbable English bobbies stood around, keeping order but not interfering in any manner, while faddists, theorists, and assorted crackpots expounded on every imaginable subject. One speaker was even asserting that he, not the late George VI, was the rightful King of England.

I walked a little further in Hyde Park and came upon a little group of people singing religious hymns. They were hymns that were familiar to me, for I used to sing them in the churches I attended in Lowes and Clinton as a boy. Before I knew it, I had drifted in with the crowd and stood there singing with them "Nearer My God to Thee" and "Jesus, Lover of My Soul." No one there had any idea that the majority leader of the United States Senate was standing there singing with them, but they welcomed me with friendly smiles. It was a warm, human experience.

When I went to Russia in 1930, nowhere on the streets or squares did I find the people either exercising free speech or singing hymns. I had a feeling, however, that they would have liked to.

Two of the most charming people I have ever met anywhere are Queen Frederika and King Paul of Greece. (I suppose protocol would require that I mention the King first, as he is the reigning monarch, but I am sure that King Paul would not object to my putting the lady first.) I met them while visiting Greece on an official mission after World War II, and was entertained by them at dinner. I sat next to Queen Frederika, and can quite understand how America fell in love with her when she and her handsome husband visited this country in 1953.

Somehow the Queen got to telling me the story of her courtship, and, in view of later developments in my own life, it rather intrigued me, as it had a certain similarity to the joke that Jane, my wife, and I enjoy, about who proposed to whom.

Frederika was attending an English-supervised college in Florence, Italy, when her cousin, Paul, came to visit her. She told me she fell in love with him immediately, but did not let him know it. He went away and she did not see him for almost a year. Finally, she sent him a wire, saying, in effect, "Why don't you come back here and visit your cousin?" He did; they saw a lot of each other, and, as Queen Frederika related to me, Paul warmed up to the situation.

One day he was taking her automobile riding in the outskirts of Florence, and, as young men will do, stopped his car on a road near a beautiful, wooded hill. They walked up the hill to a grove and sat down, whereupon he promptly proposed to her and she accepted at once.

"After a suitable interval," the beautiful Queen told me, her eyes twinkling, "I said to Paul, 'Why didn't you propose to me before we reached this grove?'

"He replied, 'Why, darling! It would have been vulgar to propose marriage to you while riding in an automobile!' "

I would like to say just a word on political axioms. I have mentioned the cliché which every politician uses, *"Always run scared,"* which actually makes pretty good sense. Another sound political axiom is, *"Never take a constituent for granted."*

I remember coming home to Kentucky once as a young congressman, all swelled up with self-righteousness because I had voted against a pay increase for members of Congress. I thought I would be pretty much of a hero to my constituents because of it. One Saturday afternoon, however, I met an old farmer, Uncle Zach Cockrell, who had come in to town from his place about fifteen miles out in the country. We backed up against the wall on the shady side of the street and talked for an hour about what had happened in Congress. Finally Uncle Zach said:

"Well, Alben, I hear that you've increased your salaries up there."

"That's true, Uncle Zach," I replied. "But I voted against it."

"You say you voted against it?" queried Uncle Zach.

"That's right," I said.

"Well, Alben," he said, shaking his head sorrowfully, "all I've got to say is that you're just a durn fool!"

It has been interesting to me to note that, although as this is written, I have been out of office going on two years, I still receive dozens of letters from people who were my constituents, asking me to do something about roads, schools, appointments, and other matters which a senator customarily takes care of. Maybe they are prophetic.

In an earlier chapter I mentioned my enthusiasm, as the originator of the "prop stop" type of national campaign in 1948, for campaigning by airplane. It is an eminently satisfactory way to campaign.

In addition to airplanes, television, of course, is playing an increasingly vital role in political campaigning. As the TV networks expand, they will carry the faces and the words of all the candidates into the most obscure corners of the country.

Despite the increasing omnipotence of television I do not believe, however, that the time will ever come when a candidate can remain at home and rely entirely on the electronic screen. I happen to be one of those who feel that the people are entitled, not only to see and hear their candidate on TV, but to be able to hear him in person and shake his hand as well.

Maybe this feeling stems from a story that a very brilliant and able, but very ugly, congressman from Kentucky used to tell on himself. He had been in Congress about eight years and was running for re-election. He went into a community where he had never been before, walked up to a man, shook hands, and introduced himself.

The fellow sized him up doubtfully and asked, "Are you the fellow I have been voting for these eight years?"

"Yes, sir," said the congressman, beaming. "I sure am!"

"Well!" said the voter. "This teaches me a lesson. I'll never vote for another man until I see him!"

CHAPTER 20

That Reminds Me—It's Time to Stop

As I PAUSE and review the ground I have covered in this volume, I am reminded of a good-humored exchange I once had on the Senate floor with former Senator Robert Reynolds of North Carolina.

The gentleman from North Carolina had a well-known proclivity for making long and discursive speeches, especially if he knew that any of his constituents were in the gallery. If he had nothing particular to say, he would go on about beautiful and interesting places he had visited throughout the world.

One day Senator Reynolds had been on his feet a long time; he had quite exhausted the natural beauties of the Far West and was headed for the islands of the Pacific. As majority leader, I had some business I wanted to get accomplished, so I tapped him on the shoulder and said:

"Senator, let me off when you get to Shanghai."

Perhaps it is time for me to start thinking about "getting off" myself.

As I said at the outset of this narrative, I have lived a full life and a good one. I have enjoyed all of it, and have been grateful for the opportunities given me for public service.

It was Speaker Reed who once defined a statesman as "a successful politician who is dead." I think that statesmanship and politics, while not necessarily coexistent in all cases, are often inseparably intertwined. No man, if his own conscience is clear, need be ashamed to list his profession as "Politics."

A great many honors—offices, medals, and awards—have come my way during my career. There have been far more, perhaps, than I have deserved, but I am grateful for all of them. If I had to choose the phrasing of any particular commendation as words that I would like to be remem-

bered by, I think I might lean toward the citation which accompanied
the Collier's Award, which I received in May 1948. In naming me as
the outstanding senator during the previous year, when the opposition
party was in power and I had stepped down from majority to minority
leader, the awards committee was quoted as saying:

> Under conditions that would have caused a less determined man
> to walk out and rest, he continued to work for his country through
> the party. . . . His good temper was as always a good influence in
> the Senate. . . . His ability in rough and ready debate, his remark-
> able capacity to argue powerfully on many and diverse issues, and
> his acceptance of demotion without a trace of venom, made him the
> Grand Old Man of the Senate last year. As his position came down
> he seemed to grow in stature . . . by his wisdom, humor and moder-
> ation, plus his devotion to the system, he has strengthened the con-
> cept of party responsibility.

Throughout my career I have tried to keep my outlook and my thinking in tune with the public interest. Yet, while striving to maintain the
flexibility demanded by the changing times and fortunes, I have attempted to remain consistent in my general aims. I hope no one can say of
me that I was like a certain candidate I once knew who made a long-
winded speech, listing in great detail all the things he stood for. At the
end of the lengthy recital he said to his audience, "Now these are the
things in which I believe, but if anyone doesn't like any of them, just let
me know and I can change."

I do not think any man in public life should have his mind fixed so
rigidly that he becomes blind to reason. Nor should anyone in public
office become merely a party hack.

I have been a loyal, regular Democrat all during my career. I believe
in the principles of the Democratic party and I have fought for them
as hard as I could fight. However, that has never precluded me from
recognizing a lot of good things emanating from the opposition. In the
periods when I was in Congress and the Democrats were in the minority I supported measures which I thought were beneficial for the people,
regardless of which side of the aisle they came from.

I believe there are certain things which are still crying for accomplishment in this country. I shall continue to raise my voice for them.

Speakers who follow the political hustings are always "pointing with
pride" and "viewing with alarm." I "point with pride" to the fact that
not once in this volume, until now, have I used the phrase, "I view with
alarm." But I shall use the term now to describe my feeling concerning

the apparent trend of the present Administration in Washington to throw back upon the states responsibility for preserving or expanding the gains achieved in the Roosevelt and Truman administrations in many fields of political, social, and economic life. For instance, there is constant talk of abandoning the government's interest in such measures as flood control, soil conservation, rural electrification, social security, benefits to education, the development of our natural resources, the improvement of our river valleys for navigation, flood control, power, and other phases of our nationwide development.

I think this concept of the government's duty and its relationship to the people is badly out of tune with the world in which we live. While these rumblings are disturbing and somewhat depressing, I doubt whether the party in power or any administration that may come into power will have the audacity to turn back the hands of the clock so as to nullify the great gains which have accrued to the American people by the progressive movements and programs which have made our government more and more the servant, and not the master, of the people.

I can recall when William Jennings Bryan was ridiculed unmercifully for his "fantastic" proposal that the Government of the United States guarantee deposits in private banking institutions. He was derided as advocating "socialistic" ideas, just as I was in my first Congressional race when I dared to come out for federal aid to highways. However, after the wholesale bank failures of the Hoover administration, Franklin Roosevelt's New Deal administration did enact federal deposit-insurance legislation. Now the people have faith in our banking system, and do not lie awake at night wondering whether they will ever get their money back should the bank fail. I do not think that even the most hidebound opponent of this measure at the time it was passed would advocate today that federal deposit insurance be canceled out.

Some officials in power talk about selling the Tennessee Valley Authority to private interests. I could write a volume on what this great agency has done for a region—and for the whole nation, for, without the TVA's power facilities, we would have been in a bad way when industrial expansion became so necessary during World War II. I shudder to think of the beating the Treasury would take if the Government should ever dispose of the TVA by sale to privately owned corporations.

Turning to a different area of current problems, I think everything within human power must be done to see that the United Nations organization is fortified and strengthened and supported, rather than sabotaged and whittled away. In my opinion it has more than justified its existence. All the hopes which were kindled by its organization in San Francisco have not yet been realized; yet, without the United Nations, there would have been infinitely more chaos and possibly another world war by this time.

Without for a moment ever relaxing in our determination to keep our powder dry we must continue to strive to reach an honorable understanding with the Soviet Union. Because of Russia's present attitude there is no easy solution for this problem, but we should never cease trying, for the pulverization of cities—and I mean American cities as well as Russian cities—under the impact of hydrogen bombs is not an easy solution either. If we cannot obtain an agreement for the abolition of atomic weapons in time of war, we should continue to strive for an enforceable agreement for world-wide regulation and inspection of the production and use of atomic energy. This our government has repeatedly proposed, but the autocrats of the Kremlin have disdained entering into such an agreement.

There are also many things still to be done in our domestic life. I am opposed to bigotry, intolerance, and discrimination. I believe in the principles which our forefathers wrote into the Declaration of Independence and the Bill of Rights of our Constitution—equal opportunities for all our people. I believe in the doctrine announced by Thomas Jefferson when he said, "I have sworn eternal hostility to any form of tyranny over the mind of man." I believe that Lincoln came as near giving an accurate definition of government as has ever been given when he said, "The function of Government is to do for the people what they cannot do for themselves or do so well."

If I were in Congress today, I would continue to work for the same goals which I supported when I was a member, including legislation which would accord to every American citizen the full enjoyment of every civil right.

I would favor the general overhauling of our national election machinery. I believe that the people should have the fullest possible participation in the selection of their Chief Executive. I therefore favor nationwide primary elections for the nomination of candidates for President and Vice President. Popular nominations and elections have been successful in the choosing of members of both Houses of Congress, in the election of governors, and, in many instances, the highest judicial offices of the state. I believe the people are capable of making equally wise selections for President and Vice President.

I believe in the two-party system in the United States. In my opinion it would be chaotic, if not disastrous, for the American people to be split into the multiparty political systems that prevail in some countries. The object of political parties is to make possible the formulation of group opinions and programs, one against the other, to be presented to the people for their consideration and their verdict.

Accordingly, when the people have chosen their presidential and vice presidential candidates through the democratic method of a nationwide primary election, the political parties should hold conventions to formulate the principles upon which their respective candidates shall stand before the people.

I disagreed completely with the facetious remark attributed to a politician some years ago when he said, "Political platforms are like the platforms on a passenger train—made to get in on but not to stand on." Political platforms, which are the pledges of political organizations to the people, should not be regarded as mere scraps of paper composed in the interest of expediency and opportunism, but should be regarded as sacred documents to be respected to the utmost detail.

These things I favor because I believe in the common sense of the American people, and because I believe they are just as capable to choose their nominees as they are to elect them after they have been nominated.

In accordance with these opinions I believe that the ancient and outmoded Electoral College system should be abolished and that the people should vote directly in all the states for President and Vice President. The Electoral College was established in the beginning of our history for the same reasons which actuated our forefathers in providing that United States senators should be elected by the legislatures rather than by the people of the respective states. Our form of government was a new experiment and those who fashioned it were somewhat doubtful of the wisdom of the people in choosing their Chief Executives and their senators. We long ago learned that the people can act with a degree of wisdom equal to that of those whom they choose. More than four decades ago we changed the method of electing United States senators by state legislatures to their selection by the people directly.

We are one people in this nation. We have our states and our state governments and they all have their local responsibilities and it is not desired that they be stripped of the power to deal with their local problems as their individual situations may require. The President of the United States is the President of all the people. He is not the President of the people of any one state more than he is President of other states. Why should not the people be allowed to vote for their choice by name on a ballot presented to them directly in every polling precinct in the nation so as to let their choice be proclaimed as the head of our nation? By this method it would not be possible for a candidate receiving a minority of the votes to be elected President through the Electoral College because of the antiquated distribution of electoral votes based upon narrow margins within any number of states.

I have always felt that the House of Representatives is too large and unwieldy and that, as a needed improvement in our lawmaking process, a reduction should be made to a number not to exceed 300. The House was never intended to become so unwieldy; but as the population of the country increased, Congress for a long time was unwilling to reapportion the country in such a way as to lose seats for any state. So, like Topsy, it just "grew and grew." Until 1913 each member of the House of Representatives had an individual desk and chair at which he could work, as is the case in the Senate, but after the census of 1910 there was no longer any room for enough desks to accommodate all members, so the desks were removed and benches were substituted.

In 1913 the growth of the House of Representatives for all practical purposes ceased. There was simply no longer any room for more members. In my judgment 300 members could represent the country as efficiently as the present membership of 431. It would likewise give individual members greater opportunity to develop their qualities as legislators. Many good and able members are overwhelmed by numbers and in most cases must wait an indeterminable period to show their mettle and their ability in matters of government.

To quote my favorite line attributed to the great American humorist, Artemus Ward, "One man has as much human nature in him as another, if not more." So I do not entertain a very optimistic opinion that the House will ever vote voluntarily to reduce its membership as I have suggested, but it could be done without an amendment to our Constitution, which requires that after each decennial census Congress shall apportion members among the different states.

These observations are not based upon any disrespect for the House of Representatives or its members. I have always held a high opinion of this body in which I served for fourteen years.

In discussing our legislative process I wish also to say that I have always opposed filibusters, which are nothing short of obstructive tactics designed to prevent a majority of the people's representatives from voting on any given measure before them. It is paradoxical for those who profess to believe in majority rule under democratic institutions to be able to kill legislation by merely talking it to death in linguistic and often irrelevant marathons. I believe in full debate of every problem that comes before any legislative body; but to deny by artifice or extraneous argumentation the right of the people's representatives to vote on any given problem is equal to denying the people themselves the right by majority rule to pass upon questions involving their welfare and their destiny.

I should like to live to see all our great river valleys improved for navigation, flood control, soil conservation, and power. Under the Constitution, Congress possesses the exclusive power to regulate commerce. All our navigable rivers are highways of commerce. They are under the exclusive jurisdiction of Congress and the federal government. No person can build a bridge or other obstruction in or across them without the consent of the federal government. They belong to the people. They should never be allowed to come under the control of private interests. If every river valley that is feasible for such development could be developed as the Tennessee Valley has been, with similar results, the standard of life throughout the nation would be immensely advanced. No such development can take place except by the federal government. This cannot be done at once; it would have to be a gradual process. But it is as legitimate a conception of the functions of government as the regulations of banks or the carrying of the mail.

I should like to live to see every American family living in a comfortable home, and every American child born and reared in an atmosphere sufficiently wholesome to guarantee an even chance for health and intellectual and moral development consonant with the responsibilities of American citizenship.

I should like to live to see the world at peace where the inventive genius of man would be utilized to improve the conditions of life throughout the world. I should like to live to see the pledge of every nation respected by every other nation because it was made in good faith and observed to the letter.

I should like to live to see the day when religious and racial bigotry and intolerance would give way to the universal recognition of the rights of every man and woman regardless of race, creed, or color.

These ideals may constitute Utopian dreams. But if civilization is to be preserved mankind must seek their consummation.

And now, speaking of filibustering, a practice in which I never indulged during my many years on Capitol Hill, I must bring myself to the recognition of the fact that I have talked a long time in this volume. There may be some who will conclude that I am engaged in a literary filibuster. In this connection I must recall what my fellow Paducahan, Irvin S. Cobb, once said to his friend, Opie Read, the humorist. Over the coffee and brandy after a leisurely dinner at their club in New York City, they were having a ruminative discussion concerning their literary works.

"Irvin," mused Opie, "I find that when I write far into the night I have difficulty going to sleep."

"Opie," said Irvin, "why don't you stop and read some of it?"

All of which reminds me again of the speech I have already told of having delivered long ago in Frenchburg, Kentucky, the county seat of Menifee County, during one of my senatorial campaigns.

I had forgotten when I started speaking, so I picked up my watch, looked at it, gave it the up-and-down trombone movement, then absentmindedly put it to my ear to see if it were running.

Back in the audience some man shouted to me, "Barkley, if your watch has stopped running, there's a calendar on the wall behind you!"

I knew how to take a hint. I drew my speech to a hasty conclusion. I think I should now conclude this narrative with the same words with which I concluded my speech to the 1952 Democratic convention.

Thank you—and good-by.

Index